British immigration policy since 1939

In the space of less than half a century, Britain has shifted from being a virtually all-white society to one in which ethnicity and race are significant social and political factors. This book traces the chronology of this transition from the Second World War, through the first restrictive legislation on immigration in the 1960s, to the development of powerful ethnic communities in modern British society.

Based on a detailed study of recently released archival material, Ian Spencer's book is unique in its coverage of post-war immigration from a historical perspective. From this evidence, Spencer contends that the settlement of black and Asian people was not welcomed at any stage by the British government. The author documents the restrictive measures which failed to prevent the rapid influx in the late 1950s and 1960s of people from a wide variety of backgrounds and nationalities who displayed considerable initiative in overcoming obstacles placed in their way.

Ian R.G. Spencer is an independent consultant working in education and equal opportunities. He is the former Head of History, De Montfort University, Leicester.

British immigration policy since 1939

The making of multi-racial Britain

Ian R.G. Spencer

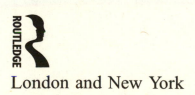

London and New York

First published 1997
by Routledge
11 New Fetter Lane, London EC4P 4EE

Simultaneously published in the USA and Canada
by Routledge
29 West 35th Street, New York, NY 10001

Typeset in Times by LaserScript, Mitcham, Surrey
Printed and bound in Great Britain by
TJ International, Padstow, Cornwall

British Library Cataloguing in Publication Data
A catalogue record for this book is available from the British Library

Library of Congress Cataloging in Publication Data
Spencer, Ian R.G.
British immigration policy since 1939: the making of multi-racial
Britain/Ian R.G. Spencer.
Includes bibliographical references and index.
1. Great Britain – Emigration and immigration – Government policy –
History – 20th century. 2. Great Britain – Politics and government –
20th century. 2. Great Britain – Politics and government –
1936–   . I. Title.
JV7633.S64   1997   96-9867
325.41′09′045 – dc20   CIP

ISBN 0–415–13695–4
ISBN 0–415–13696–2 (pbk)

To
SULEMAN PREMJI MAWANI
(1912–1995)

Contents

Figures

Tables

Abbreviations

BCWS	British Caribbean Welfare Service
CAB	Cabinet Office
CM	Cabinet Minutes
CO	Colonial Office
CRO	Commonwealth Relations Office
CRC	Community Relations Commission
H.C. Debs.	House of Commons Debates
H.L. Debs.	House of Lords Debates
HO	Home Office
IWA	Indian Workers Association
LAB	Ministry of Labour
MT	Ministry of Transport
[PPS] PS	[Parliamentary] Private Secretary

Preface

It hardly needs to be said that the making of multi-racial Britain is a very important subject. It is concerned with nothing less than a rapid and quite unprecedented demographic and cultural transformation of British society. In the space of half a century, between 1940 and 1990, communities of Indian sub-continental, Caribbean and African origin have grown from a small fraction of 1 per cent of the total population of Britain to almost 6 per cent. Within another generation it is likely that Asian and black Britain will comprise about one-tenth of the whole population. The consequences of the migration have been – and will continue to be – profound, eventually transforming the way Britain sees itself and is seen by others. My hope is that *British Immigration Policy since 1939* will contribute to the growth in understanding of how and why this came about.

The transformation of Britain from an all white to a multi-racial society, in the course of the second half of the twentieth century, has attracted a great deal of media and academic attention. In academe the writing on the subject and most of the exchanges have been dominated by sociologists, anthropologists and political scientists, perhaps necessarily because most historians disqualify themselves from the study of the very recent past. Not that social scientists have always eschewed the historical approach – Ballard, Deakin and Layton-Henry, to give a few examples, have had much of value to say about the history of Asian and black immigration. In so far as historians have interested themselves in immigration as an aspect of modern British history, they have tended – as exemplified by Colin Holmes' excellent 1988 book *John Bull's Island: Immigration and British Society, 1871–1971* – to see Asian and black immigration as part of a larger pattern of movement, or to examine the long-term history of black immigration to (and settlement in) Britain as, for example, in Peter Fryer's *Staying Power: The History of Black People in Britain* (1984). The journal *Immigrants and Minorities* has emerged in the last decade as the place in which historians interested in all aspects of the history of British immigration and settlement can publish their views. This present volume does not adhere to either of these approaches. It is focused on immigration into Britain in the second half of the twentieth century of a myriad of communities from the Indian sub-continent, the Caribbean and Africa – 'coloured' immigration as it was called in the 1950s or 'New Commonwealth' immigration as it was more politely labelled in the 1960s and 1970s. Put another way, this book examines aspects of the history of the immigration and settlement of most of the 'ethnic' groups the government thought were important enough to be counted in the census of 1991.[1] Of course, Britain has for many centuries been both multi-ethnic and multi-cultural; only recently has it become multi-racial, in the sense that only in the second half of the twentieth century have groups, who are perceived to be different from the existing settled population by the colour of their skin, settled in Britain permanently and in significant numbers.

The time is now right for such a work. The Census of 1991 provided the basis for the construction of a much more detailed picture of the history, character and demographic importance of contemporary Asian and black communities, and their immigration and settlement. Not only is the population that derives from this immigration of increasing importance both in terms of its number and its influence in British society, but the issues and challenges raised by its permanent presence – such as those about discrimination and racism, equal opportunities and positive action, cultural identity and pluralism – are of increasing importance in the lives of all residents of the British Isles. In the recent past, government papers on the critically important Commonwealth Immigrants Act of 1962 have been opened up under the thirty-year rule, making it more rewarding for historians to engage in the debate about the origins and causes of the transformation of Britain. Incorporating material gathered from official papers and insights gleaned from the copious materials published for an academic readership, this book attempts to contribute towards an understanding of the making and application of the British government's immigration policy as it affected Asian and black immigrants and settlers in the twentieth century. Of course, government policy alone did not make multi-racial Britain. In fact the growth of a substantial minority – which was distinct, by virtue of various combinations of physical appearance, culture and religion, from the majority of the population – was quite contrary to the aims of British policy throughout the twentieth century. In so far as multi-racial Britain was an outcome of British policy, it was an unintended one. Yet with the benefit of data from the Census of 1991 and from a perspective of the late 1990s it is clear that governmental actions and behaviour have done much to give shape to Asian and black communities, as an examination of, for example, the peculiar and particular age distribution profiles of different communities will confirm.[2]

The book is based on the proposition that the essential elements of the history of Asian and black immigration into Britain are fourfold:

- it was a migration, or rather a series of migrations, whose origins are to be found in the period just before, during and just after the Second World War and whose key stages of growth were contained in the ten years either side of the 1962 Commonwealth Immigrants Act
- it was a migration which the British government did not welcome at any stage, but which it was both unwilling and then unable to prevent
- it was not one migration but a series of broadly related migrations of culturally distinct and diverse communities from widely scattered parts of the Commonwealth and Empire which started and ended at different times over the latter half century, and
- it was a migration neither of recruits nor of an underclass but of people from a range of social and educational backgrounds who displayed considerable initiative, self-confidence and courage in financing their endeavour and then overcoming the obstacles placed in their path by an unwelcoming government and society.

The migration has provided Britain with a set of communities with qualifications at least equal to, and aspirations considerably greater than, those of the indigenous population. The communities contain a vast diversity of language, culture and religion. Their only common attributes are that they differ in outward appearance from the 'white' native population and experience the discrimination which is systematically directed at physically and culturally distinct newcomers. Only the first two of these propositions is examined in any detail here, this book being part of a larger, continuing project.

This book is not intended to be a comprehensive study of the making of multi-racial Britain. Many important aspects of the subject are not dealt with here and many valuable perspectives – not least those of the immigrants themselves – are largely excluded. As a study of the making and implementation of immigration policy it offers revisions which challenge some of the orthodoxies, both old and new, about the history of Asian and black Britain. It begins to suggest alternatives to established beliefs and assumptions about the reasons for – and character and chronology of – Asian and black immigration, and the policy and attitude of the British state towards it. Its chronological focus is the Commonwealth Immigrants Act of 1962 which, it is argued, was of considerable importance in both making – and then providing a basis for limiting the growth of – multi-racial Britain. The importance of the 1962 Act justifies the detailed study of the origins and background to the Act found in Chapter 4.

But there is a practical reason for the chronological bias of the book, which is no less important. Serious historical study can only proceed on the basis of reasonable access to a range of sources and, in a work that concentrates on official attitudes and policies, that means official sources. In the central chapters I have relied heavily on government papers released under the thirty-year rule by the Cabinet, the Dominions, Colonial and Home Offices and the Ministries of Transport and Labour. The tardy release of official papers makes it difficult to pursue the story much beyond the early years of the 1960s. Chapter 5, which covers the period 1962–91, depends very heavily on other writers' published work. Though it may not be either obvious or welcome to them, my greatest debts are owed to Roger Ballard, Nicholas Deakin, Zig Layton-Henry and Tariq Modood.

As the difficulties related to the choice and inclusion of a Census question indicate, the selection and use of terminology referring to race, colour and ethnicity is sensitive, difficult and subject to fashion. Generally, I have avoided using the term 'race' or 'racially'. Races do not exist and persistent use of the term as a category supports the contrary impression. This book is about the immigration of groups from the Indian sub-continent, the Caribbean and Africa, groups who were thought to be 'a problem' because of the colour of their skin. Until well into the 1960s, these communities were usually referred to as 'coloured', but by the mid-1970s the term 'black' was being widely used as the collective term for all non-white communities. In turn, 'black' has given way to 'black and Asian'. 'Black' is widely rejected as a descriptive term by most people whose origins lay in the Indian sub-continent but is broadly accepted, if sometimes only in a hyphenated form, by people whose origins are Caribbean and African. It is in the latter sense that it is used here. 'Coloured' is employed in inverted commas where the text refers to official perceptions during a period when this construction was widely employed.

'Asian', though less than satisfactory, is widely used in contemporary discussions to denote the Indian, Pakistani and Bangladeshi derived communities. Of the possible alternatives 'South Asian' is accurate but is widely understood only by academics and Americans, 'Indian' is plainly unacceptable to people of Pakistani and Bangladeshi origin and 'Indian sub-continental' is too clumsy. 'Asian' is likely to be the least misunderstood as well as the least offensive. My adoption of the collective term 'Asian and black' recognises the large and increasing numerical superiority of communities from the Indian sub-continent.[3]

1 The origins of multi-racial Britain

A TWENTIETH-CENTURY STORY

The black soldiers who comprised a small part of the Roman armies that invaded Britain, the African slaves who were not freed by Mansfield's much misunderstood judgment of 1772 and the Asian and black seamen who lived in multi-racial dockland communities are evidence of a long-standing element of racial diversity in Britain. London, for three centuries the metropolitan centre of a vast worldwide Empire and successor Commonwealth, was host to countless visitors and residents from it. The idea that Britain has for long been a multi-racial society is one that has been widely aired and is now widely believed, fostered principally by liberally minded people associated with spreading and reinforcing the multi-culturalist approach to education and race relations.[1] In their campaign for the acceptance of the highly laudable idea that Britain is a multi-racial and multi-cultural society which should recognise and respect the cultures of minority ethnic communities, the 'discovery' of the 'hidden' history of the Asian and black presence in Britain provided a heritage and even a legitimacy for contemporary settlement. The long history of the Asian and black presence in Britain then made even more inexcusable the racist response that greeted Asian and black settlement in the latter half of the twentieth century.

Historians had already taken up the challenge of providing an account of the past against which contemporary movements and issues could be discussed. In their effort to supply historical background for the post-war Asian and black presence in Britain many writers asserted or implied that Britain had always been a multi-racial society. In recent years the works of Folarin Shyllon, Rosina Visram, Peter Fryer and Ron Ramdin, for example, have done much to illuminate the early history of Asian and black people in Britain but, perhaps unwittingly more than deliberately, have left the impression that those communities were more important historically than they were.[2] Residents of late eighteenth-century England would surely have been rendered speechless with incredulity by the recent claim of a historian that, by 1772 – considered by many to have been the apogee of black society – Britain had 'ceased to be a white man's country'. At that time blacks were, perhaps, a fraction more than one in a thousand of the population.[3]

It is clear from even a cursory glance at Britain's past that it has become a multi-racial society only very recently. Whilst prejudice has, no doubt, tended to suppress the history of Asian and black Britain, another important part of the explanation for the fact that it has remained hidden is that, until the last thirty or forty years, the size of the Asian and black communities has remained very small, their location scattered and their influence slight. Over the three centuries down to the Second World War the Asian and black population fluctuated in size, probably reaching a more sizeable proportion of the population as a whole in the latter half of the eighteenth century before declining. Contemporary guesses then – at the size of a population notoriously difficult to estimate – put the largely slave-related black population of Britain at anything between 10,000 and 40,000 and London's black population most often at 20,000. Recent research indicates that the size and composition of Britain's black population was quite volatile but that a figure upwards of 10,000 for the late eighteenth and early nineteenth century is most likely to be accurate.[4] After the abolition of the slave trade in 1807 very few black people were brought to Britain and inter-marriage by the largely male black population appears to have been the cause of its visible decline. By the outbreak of the First World War the size of the permanently settled black population had fallen to 'several thousands'.[5]

It is certainly the case that Asian and black residents played an interesting and occasionally important part in British society through the centuries. Much has been made of exceptional individuals of the nineteenth century – such as William Cuffay, the Chartist leader, Samuel Coleridge-Taylor, the composer and conductor, and Mary Seacole, the nurse – but it would be an exaggeration to say that collectively their part in British life was of any great significance. The most eminent Indians in public life were the four Indian members of Parliament, Dadabhai Naoroji (1892–5), Mancherjee Bhownagree (1895–1905) and Shapurji Saklatvala (1922–3 and 1924–9) in the Commons and Baron Sinha of Raipur (1919–28) in the Lords. Abdul Karim, Queen Victoria's moonshee, was not without influence in the last years of the nineteenth century. However, better known to a much wider public were Ranjitsinhji, Duleepsinhji and the two Nawabs of Pataudi who collectively brightened many an English summer. For the period up to the Second World War the Indian population of Britain has been characterised as one comprising ayahs, lascars and princes; additional categories might be added for students and pedlars.[6] However, for the very large majority of members of these groups, permanent settlement in Britain was never in view. Princes, after spending the hottest months of an Indian summer at the Savoy or the Dorchester – or students, after three or four years of the rigours of the London School of Economics or the privileged enclaves of Oxbridge – would almost always return to India.

The main concentrations of Asian and black settlement were to be found in the multi-ethnic dockland areas of seaports such as London, Liverpool, Cardiff, South Shields and Glasgow. The community in London's dockland appears to have sixteenth-century origins. Though substantial foundations for most of the communities were laid in the latter half of the nineteenth century, when they began to take on the appearance of permanency, many of their members remained transients, living in Britain between seagoing jobs. The development of the steamship, the emergence of the 'tramp steamer' and the huge expansion of Britain's overseas trade supported a very large and rapid increase in maritime employment opportunities to which seamen from the Empire had access, even if it was largely on the bottom rungs of the new ladder. Largely as a consequence of the First World War and the economic conditions that followed it, increasing numbers looked for jobs ashore and formed permanent relationships with local women.

People who derive from the Indian sub-continent, Africa and the Caribbean were, until very recent times, a tiny fragment of the permanent, settled population of Britain – a fraction of one per cent of the whole – until the changes in migration and settlement patterns in the 1950s. For an era when the census did not identify race or ethnicity, it is very difficult to assess accurately the size of minority communities of any kind. The problems of estimation are made more complex by definitional difficulties relating to the identification of race and ethnicity and to the nature of permanence. As recently as 1939 the permanent Asian and black population of the United Kingdom was officially estimated at about 7,000 people.[7] Even allowing for a large degree of inaccuracy in an estimate based on police reports, it would be stretching the definition of 'multi-racial' to absurd limits to apply it to Britain at a time when its Asian and black population was so small and so concentrated, and largely temporary. In the early 1950s half of Britain's population had never even met a black person. Until the mid-1950s the large majority of cities in Britain remained almost entirely white, as did most parts of the few major cities in which Asian and black settlement was a feature. In the leafier suburbs of London in the late 1950s, non-white people were still such a curiosity that it was not unusual for them to be stopped by local people curious to know about their background.[8]

Without denying in any way the presence in Britain of small, isolated Asian and black communities of very long standing, care must be taken not to place the inception of multi-racial Britain too far back in time. The appearance in most major towns and cities Britain of permanently settled, substantial minorities – clearly distinguishable by appearance, traditions and customs and practice from the very large majority of the population – is a development of the very recent past, of the late 1950s and succeeding decades. If the sharp decline in Asian and black movements into Britain that occurred at the end of the 1950s had not been reversed, or if legislation had been introduced at that chronological point effectively to prevent further significant inward movement, Britain would not have become a multi-racial society. At the start of the 1960s, the Asian and black population of Britain still represented only about 0.25 per cent of the whole. By the time the Commonwealth Immigrants Bill became law in 1962 that population had doubled and was set to increase further. If there was a watershed in the growth of Asian and black communities in Britain it occurred in those years immediately before and after the Act. Before it the size of the Asian and black population was tiny and its presence was regarded by many, some of the minorities included, as temporary. After the 1962 Act the communities continued to grow rapidly and quickly began to regard themselves and be regarded by others as a permanent part of British life. By the late 1960s, for the first time in British history, non-white communities of a significant size had established themselves in many of the major cities of the north and Midlands, a basis on which, over the next two decades, these communities were to make themselves into major players in local politics and economies and become a manifest influence on the formation of national culture.

However, any study of the making of multi-racial Britain must give some attention to the origins and early history of Asian and black Britain, particularly in so far as early settlements were to a limited extent significant in providing the foundations for the major migrations of recent decades. Pioneer settlers from Jullundur/Hoshiapur, Sylhet and Mirpur first established themselves, even if not on a permanent basis, in the period 1850–1939. Also, for the purposes of this study it is important to examine the policy of the British government towards those small numbers of Asian and black migrants and settlers. Before the substantial inward movement of the post-Second World War period began, official policy displayed a clear hostility towards the settlement in Britain of non-white communities of any significant size. Whilst it can be said with the highest degree of certainty that Britain became multi-racial against the wishes of successive governments, it can only be hypothesised that multi-racial Britain might have been created rather earlier without such consistent opposition to the formation of Asian and black communities. Perhaps this hostility provides part of the explanation of why Britain, at the centre of a vast multi-racial Empire within which there was apparently free movement, did not become a multi-racial society sooner.

THE FIRST SETTLED COMMUNITIES, 1850–1939

No doubt sailors of a wide range of ethnic origins have been a feature of many major British ports for centuries. Cardiff, Liverpool and London, with long-standing connections to the Caribbean, West Africa and India, had already, by the middle of the nineteenth century, acquired a diverse multi-racial population with deep roots. Although seamen from the Indian sub-continent had been recruited since the seventeenth century, it was the large-scale expansion of the British shipping industry in the latter half of the nineteenth century that brought much enlarged communities of mainly transient seamen from Africa, the Indian sub-continent, China, the Middle East, the Caribbean and Malaya to British ports. Lascars, krus and seedees, as sailors from India, West Africa and the Middle East were popularly known, were employed mainly in roles which required no skills of seamanship – firemen and coal trimmers, cooks and stewards – though lascars were often employed as deck ratings, and seedees very seldom as cooks and stewards. The requirements of the imperial myth of white supremacy combined with racial stereotyping to ensure that, whereas the engine room could contain all races, the officers' mess was a white-only preserve.[9]

It is perhaps worth asking what controls there were on lascars settling in Britain and why lascars did not figure more prominently among settled dockland communities before the Second World War. During the Napoleonic Wars, when the number of lascars coming to Britain increased substantially – on occasion over a thousand were housed in the barracks set aside for them – a Parliamentary Committee of Inquiry was set up to examine their plight. It recommended both better conditions for the men but also stricter regulation of them while ashore and tighter controls to ensure that they returned to the sub-continent. The 1823 Merchant Shipping Act which resulted from the inquiry made it compulsory for shipowners to provide customs authorities with a list of their 'Asiatic' sailors. The Act made owners liable to a fine if Asiatic sailors were left in port and it made the East India Company responsible for their repatriation, a charge which it could in turn levy on the shipping company. Recruited in India since 1855, on contracts which required the employer to repatriate the sailor to the original port of embarkation in India (usually Bombay or Calcutta), lascars were often required by their company to change vessels in British ports. From 1871 the Board of Trade appointed to each major port in Britain a 'Lascar Transfer Officer' (a function of the office of the Superintendent of Mercantile Marine), a post created and maintained largely in order to oversee this transfer and to prevent 'leakage' of lascars into permanent or semi-permanent residence. From 1858 the India Office paid the Strangers' Home (a charitable institution which offered cheap shelter to Asiatic and African sailors) £200 a year to maintain lascars prior to them finding a vessel on which to return to India. Though as a group among seamen the lascars appear to have been uniquely well supervised, the vagaries of war and an abundance of employment opportunities led to lascars taking up jobs ashore on Merseyside and Clydeside in the last years of the First World War. It has been suggested that Indian sailors stranded in Glasgow at the end of the war and unable to find employment on east-bound liners were forced to look for work in the local iron and steel industry. Attempts by the shipping companies through the local Mercantile Marine Offices to secure the return of the lascars to sea were neither immediately nor entirely successful.[10]

Until almost a decade after the end of the Second World War the most substantial part of the settled Asian and black population of Britain was still occupationally related to the sea.[11] Although its growth was stimulated significantly by the two world wars, the settled dockland communities remained very small. In Liverpool the combined size of the black and Chinese populations in the inter-war years was considerably less than one thousand. Cardiff's minority population was much larger and more ethnically diverse, possibly due to the attractiveness of its clement climate but much more likely because Cardiff was a centre of the tramp trade and a seaman with his home base there was likely to get more regular employment. In 1930 the total 'coloured' population of Cardiff, including those at sea and those ashore, was just over two and a half thousand, three-fifths of whom were Arabs or Somalis. Its African and Afro-Caribbean population was in the region of seven hundred, with the largest number of Africans coming from Sierra Leone whilst Barbados and Trinidad were the best represented of the Caribbean territories. Many of the settled seamen were married or in permanent relationships with local women and by the outbreak of the Second World War several hundred children resulting from those unions had swollen the size of the community.[12] Overall, in the dockland settlements before the Second World War, the largest of the Asian and black communities was Arabic-speaking, often referred to as 'Adenese' or 'Somali' and deriving mostly from Yemen or, to a much lesser degree, from the Aden Protectorate and Somaliland. When 'coloured' seamen were forced to register as 'aliens' in 1925 almost 7,500 were recorded, though this did not represent an accurate count of all Asian and black seamen, at sea and ashore, operating from British ports.[13]

Even though for most of the community, foundations were laid and first built upon during the period of rapid development of modern shipping from the mid-nineteenth century, the most dramatic period of growth took place during and immediately after the First World War. The war gave a considerable boost to the Asian and black population of Britain. The impetus was provided by the recruitment of large numbers of merchant mariners of European origin to the expanded Royal Navy, the requisitioning of many ships with black crews for Government work (their discarded crews being left behind in British ports) and the formation of labour battalions abroad for wartime service in Britain and who were subsequently 'demobbed' (demobilised) in Britain. Men were brought from the colonies to work in munitions and chemical factories in Manchester and elsewhere. It appears that at the end of the war, with the closing down of wartime industries, many men found themselves in – or they made for – seaports such as Cardiff where there were, temporarily as it transpired, some employment opportunities. Taking into account both men at sea and people ashore it is unlikely that there was a great change in the total size of the Asian and black dockland communities in the period between the wars. However, the size of the communities actually ashore almost certainly grew quite significantly, primarily as a consequence of the very high rate of unemployment that persisted in the dockland areas after the initial, and very brief, post-war boom. This was caused by the long term depression in the British shipping industry, a shift from coal-fired to oil-fired power (which disproportionately affected Asian and black seamen) and discrimination against 'coloured' seamen by both employers and unions.[14] Numbers were boosted from the 1920s by the arrival of small numbers of men, mostly from Punjab, who intended to make a living in Britain. Some of them were soldiers who had served in Europe in the First World War, others were relations and friends of seamen who had knowledge of conditions in Britain.

Research in Scotland has provided an account of the early phases of settlement of a mainly seamen-derived Asian community in Glasgow that may be taken as broadly representative of developments in many other major seaports. Long waits between engagements and some desertions created the basis for the permanent South Asian population in the middle decades of the nineteenth century. Several boarding houses established towards the end of the century provided the first discernible focal point for the largely transient community and probably attracted a small number of men who had been brought over from India as servants and had subsequently left service. Asian and black seamen were numerous enough by 1919 to attract the violent attention of rioting Scottish seamen. Unable to find work in Glasgow, a few drifted away to seek employment in the coal mines, and iron and steel plants, of Lanarkshire. In the 1920s a new phase of permanence began with the arrival from India of small numbers of men (not seamen themselves but usually related or known to seamen) looking for economic opportunities in Britain, now that prospects in Australia, Canada and the USA had been closed down. Indians – Arraein Muslims from Nakodar (Jullundur District) and Jagraon (Ludhiana District) in Punjab – first appeared on the Glasgow Valuation Rolls in the mid-1920s, quickly followed by Sikhs from the same area. Men from Faisalabad District – a canal colony area in which families from Jagraon had settled, following the large-scale development of irrigation – joined in later. Some arrived as one-trip seamen and most, after arrival, tried to make their living as pedlars. By the end of the 1920s the permanent Indian population of Glasgow was about a hundred and tiny communities had been seeded in Edinburgh and Dundee. Within a decade the pedlar population of Scotland had grown to about 300 and was beginning to attract the attention of the government. Nor was it only seaports that began to develop small, largely pedlar communities of Indian sub-continental origin in the inter-war years. Birmingham, for example, was home to about one hundred pedlars the first of whom took up residence in 1931.[15]

GOVERNMENT POLICY AND THE GROWTH OF COMMUNITIES, 1919–39

During the years between the two world wars, government applied a *de facto* immigration policy which was specifically directed at limiting the growth in numbers of 'coloured' seamen, whose communities had already become established in a number of UK ports. The policies of these years were limited in their application, but in several ways they were the clear predecessors of those developed after the Second World War. Officials admitted privately that their intention was to limit the number of 'coloured' people settling permanently in Britain, yet neither before nor after the war, indeed not until 1962, was policy the outcome of publicly debated legislation. The policies were implemented without any public announcement through administrative measures, by government circulars, by intergovernmental arrangements or by confidential letters from the Home Office to Chief Constables. At the same time the imperial rhetoric of 'equal rights for all British subjects' and *civis Britannicus sum* was maintained. The policies of the inter-war years constituted an undeclared immigration policy whose clear intention was to keep out Asian and black settlers.

The most frequently repeated justification – and probably the most important reason – for these policies was fear of a repetition of the serious outbreaks of inter-racial violence that had occurred in 1919: in Glasgow in January, in South Shields in January and February, in London in April, and in Liverpool, Cardiff, Barry and Newport in June. These disturbances were not the first examples of collective racial violence in Britain. There had been clashes in the 1870s, and in 1911 Cardiff's Chinese community had been attacked. But taken collectively, the disturbances of 1919 were far more serious than any previous episode.[16] They resulted in five deaths and many serious injuries, the cordoning-off of areas in which the communities lived and many hundreds of people being taken into protective custody. The most serious outbreak occurred in Cardiff where the largest Asian and black community lived. Whatever the cause of the disturbances – and clearly the wartime disruption of the economy; the strains imposed by rapid demobilisation; competition for jobs, housing and women; and the impact of, and response to, discriminatory practices all played a part – they were not unique to the first half of 1919.[17] Tensions affecting dockland areas were sharpened by the continuing decline of the British merchant shipping industry in the inter-war years: in a stagnant world market, it continued to shrink and with it the jobs that had drawn the Asian and black population to the ports. Shipping companies facing a difficult market tried to cut costs by recruiting firemen and stokers in colonial ports; such employees did not have to be paid at the National Maritime Board rates that applied to sailors, whatever their colour, hired in British ports. Asian and black sailors in British ports faced the resentment of their white colleagues who identified them as less expensive competition for what they regarded as their jobs.

The disturbances of 1919, allied to evidence of continuing high levels of 'coloured' unemployment, together with assumptions about the propensity of dockside populations to become involved in crime and violence, predisposed the local and national authorities in their approach to dockland communities to place a strong emphasis on the need to establish control. That the riots were largely the consequence of white attacks on multi-racial dockland communities was not a matter of importance to the authorities. Their analysis was straightforward and functional: if the Asian and black dockland communities had not existed the riots would not have occurred. Remove or restrict the size of the multi-racial communities and the likelihood of further disturbances would be removed or at least restrained. The newspapers at the time of the rioting expressed much enthusiasm for segregation and repatriation.[18]

Repatriation was one of the government's preferred solutions but it foundered on the resistance of its intended victims and the unwillingness of any of the relevant ministries to take financial responsibility for the process. Government lacked the legal powers to coerce seamen, and the India Office and Colonial Office were both sensitive to the possible political repercussions of pressing the question too hard. In 1919 local committees were formed to encourage the movement, and the Ministry of Labour agreed to pay volunteers a £5 resettlement grant. In most areas very few came forward, though from Cardiff 500 Adenese seamen were eventually repatriated out of a total of probably 600.[19] There were campaigns in 1920 and 1921 and the effort was renewed with the onset of the Great Depression when competition for jobs, and therefore the prospect of disorder, increased significantly. To some degree there were official attempts to withhold financial assistance and social support in order to encourage return. Cardiff, as one of the few centres willing to provide poor relief, saw its unemployed 'coloured' population grow during the Depression. When central government was approached for assistance by local relief authorities it offered assistance for repatriation.[20] Overall, repatriation was a failure.

The 1905 Aliens Act (almost always so called, but more correctly the Aliens Order), inspired by the arrival of large numbers of mainly Jewish migrants from eastern Europe, was the first legislation designed to limit entry to the United Kingdom. The anxieties of the war led to the Aliens Restriction Act of 1914 which was extended into peacetime by the Aliens Act of 1919. In 1920, by the Aliens Order, the government tightened up the supervision of aliens living in Britain and further restricted the settlement of alien immigrants who were unable to provide proof that they could support themselves.[21] Apparently, none of these provisions applied to British subjects. However, under the Aliens Order of 1920 coloured seamen could be refused permission to land by immigration officers unless they could prove that they were British subjects, that they had signed on for a round trip in a UK port or that they were permanently resident in Britain. Evidently, the Home Office was responding to the agitation of the seamen and to fears that adding to the number of unemployed 'coloured' seamen in British ports would encourage a repetition of the disturbances of 1919.[22] The expectation of further racial conflict, should the 'coloured' population of docklands continue to grow, almost certainly played its part in the decision of autumn 1920 to refuse permission to land to 'Arab seamen' who arrived as passengers without proof of British nationality. Initially the bar was intended to apply to Arabs from the Protectorate of Aden, who technically may not have been British subjects – definitions were not universally agreed – but it was steadily extended to cover all 'coloured' seamen who could not prove their nationality.[23]

The Order was, however, quite ineffective in controlling further inward movement, particularly of Arabic speaking sailors. The continuation of very high unemployment levels induced the unions, allied to various local authorities responsible for welfare and for law and order, to press for further restrictions. The Special Restriction (Coloured Alien Seamen) Order of 1925 brought all sailors under the provisions of the Order of 1920 and was applied to all coloured seamen irrespective of their citizenship and nationality. Under the Order the police were empowered to arrest an alien without a warrant. Those subject to the Order were obliged to register with the police and to obtain and carry an alien seaman registration certificate (in effect, an identity card). The onus of proof of identity was placed on the sailor. The continuous discharge book containing a record of previous voyages was the record that most sailors carried; but such books – together with certificates issued by British consuls or ships' masters, birth certificates or passports issued more than two years ago – were all declared to be unacceptable as evidence of British identity. In effect, the 'coloured' seaman, in order to avoid being obliged to obtain an alien seaman registration certificate, had to be already in possession of a recently issued passport. Very few were so equipped. The Order was applied to all coloured seamen, initially in thirteen major ports but extended in 1926 to all ports, with the result that it became virtually impossible to be 'coloured' and British at the same time. It was even applied (in Glasgow) to sixty-three pedlars. Many 'coloured' seamen (and pedlars) were British subjects yet almost all were forced to register as aliens and to report regularly to the police.[24]

There were some important exceptions. Many of the West African seamen in Britain had arrived on ships belonging to Elder Dempster, a Liverpool-based company which held a virtual monopoly of shipping freight and mail between Britain and West Africa from before the First World War until the 1930s. They arranged with the Home Office a separate registration system for West Africans serving on their ships, the specific objectives of which were to prevent Elder Dempster seamen moving into other employment, to limit claims for unemployment insurance and to allow the immigration authorities in Liverpool more secure control over West African sailors. The arrangement provided a mechanism of co-operation between the company and the immigration officials which enabled the latter to prevent the settlement of the 'work-shy and troublesome' and thereby reduce the number of Africans living ashore. The Home Office was of the view that: 'Their presence in the United Kingdom is socially very undesirable and gives rise to "trouble". The police are very anxious to get rid of all except a handful who have acquired permanent domicile.'[25]

For the purposes of this study, the effect of the 1925 Order on intending settlers from the Caribbean, Africa or Asia was even more significant. The right to register applied only to those who were resident or at sea in April 1925. 'Coloured' persons arriving after April 1925, if they were British, would be very unlikely to be able to prove that they were; if they were not British – or could not prove that they were – they would be refused registration, unless they were properly signed on from a British port and, could therefore establish the right to land. In effect, the government had designed an immigration control with the force of law that sharply restricted the right of entry for settlement to the United Kingdom of Asian and black British subjects.[26] Neither the police nor the unions were entirely happy that the scheme was being enforced rigorously enough and they continued to press for a tightening up. In 1930 these efforts, their effects deepened by the impact of the Great Depression, led to further disturbances in Cardiff and South Shields.[27] The effect of the application of the order was felt very gravely after the passage of the British Shipping (Assistance) Act of 1935 under which subsidies could only be claimed by companies employing substantially British crews. 'Coloured' seamen, most of whom were now unable to prove their British nationality, were excluded from employment by shipowners who wanted to enjoy the government subsidy. Of the 690 unemployed firemen on the Cardiff Docks Register in June 1936, 87 per cent were 'coloured'.[28] There was a major rush to apply for naturalisation papers (despite the £9 charge) and a concerted and partly successful campaign by an alliance of groups representing 'coloured' seamen to change the subsidy arrangements.

In the inter-war years the government developed another method of keeping out British subjects they did not want, which was of greater long-term significance than the Aliens Order. The British government caused various of its overseas agencies to restrict the issue of travel documents, and in particular to refuse to issue them to certain classes of persons that it wished to keep out. The 'problem' of an influx of immigrants from the Indian sub-continent was apparently first detected in the mid-1930s when the Home Office noted that the police were experiencing increasing difficulty in keeping track of Indian pedlars and seamen. Their response was, in the words of the Home Office, 'to take steps to restrict, as far as may be possible, the grant of passport facilities'.[29] The result was an agreement which was to last until well into the post-independence era and one that the British government attempted to develop and tighten as the number of those from the sub-continent seeking to settle in the United Kingdom rose slowly in the late 1950s. From the mid-1930s, the Government of India – which then administered what is now Pakistan and Bangladesh as well as India – agreed to refer to London for comment all applications for passports to visit the United Kingdom that were received from illiterate or unskilled Indian subjects. To be successful, the applicant was required to obtain a sponsor in Britain who could provide guarantees of maintenance and repatriation. The reliability of the sponsor and the availability of reputable and permanent local employment were checked by the police in the United Kingdom. The final decision, however, rested with the government of the sub-continent. As a Home Office official put it in the 1930s, the object of these long-standing arrangements was from our point of view to control the entry into the United Kingdom of Indians and Pakistanis who may tend to become pedlars or to resort to undesirable methods of earning their living'.[30] In a parallel move in 1935 the Aden authorities were instructed to refuse to issue seamen with Certificates of Nationality and Identity which would have enabled them to travel to the United Kingdom in search of work. Exceptions were to be made for those who had very recently either been resident in Britain or had worked on British ships. The limitations were to apply to both British subjects and British protected persons.[31]

The parlous state of the shipping industry through most of the inter-war years, the discrimination and poor treatment meted out to 'coloured' seamen and the implementation of what was, in effect, an immigration policy that restricted entry of Asian and black people to Britain all provide an explanation for the slow growth of Asian and black Britain following the acceleration associated with the First World War. The public identification of communities which suffered extremely high levels of unemployment, together with poverty and dependence on government assistance, was hardly surprising and their stigmatisation by association with 'moral' problems was not far behind.[32] In 1939 the economic position of the Asian and black dockland communities was still very weak: in Liverpool, for example, three-quarters of the families of white seamen benefited from earnings compared to 40 per cent of black seamen's families.[33] However, by 1939 the demand for sailors had begun to increase and the Second World War was, to a considerable extent, to see a replication of the conditions of the first. Suddenly, Asian and black British subjects were needed again for the purposes of imperial defence in time of war. War service or even temporary residence to help with the war effort was acceptable, even welcomed. Permanent residence was another matter; the official mind was always hostile to the settlement of people of colour in Britain. This was entirely at one with the attitudes of the post-war era of the so-called 'open door' immigration policy.

THE SECOND WORLD WAR

During the Second World War the Asian and black diaspora spread from the seaports to the industrial towns of the Midlands and the north, and

temporarily to the air bases of the south and east and even to the forests of
Scotland. The Second World War itself was a period of particular
significance in forming the specific ethnic and cultural character of the
multi-racial Britain that developed in the second half of the twentieth
century. Of the major ethnic and cultural groups that now comprise the
overwhelming majority of contemporary Asian and black Britain – Indian
(Punjabi and Gujerati), Bangladeshi, Pakistani, West Indian, West African
and Chinese – four experienced a key stage in their modern development
in Britain during the Second World War. Those groups – Sylhettis from
Bengal, Muslims from north-west India, West Indians and West Africans –
now comprise about half of the Asian and black population of Britain.[34]
As we have seen, the origins of each of the groups, as well as those of the
Sikhs from Punjab, can be traced to earlier periods but the Second World
War experience was critical in converting their presence in the United
Kingdom from one that was very small-scale, largely transitory and
essentially peripheral, to a more substantial and permanent position. As a
result of the increase in their size during the Second World War and an
increasing propensity to settle permanently in the post-war years, West
Africans became the largest of the Asian and black groups in Britain until
overtaken by the surge in immigration from the Caribbean in the mid-
1950s.[35] Sikh and Muslim pedlars were a not uncommon sight in Britain in
the 1930s and their growing presence, even if not a permanent one, had
caused the British government to introduce controls over the issue of
passports.

Two of the groups whose roots in Britain were greatly strengthened
during the Second World War – Muslim lascars from Punjab and Kashmir
in the west and those from Sylhet in the east – had been recruited for many
decades to crew vessels sailing from Bombay and Calcutta. Protective
Government of India latitude restrictions and employer/union agreements
generally prevented the engagement of lascars on routes from Britain other
than those to and from Indian ports. As we have seen in the case of
Glasgow, there is evidence of small numbers of Indian sailors settling
permanently in Britain before the Second World War. Several Sylhetti
homes had been established in East London by the 1920s and they
apparently acted as a focus for visits from Indian sailors docked in
London. The first Sylhetti restaurant in London dates from 1938
(*Veeraswamy's* and *Shafi's* were both started in the 1920s though not by
Sylhettis) but by 1946 there were twenty in the capital.[36]

In the inter-war years few sailors from Africa, Asia or the Caribbean
allowed their vessels to sail from British ports without them. Employment
opportunities were limited, mainly to the clothing trade and large hotels, in
the boiler-rooms or as kitchen porters. The sparseness of employment

opportunities – and opposition from employers and unions to the employment of 'coloureds' when white workers were available – explains why so many of those seamen who decided to stay appear to have tried their hand as pedlars. Yet enough did so to persuade the government to instruct Chief Constables to examine applications from lascars and 'other coloured seamen' with special strictness and slowness to discourage desertion from the articles under which lascars were employed and the irregular landing of coloured seamen.[37] In peacetime, shipping companies had less difficulty enforcing lascar articles but war changed all of this. During the Second World War numbers of settling lascars again grew to a level significant enough to cause considerable concern both to local Chief Constables and to the Home Office. The underlying reasons for the increase in lascar settlement were that in June 1939 the Government of India relaxed its latitude restrictions on the employment of Indian sailors and that, as a result of the peculiar conditions created by the war, far more lascars were employed in the British merchant marine and, therefore, far more lascars crewed vessels called at British ports. During the war Indian sailors were viewed as replacements for the large number of merchant mariners recruited into the greatly enlarged wartime Royal Navy. Their numbers almost doubled between 1939 and 1943. A significant number of lascars were subsequently stranded by the loss of their vessels to enemy naval and aircraft actions. Many Indian-crewed vessels were torpedoed off the British coast and others were bombed while in harbour. Ample labour opportunities were also available during the war years, in munitions and other factories, and many of these stranded sailors elected to take those opportunities to earn money in what must have seemed a safer setting. The Indian population of many industrial towns rose significantly during the war years.[38]

Certain changes in the administration of entry rules may also have affected the numbers finding work in Britain during the war. In 1942 the Colonial Office, for long critical of the employment of the 'colour bar' in the application to 'coloured' seamen of the 1925 Special Restriction (Coloured Alien Seamen) Order, made strong representations to the Home Office. As we have seen, under this regulation of the 1914 Aliens Registration Act, any 'coloured' seaman who could not produce documentary evidence of his national identity could be, and apparently often was, either registered as an alien or refused entry. Revised instructions were issued to immigration officers to use their discretion in favour of the claimant to British or British protected status, even if they had no documentary proof of identity. Despite this change the Immigration Branch of the Home Office remained hostile to the idea of unrestricted entry for all classes of British subject.[39] Indeed, the major thrust of the discussion about courses of action to be taken in response to the increased numbers of sailors who were settling in the United Kingdom was exclusively towards trying to discover ways of limiting the numbers of those who could settle and of reducing the number of those who were already in Britain. Midlands towns, particularly Coventry and Birmingham, appear to have been the most popular areas of settlement; 800–900 were already residing in these two cities by the middle of 1943, a sufficient number for their Chief Constables to refer to the sailors as 'a problem'.[40]

A wide range of possible measures to deal with the 'deserters' was examined. From January 1943 no seaman was entitled to a National Registration Identity Card. This card enabled the holder to receive coupons for rationed items. In Coventry the local Registration Office refused to issue identity cards to Indians on the grounds that they were all seamen. An addition to the Defence Regulations that would allow the police to 'collect the deserters in batches and ship them back to India' was briefly contemplated. Scotland Yard had apparently prepared for such an eventuality by keeping a central register of all deserting seamen. A senior policeman argued that despite all the extra work such an action would entail, the police were 'very willing' to take on the task 'since it would relieve them of a burden in the long run'.[41] Recourse to the courts was also considered, but there were major difficulties in proving desertion as it was necessary to produce a copy of the ship's Articles and to bring the sailor to court before the expiry of his agreement.[42]

There is little doubt that the sailors who settled in ports and moved inland during the war provided the basis for the post-war development of the Bangladeshi and Pakistani communities in Britain. As they developed in the 1950s and 1960s, Bangladeshi and Pakistani communities often owed their origins to a tiny number of early pioneers. So strong was the process of chain migration that a population of several thousand could be derived from a very small number of kinship groups related to perhaps only a handful of villages. The original migrant would invariably have been financed by a group of close kin and when successful that migrant would have used his savings to help one of his close relatives to join him. They would soon be in a position to sponsor other members of their kinship group whom they would also help with jobs and accommodation on arrival. A study of the 2,000-strong Pakistani community in Oxford reveals that almost all the migrants there can be accounted for by just two chains, one of which began with a man who had settled in Glasgow during the Second World War.[43]

Many of the sailors may have returned to sea at the end of the war, particularly if their employment in war-related industries ceased after the end of hostilities. However, it is likely that a substantial proportion of these men came back to Britain following the partition of the Indian Empire in 1947. The partition had an extremely damaging effect on both communities by locating their place of residence and the port in which they gained employment in different countries. Sylhet became part of East Pakistan while Calcutta became part of India; the families of Muslim sailors recruited in eastern Punjab fled to the new state of Pakistan and Mirpur formed part of Pakistani-ruled Azad Kashmir while Bombay was sited securely in India. The income and remittances of the Sylhetti and Muslim Punjabi sailors, upon which their families no doubt depended, were threatened once new employment laws which restricted employment opportunities to nationals of the new states could be made to work. Sailors from both Muslim districts had to seek new sources of earnings. Wartime experience in Britain provided a certain guide.[44]

Whereas Sylhettis and Mirpuris took advantage of wartime opportunities to settle in Britain, West Indians were – with some imperial reluctance and after considerable delays – directly recruited in substantial numbers for wartime work in Britain. It is difficult to estimate with accuracy the number of people of Caribbean origin recruited for service in Britain. The history of particular groups has been researched, but no study has been made of the Caribbean contribution to the war effort in the United Kingdom as a whole.[45] One thousand technicians and trainees were recruited for service in war factories on Merseyside and in Lancashire, 1,200 British Hondurans as foresters in Scotland and an unspecified but smaller number for the merchant marine. In one scheme 200 trainees were recruited from seven different territories in 1941 for work in munitions factories. They were contracted to work for the duration of the war and, after three to five months at a government training centre in the United Kingdom, were paid at the same rates as British workers, though with an additional expatriation allowance (£1 per week) paid to their families in the Caribbean.[46] The number recruited for military service, mainly to the RAF, was 1,350 from British Guiana, 10,270 from Jamaica, 800 from Trinidad and smaller numbers, probably not exceeding 1,000 in all, from other Caribbean islands.[47] The interdepartmental Overseas Manpower Committee considered the possibility of organising the very large number of unskilled volunteers who were apparently available from the Caribbean for service in Britain but concluded that the costs and risks of transatlantic travel were too high. One vessel carrying Caribbean volunteers had already been sunk off Bermuda and US troops were beginning to embark in large numbers for European service.[48]

There is much evidence to suggest that although most of those who worked in Britain during the war were encouraged to return to the Caribbean, their wartime experience was crucial in forming their determination to settle in Britain after the war. Only a third of the 1,000 civilian recruits agreed to accept the government's repatriation terms; most of the rest stayed on in Britain. Just over half of the Honduran foresters accepted repatriation; most of the rest settled down in Scotland and the north of England. Despite an apparent determination that no 'appreciable number' of West Indian servicemen should receive their discharge in the United Kingdom, of the 10,000 or so Jamaican servicemen only about two-thirds were demobbed in Jamaica. Many of those who arrived on the first boats bringing immigrants from the Caribbean to the United Kingdom after the war were ex-servicemen and volunteers who had worked in Britain during the war. For example, the SS *Almanzora* which left Jamaica in late 1947 carried ninety former members of the RAF and ex-munition factory workers; and about two-thirds of the settlers who arrived on the *Empire Windrush* in June 1948 had already seen service in Britain during the war. As the war grew more distant the proportion of immigrants who were veterans of the war declined. On the MV *Georgic* which arrived in June 1949 only twenty-six of the 163 male Jamaican immigrants were in this category. James Griffiths, the Colonial Secretary, reckoned in 1950 that of the 2,000 or so immigrant workers who had arrived from the West Indies 'a large number' had served in the RAF during the war and were using their gratuities to pay the cost of the passage to the United Kingdom.[49] The returnees formed the core of those coming to Britain in the post-war decades.

The demobilisation of Caribbean servicemen was half completed when news of the employment of Polish and Italian workers in post-war Britain reached the Caribbean. Ex-servicemen from several territories were active in petitioning their governments to make employment opportunities available for them. Those governments in turn pressed London, quite unsuccessfully, to use Empire rather than European sources to satisfy its labour needs.[50] To add to the pressure, the resettlement of servicemen was not going well. The Resettlement Department in Jamaica, which had by far the largest task relating to the reintegration of servicemen, was operating in an unsatisfactory manner; aspects of its work were described as 'deplorable'. Most returnees faced almost certain unemployment. A senior Colonial Office official, J.L. Keith, was dispatched to the Caribbean in July 1947 to discuss the linked problems of the resettlement of ex-servicemen, unemployment, and what appeared to be an impending flood of immigration to the United Kingdom.[51]

Welcome though their help may have been in wartime, there was evidently no place for skilled West Indian workers as residents of peacetime Britain. As Chapter 2 will show, there is plenty of evidence, from an examination of the treatment of Caribbean technicians and trainees recruited in Jamaica and Barbados to work in factories in the north-west of England during the war, to suggest that officials were keen to prevent their permanent settlement in Britain. That was so at a time when the British economy was desperately short of skilled and semi-skilled labour and was about to begin to encourage large numbers of European volunteer workers to come to Britain. Wartime experiences, predominantly Jamaican ones, provided the foundation for the gradual growth of Asian and black Britain in the post-war decade. By comparison, the Mirpuri and Bangladeshi communities grew very slowly, perhaps owing to the difficulty of obtaining travel documents and the expense of the journey measured by earning power both in Britain and in South Asia. In the early stages of their growth both of these South Asian communities were virtually all-male and neither appeared set on permanent settlement. But the wartime pioneers were the basis on which, through the importance of kin and the process of chain migration, the communities were eventually to establish themselves permanently in Britain. Britain's minorities are not a representative cross-section of the population of the Empire/Common-wealth or even of those territories from which movement to Britain occurred. They derive from particular small parts of a limited number of countries. The explanation for this is to be found partly in the experience of war. For communities from the Indian sub-continent the combined experiences of war and partition expanded opportunities and provided motivation for specific communities; the strength and importance of kinship ties did the rest.

The set of the official mind was always opposed to the permanent settlement in Britain of Asian and black communities. That the Asian and black population of Britain failed to grow significantly between the wars was, in part, the result of depressed economic conditions but was due also, in no small measure, to the various administrative measures applied by both the British and Indian governments. Taken together they comprised an undeclared immigration policy aimed at restricting non-white settlement. During the two world wars their contribution to the war effort was welcomed. After the First World War the enthusiasm for repatriation and the application of orders to restrict permanent settlement in Britain to 'coloured' seamen who were British are evidence that wartime contributions were considered insufficient to modify the official determination to prevent the development of Asian and black communities in Britain. After the Second World War a similar pattern was repeated. Repatriation was again favoured, and a battery of administrative measures were applied, this time in a period of full employment when labour was being sucked in from Ireland and Europe at a rapid rate. As we shall see, during the lengthy and frequent discussions between 1948 and 1961 at Cabinet, ministerial and official level about how (not whether) to limit Asian and black settlement in Britain there was not a single echo of the wartime origins of the movement, or recognition of the extent to which the origins of 'the problem' lay in Asian and black responses to Britain's wartime needs.[52] At the end of the Second World War Britain was not, and never had been by any reasonable definition of the term, a multi-racial society. That it became so within a generation of the end of the Second World War owes a great deal to developments that occurred during the two wars but nothing to official approval or encouragement.

2   Immigration policy in practice, 1945–55

THE MYTH OF *CIVIS BRITANNICUS SUM*

In Chapters 3 and 4 the political debate about the need for controls on the entry of 'coloured' British subjects to the United Kingdom is examined. Whilst that debate continued the British government consistently applied a policy that sought by a wide range of different means to keep down the number of Asian and black British subjects who were able to enter and settle in Britain. These policies were pursued through a period of economic recovery and expansion when the British economy sustained full employment, in an era of net emigration when the size of the 20–44 year old population was reckoned to be falling by 100,000 a year and at a time when immigration from Ireland was running at far higher levels than immigration from the Asian and black Empire (or later Commonwealth). Throughout this period the British government continued to subsidise emigration schemes to the 'white' dominions.[1] This chapter examines British immigration policy in practice, the methods it developed and employed, and the attitudes and assumptions that underlay the hostile approach to Asian and black immigration.

To all outward appearances, during this first post-war decade, British subjects from all parts of the Empire/Commonwealth remained free to enter the United Kingdom as and when they pleased. However, in practice, rather than in theory, British immigration policy operated in a way that was intended to make it difficult for Asian and black British subjects to settle in the United Kingdom. The British government throughout this period adhered to a racially discriminatory immigration policy. It is clear that restrictions on the movement into Britain of people from the Indian sub-continent, Africa and the Caribbean were a reflection of widespread underlying assumptions about the general undesirability of the settlement of physically and culturally distinct groups. In this respect there is a clear continuity of policy between the inter-war and post-war periods. During the first post-war decade informal and generally invisible methods of regulation almost certainly had a significant impact on levels of immigration and settlement. Debates at the official level and policy in operation reveal much about the discriminatory nature of British immigration policy.[2]

Over the decade 1945–55 there were a number of key changes in the relationship between Britain and the Empire/Commonwealth which, in theory, made the control of immigration from within that Empire/Commonwealth more problematical for the United Kingdom. The most important was the shift towards self-determination of territories whose policies towards the migration of their populations had previously been under firm control from London. In this respect the Indian sub-continent moved swiftly to partition and independence in 1947 and the Caribbean territories, including the islands of Jamaica, Barbados and Trinidad, gained a substantial degree of autonomy. London should have found it increasingly difficult to control the movement of populations within the Empire/Commonwealth by the use of administrative arrangements that required the co-operation of other governments. Independent and self-governing territories obviously began to make decisions which affected migration according to their own – rather than London's – interests. In theory, for example, passports would become more freely available if issued in India and Pakistan by the newly independent governments; their issue was now outside London's control. Nonetheless, the British government persisted in seeking – and succeeded in finding – a variety of ways to hinder the movement of British subjects from the Caribbean, the Indian sub-continent and Africa to the United Kingdom, including the maintenance of arrangements which had their origin in pre-war colonial days. Their degree of success was limited. Eventually after extensive, and for a time successful, efforts to revive informal, administrative controls the Commonwealth Immigrants Act of 1962 was introduced to provide a legal framework which would enable the British government to restrict the settlement of 'coloured' colonial and Indian sub-continental British subjects for itself.

One of the cherished illusions of apologists for the Empire/Commonwealth was that all British citizens – irrespective of their place of residence, colour or religion – enjoyed full and unimpeded rights to enter and settle in the United Kingdom. Foreigners, on the other hand, were subject to the restrictions stemming originally from the Aliens Act of 1905. British politicians and civil servants, and most writers on Commonwealth affairs, continued throughout the 1940s and 1950s to boast that Britain alone of the white countries of the Empire/Commonwealth managed to hold out against discriminatory practices and maintain freedom of entry to the United Kingdom for all British subjects, irrespective of race. A classic, if tear-stained, statement of the official position was made by Henry Hopkinson, the Minister of State at the Colonial Office, in a House of Commons debate in 1954:

> As the law stands, any British subject from the colonies is free to enter this country at any time as long as he can produce satisfactory evidence of his British status. This is not something we want to tamper with lightly. . . . We still take pride in the fact that a man can say *civis Britannicus sum* whatever his colour may be and we take pride in the fact that he wants and can come to the mother country.[3]

The ideals of the emerging Commonwealth, with its new members drawn from the newly independent colonies of Asia and Africa, emphasised the equality of all, irrespective of colour or religion. Yet, as the first chapter has illustrated, it is clear that Britain, well before the beginning of the Second World War, had already begun to adopt practices that were intended to limit severely the right of entry and settlement in the United Kingdom of British subjects who were not themselves emigrants from Britain to the Empire/ Commonwealth or the descendants of those emigrants – that is, to exclude those who were generally non-white and who were often not English-speaking.[4] With the collusion of some of the emerging and newly independent governments of the Empire/Commonwealth after the war Britain continued to try to constrain the entry to Britain for settlement of non-white British subjects resident in those countries. In theory, all British subjects were free to enter the United Kingdom for any legal purpose, including settlement. In practice, some subjects found this right much more difficult and expensive to exercise than others.

THE ISSUE AND ENDORSEMENT OF TRAVEL DOCUMENTS

The most effective and, for officials and politicians, the most popular measures that were used to restrain 'coloured' settlement were applied in the countries of origin of the prospective migrants. The proud boast that a British subject, no matter what his or her background, could freely enter Britain could remain technically true if it was the ability of the prospective migrant to leave the country of origin that was adversely affected. As we have seen in Chapter 1, it is clear that controls on the issue of passports and other administrative devices were widely used in the inter-war years to deter colonial subjects from embarking on emigration plans.

Cyprus provided a testing-ground for a set of practices that were widely applied in the Indian sub-continent. Oakley's study of Cypriot migration to the United Kingdom in the inter-war years reveals a clear pattern of British obstructionism.[5] The first response to the perception of Cypriot settlement in the United Kingdom as a problem in the 1930s was to introduce the requirement that Cypriots leaving the island should enter into a security bond indemnifying the government of Cyprus against costs it might incur on behalf of the migrant, including repatriation expenses. Pressure from London to convert this bond into a £50 cash deposit was resisted by the colonial authorities. As a result of further pressure from London, from 1935 intending migrants 'of the poorer classes' were required to produce an affidavit of support, a document which contained a promise from a person resident in Britain that they would support the migrant until they had found work. Migrants from Cyprus were supposed to have their passports endorsed in Cyprus for settlement in Britain. How effective these measures were in restraining the flow of movement from Cyprus to Britain is difficult to say. It is clear that the obstacles were evaded or overcome by, for example, intending migrants making an initial journey to Greece. Although it was not widely known among intending migrants in Cyprus, the administrative requirements lacked the legal force to prevent entry to the United Kingdom. A port official in the United Kingdom could not prohibit the entry of travellers from Cyprus who were able to identify themselves to the satisfaction of port officials.

Broadly similar administrative arrangements were made from the 1930s with colonial and post-colonial governments in India and Pakistan and with colonial governments in post-war West Africa to restrict the flow of settlers to the United Kingdom. In precisely the same way only the 'poorer classes' were the target of the measures, the requirement of passport endorsement was used to limit emigration and the edifice of measures rested on the assumed and continuing ignorance of the potential immigrant of just what the British immigration authorities would require. They involved deception by omission: the intending emigrant was clearly not informed of his right of free entry to the United Kingdom. It was entirely legal in the colonial context to require a British subject leaving a territory to possess a valid passport properly endorsed, but to employ the control of passport issue and endorsement to regulate the exit only of certain classes and ethnic groups who wished to go to Britain stretched to breaking point the claim that all British subjects had the right to enter the United Kingdom freely. The restrictions applied differentially: they were applied only to the poorer classes from the Asian and black Empire/Common-wealth and then only by the colonial and Commonwealth governments that were prepared to co-operate. In a technical sense Britain kept its hands clean; it did not discriminate at the point of entry. Some of its colonial authorities and its Commonwealth allies discriminated at its suggestion and on its behalf at the point of departure.

Because of their nature it is difficult to say with any precision what effect these administrative methods might have had on the flow of immigrants to Britain. Though clearly other factors were also involved, it may not be entirely without significance that the areas of the Empire/ Commonwealth in which they were applied by co-operative governments were areas from which migration, having started during and after the war, did not develop with any speed. In West Africa migration slowed following an initial post-war spurt when the governments began to require persons, applying for passports to come to the United Kingdom, to provide deposits and sureties to cover the cost of repatriation. The experience of Jamaica, whose governments refused to apply the constraints, may be compared with those of India and Pakistan, whose governments co-operated with London.[6] From both areas contacts had been established and developed during the Second World War that laid the basis for potential migration in the post-war period. In India and Pakistan there is some evidence that these arrangements may well have been of considerable importance in keeping down the number of people travelling from those countries to Britain for settlement until well into the late 1950s.[7] The best evidence for their effectiveness probably comes from the concerted, immediately successful (though eventually unavailing) effort in the late 1950s to assert firm control over movement from India and Pakistan.[8]

In both Pakistan and India after 1947 intending emigrants could, in theory, apply for a passport either to the British High Commission or to their own government passport offices. Applications for passports made to the British High Commissions in the sub-continent were, in practice, generally accepted only from people who were white. Successful applicants were almost always either citizens of the Irish Republic, Europeans naturalised in India or persons accepted for registration under Section 12 (6) of the British Nationality Act of 1948. This section of the Act referred to people who were direct descendants of those born or naturalised in the United Kingdom, who intended to reside in the United Kingdom and who had close associations with the United Kingdom or colonies. In theory and in law, British passports could be issued to all British subjects, but in practice this power was used 'sparingly'. British passports were not issued to persons who already possessed an Indian passport; those possessing a British Indian passport could not exchange it for a British subject passport on renewal 'unless there was some very good reason for doing so'. In practice, Indian passport applicants to the British High Commissions in the sub-continent were either refused or were referred to the British government; white British applicants were issued a British passport.[9]

Anglo-Indians and Anglo-Pakistanis, who claimed descent from an ancestor born in the United Kingdom (as well as ancestors born in the sub-continent) – and who in quite considerable numbers sought entry into the United Kingdom in the years immediately following independence – were generally refused British passports. In the first years after independence it is clear that sympathetic officials at the High Commissions in India and Pakistan assisted the passage to Britain of small numbers of members of these communities by the issue of travel documents and by the use of small sums of money at the disposal of the High Commissioners. A small resettlement scheme was even contemplated. However, by 1950 it is clear that officials in the High Commissions of the sub-continent were refusing Anglo-Indian and Anglo-Pakistani applications for passports unless the applicant was able to produce documentary proof of direct descent from an ancestor born in the United Kingdom. In the large majority of cases no such proof could be provided. In 1954, 'in view of Ministers' concern about the influx of coloured persons into this country, many of whom, including Anglo-Indians, were likely to become dependent upon National Assistance', the High Commissions were directed 'to tighten up the qualifications for the grant of assistance and to severely reduce the funds available for this purpose' even though the Anglo-Indians and Anglo-Pakistanis 'may be technically our fellow citizens.'[10] London told its men in the field that it would be reluctant to see any approach to the Pakistani or Indian authorities about the lifting of restrictions on passports to British subjects in these categories 'however harshly it might bear on individuals'.

Finally, any consideration of an officially sponsored resettlement scheme was to be given up.[11] As an official in the Commonwealth Relations Office, who was clearly a master of understatement, put it to a colleague stationed in New Delhi: 'We are not, as you will appreciate, anxious to go out of our way to assist Anglo-Indians and Anglo-Pakistanis to come to this country'.[12] Officials were totally unsympathetic to the plight of Anglo-Indians and Anglo-Pakistanis whose privileged position under the Raj in, for example, the railway and postal services, was coming under pressure and who were, therefore, looking for alternative sources of employment. Officials did not think that they would be useful in Britain and hence:

> We should not be displeased to see Anglo-Indians experiencing difficulty in obtaining travel documents to emigrate from India – which is of a piece with our wish to see the Government of India (and the Government of Pakistan) maintain or even strengthen their procedure for granting passports to people who wish to settle here.[13]

After independence in 1947 the governments of India or Pakistan were neither of them quick to set up their own passport offices; priorities lay elsewhere. From the start, both of the newly independent governments accepted the need to impose a financial guarantee or repatriation bond on anyone applying for a passport for the purpose of going to the United Kingdom. In the case of Pakistan the deposit was introduced at 1,100 rupees which increased by stages to Rs.2,500 by 1958. The Indian Government agreed that if an Indian passport was to be issued for travel to the United Kingdom and colonies it should be endorsed by the Indian passport authorities only after they were satisfied that the applicant had sufficient funds to support a reasonable standard of life in Britain. In practice the High Commission referred cases in which there was a doubt to the Home Office for a police report. In 1952, 545 such cases were referred and 294 (or 54 per cent) of the reports that were returned to India were unfavourable.[14] A Commonwealth Relations Office official recorded as late as 1954 his satisfaction with 'the restrictions imposed by the Pakistanis on the issue of Pakistani passports which . . . operates to the advantage of the United Kingdom in keeping down the number of undesirable Pakistanis who come to this country'.[15] He noted that the British government was still pressing West African and West Indian governments to introduce similar restrictions.

This method of control was not without its very considerable difficulties. One major problem for the authorities was the forgery of passports or of endorsements on legal passports by travel agents in India and in Singapore. The practice of the forgery of endorsements was drawn to the attention of the Indian authorities who undertook to reorganise the procedures to make evasion of control more difficult. The restrictions on the issue of passports created not only a cottage industry for the forgery of endorsements but stimulated the production of forged passports on a quite large scale. By its very nature the scale of the trade is impossible to estimate accurately. It has been estimated that 70 per cent of the 17,300 Indians entering Britain between 1955 and 1957 did so on invalid documents. Of course, the restrictions, and therefore the apparent need for forged documents, meant additional costs for the migrant, imposing either a less direct and more costly journey to Britain and/or quite substantial payments to an intermediary and to the forger. This certainly had the effect of considerably limiting the number who could afford to migrate.[16]

There were other loopholes which made it difficult to control entry to Britain from India and Pakistan by the endorsement method of controlling exit from those countries. Underlying the problem facing the authorities were the two central facts that immigration officers in Britain had no power to prevent entry to people who could provide reasonable proof that they were British subjects and the total insistence that the appearance of non-discriminatory practice by British authorities, as between British subjects, be maintained. The first loophole opened up when Indians and

Pakistanis discovered that if they travelled first from the Indian sub-continent to a second country, they could then proceed without hindrance to the United Kingdom. For the purpose of entry to Britain the British traveller was not required even to possess a valid British or Common-wealth passport, let alone one that was properly endorsed by the Indian or Pakistani government. The effectiveness of the endorsement procedure rested essentially on the ignorance of the prospective immigrant as to what was required on arrival in the United Kingdom. But people who made a living organising immigrant movements from the sub-continent to the United Kingdom were certainly aware that, though the Indian and Pakistani authorities might well refuse to endorse a passport for the United Kingdom, and at the departure airport refuse permission to embark to anyone whose passport was not properly endorsed, they were less scrupulous about approving travel to, for example, the Holy Places for the Hadj or Indonesia or Thailand. From those second countries prospective immigrants could embark for the United Kingdom without fear of difficulties at either the airport of departure or arrival.

It might be worth digressing briefly to speculate upon, and then illustrate the possible impact of these practices on the intending migrant. In effect it put many immigrants from India and Pakistan at the mercy of organisers or travel agents who had the knowledge to circumvent the restrictions in a perfectly legal manner. If he did not already appreciate the futility of applying for permission to go to Britain, an intending emigrant who did not possess money and/or qualifications would almost certainly be rebuffed by the passport office. An entrepreneur who knew the rules about departure from India and Pakistan and entry to the United Kingdom could, and no doubt did, exploit the knowledge to his advantage and the emigrants' cost. Though it fits just outside the time-span of this chapter, the particularly interesting account that follows is of a journey by an organised party of immigrants from Pakistan and illustrates the impact of the passport issuing and endorsement policy. There is little doubt that their journey had many parallels in the post-war decade.

The intending emigrant, a Punjabi Muslim from Rawalpindi District, having made known his desire to travel to Britain, was approached in early August 1957 by an agent who charged him Rs.5,500 (£300) for a guaranteed passage. After a three-week wait in Karachi with eventually twenty-two other migrants, he received a 'pilgrimage passport' valid for travel to the Holy Places made out in a bogus name. He then embarked on a small steamship for a week's journey to Basra. The first task on arrival was to go to Lloyds Bank where each received £40 worth of dinars which was at once handed over to one of the agents who had arrived by air before the party. After staying in a hotel in Basra for four days the group travelled by train to Baghdad where they were again lodged in a hotel, this time for a further six weeks. In Baghdad the pilgrimage passports were deliberately lost – left in a taxi by one of the accompanying agents – and replaced by international passports issued by the local High Commission for Pakistan. From Baghdad the party moved on to Syria and then, after two more weeks, to Lebanon, eventually arriving in London by Air India from Beirut in mid-November, the journey having taken a total of three and a half months. The migrant arrived with £2 in his pocket and was accompanied to Birmingham and later to Bradford by one of the agents. As additional precaution against official harassment an endorsement for the United Kingdom was forged into the immigrant's passport, probably in Syria, and he was provided in Karachi with a false declaration from a Commissioner of Oaths in Birmingham to the effect that he was required to come to Britain to work as an assistant salesman for a non-existent Midlands firm. The agents clearly did not know the rules of entry either and put their clients through an incredibly lengthy and almost totally unnecessary ordeal.[17]

The position for any of the millions of British subjects of Indian or Pakistani origin, living in British colonies and who might wish to travel to Britain, was very similar to those from the sub-continent. They had to go through the same process as in India or Pakistan to obtain an endorsement. Alternatively, under Section 6 (1) of the British Nationality Act, any British subject was entitled, after twelve months' residence in a colony, to apply for a British passport. The request for endorsements and passports by Indians and Pakistanis in the colonies caused embarrassment to colonial authorities who were clearly expected to act on behalf of the Governments of India and Pakistan. In other words, British officials were being asked to treat British subjects of different ethnic origins in different ways. Perhaps the embarrassment, and the potential for damaging revelation, was present in equal proportion. As one Home Office official put it, concerning a case that had arisen in Singapore (a Malayan Air Force officer of Punjabi origin had applied to come to the United Kingdom):

> All British subjects are free to enter this country as and when they wish. Unless the authorities in Singapore control the issue of UK and colonies passports to *all* citizens of the UK and colonies resident there, it would seem to be undesirable to attempt to restrict the movement of a particular class of UK and colonies citizen, attractive though the idea might be.[18]

It was acceptable for Indian and Pakistani officials to discriminate on behalf of the British government, but it was unacceptable for British officials, even those stationed in the colonies, to do so.

The frustration this caused to Commonwealth Relations Office officials, bent on keeping the number of Indians and Pakistanis entering Britain to a minimum, was almost audible in their memos and despatches. A case that attracted some official attention was that of Asa Singh who travelled to Kenya on an Indian passport and, after twelve months in the colony, applied for a British passport:

> If the Kenyan authorities eventually agree to the endorsement of the passport for the UK, I do not see how we can prevent this person from joining his illiterate brethren in the UK. . . . As persons from the Punjab think nothing of waiting two years before they can obtain a passport and scrape enough money to travel to the UK, it seems to me they will not hesitate to follow Asa Singh's example, solely to avoid the difficulties which they know exist in obtaining Indian passports.[19]

The solution lay either in persuading the Indian government to limit the issue of passports to their citizens who wished to travel to British colonies or in pressing colonial governments to be more strict about registering for residence people whose intention it was to move on to the United Kingdom. Neither was considered to be a practical course of action.

As immigration officials in Britain did not require an official passport, to facilitate entry to the United Kingdom the British High Commissions could also issue British subjects with a temporary travel document called the Emergency Travel Certificate which was valid for 12 months. It appears that up to 1954 they did so in small numbers mainly to British subjects who were white and born in India or Pakistan but who had been refused passports by the Indian or Pakistan authorities. The Commonwealth Relations Office became extremely concerned lest these facilities be granted to British subjects who were not white. On discovering that Emergency Travel Certificates might have been issued to 'persons of non-European race' in Karachi, strong disquiet was expressed:

> Thus it appears that while we are pressing Colonial Governments in West Africa and the West Indies to impose restrictions on the flow of coloured people to this country, in Pakistan we are doing our best to counteract the Pakistan Government's restrictions on this flow.[20]

Policy on the issue of Emergency Travel Certificates was swift to change. Within a couple of months the High Commissions in New Delhi and Karachi had been instructed 'in view of the present considerable feeling in some sections of the public and among ministers about the number of British subjects not of European race who are at present finding their way into this country' to refrain from issuing emergency documents to persons who were not of 'pure European race' and who were not citizens of the United Kingdom and colonies, for the purpose of proceeding to the United

Kingdom for permanent settlement. This would apply even if the applicant 'may be technically our fellow citizen'. Documents would be issued only if the High Commission was satisfied that the applicant had either sufficient means to support himself and his family, reasonably assured prospects of employment which would enable him to do that, or a near relative in the United Kingdom who was willing to support the applicant and his family indefinitely. Cases of doubt were to be referred to London.[21]

With the arrival of the first post-war immigrant parties from Jamaica in 1947–8 the question of immigration from the Caribbean to Britain became an issue for the British government. Officials considered whether arrangements similar to those operating with the Indian sub-continent could be made with relevant colonial governments. In 1950 the Colonial Office asked colonial governments to consider whether it would be possible to control the issue of passports to those 'whose financial position was not sound' and to those who were not in regular employment. The response varied from those colonial governments which were prepared to go along with the British government's suggestion to those governments, like that of Jamaica, which were most reluctant to impose any limitations at all on the issue of passports. The Jamaican colonial government took the view that it should follow the pattern set by the UK government – which specified that only fugitives from justice and lunatics were disqualified from holding passports – and refused London's request to turn down applicants who patently did not have the means to support themselves in Britain. The Governor of Jamaica was faced with very considerable problems of domestic unemployment and displayed some regard for the rights of his British subjects, many of whom had contributed to the recent war effort. The Government of Trinidad, not a significant source of migration, was more accommodating but it only undertook to delay the issue of passports until proof of passage could be produced. West African governments, however, concurred.[22] It is clear that the Colonial Office exercised its muscles in an attempt to achieve the co-operation of colonial governments. Attempts to persuade governments, many of which were enjoying the newly increased powers of elected assemblies, to use those powers in ways damaging to the colony's own economic and political interests were, in the longer term, bound to be unsuccessful.

> The view of the Colonial Office is that they have gone far enough in pressing Colonial governments to restrict the issue of passports and that with the present tendency to give more power to unofficial majorities in Colonial governments it may be difficult to maintain even present restrictions.[23]

PUBLICITY AND PASSAGES

Unable to persuade the Caribbean governments to restrict the issue of passports, the British government looked to other means at its disposal, often accompanied by the use of unequivocal language, to persuade the island governments to limit the access of their subjects to the United Kingdom for settlement. Much of this work was done by publicising the difficulties facing potential migrants to Britain. An official film was made for distribution in the Caribbean showing the very worst aspects of life in Britain in deep mid-winter. Immigrants were portrayed as likely to be without work and comfortable accommodation against a background of weather that must have been filmed during the appallingly cold winter of 1947–8. The Colonial Office, for example, sent Caribbean governments copies of figures of unemployed colonials in the United Kingdom, figures expressly collected for the purpose of dissuading further entry.[24] In the aftermath of the arrival of the *Empire Windrush*, Creech Jones tried to assure his Cabinet colleagues that he had done all he could to prevent 'these influxes':

> Not only has the position about employment and accommodation in the United Kingdom been explained by me to the Governors in correspondence but a senior officer of my Department visited Jamaica and certain of the other West Indian Islands last year and made great efforts to explain the difficulties at this end and to discourage people from coming over to this country on the chance of finding work. There was ample publicity in the Jamaican press of the difficulties men might meet if they came to England. Before the party of 417 left Jamaica they were warned by the Jamaican Government about the difficulties which would beset them on their arrival in this country.[25]

In 1950 the Secretary of State for the Colonies, alarmed by the arrival of the first charter flight carrying unsponsored immigrants from Jamaica, expressed his 'serious concern' to the Governor of Jamaica. He requested that a notice entitled 'Warning to intending migrants from Jamaica to the United Kingdom' be distributed as widely as possible in the colony. In a bid to deter intending emigrants to the United Kingdom it described conditions of poverty and misery and warned that both accommodation and jobs were difficult to find. It set down three 'absolute essentials for success in the United Kingdom': possession of proper qualifications to do work which was in demand; possession of enough money to live on until employment could be found; and a definite offer of accommodation in the area of intended settlement.[26] There is even some indication in the public record that the British Government attempted to restrict movement from the Caribbean by denying cheap sea passages to Jamaicans who wished to come to Britain to work. In 1948 the Jamaican shipping agent for the *Reina del Pacifico* had apparently been ordered by Head Office in London to decline to accept reservations for the one hundred available third-class berths from men seeking employment or from women wishing to meet relatives in the United Kingdom. The Governor of Jamaica was moved to administer a plainly worded rebuke to his political masters in London: 'The whole question of denial of passages in cases of British subjects is fraught with difficulty and from Jamaica's point of view cannot be supported'. Seeking to avoid local political difficulties, he suggested that the Colonial Office issue a statement explaining their action. They denied ordering the shipping company to refuse or restrict the sale of passages.[27] There were other ways to skin a cat. In these early years colonial immigrants from the Caribbean often arrived on troop transports which, otherwise returning empty to the United Kingdom, were able to offer low fares. In May 1950 the Director of Sea Transport decided that fare-paying civilians would not, in future, be allowed to travel in the troop deck of troop transports except for properly organised and controlled government parties, of which there were none. In future, immigrants from the Caribbean would have to pay the full fare in an ordinary vessel.[28]

STOWAWAYS, ONE-WAY SAILORS AND UNEMPLOYED SEAMEN

The issue of how to prevent the settlement in Britain of 'coloured' arrivals who were British subjects exercised the minds of government ministers and officials when it became clear after the war that the 'coloured' population of Britain had been growing during the war years – and was continuing to grow in the immediate post-war years with the inflow of stowaways and 'one-trip' seamen mostly coming from West Africa and the Caribbean. Indeed, in the seven or eight years following the end of the war far more thought and effort was expended on the issues raised by stowaways and unemployed seamen than on the movement of immigrant fare-paying workers from the Caribbean. Though by its very nature such a source of migration was difficult to quantify, estimates put the number of British subject stowaways entering and staying in the country at 2,141 for the five-year period 1946–50 inclusive, about the same number as for immigrant workers from the Caribbean over the same period. The largest number of arrivals were Jamaicans in Bristol and London, and West Africans in Liverpool, London and Hull.[29]

During and immediately after the war seamen from West Africa, Jamaica, Aden, the Yemen and Somalia had arrived as one-trip seamen, often filling in vacancies on vessels caused by the exigencies of war. By this route, it was reckoned, several thousand 'coloured seamen' had settled in Britain in the early and mid-1940s. The movement continued after the end of the war. In the light of subsequent levels of migration the figures for the early post-war years were tiny; but in the context of the small scale of the 'coloured' population at the time, and against a background of a very slow rate of immigration in previous decades, the level was regarded as significant. But what appeared once again to invigorate policy was the link made in official minds between the growth of 'coloured' communities and the increasing possibility of public disturbances. The feeling was reinforced by inter-racial violence in Liverpool (31 July–2 August 1948), Deptford (18 July 1949) and Birmingham (6–8 August 1949), all of which incidents involved 'coloured' immigrants of maritime backgrounds.[30] From late 1947 the government set out in a more determined way to stop the growth and, if possible, reduce the numbers of 'coloured seamen' settled in British ports.

Where seamen and stowaways were concerned, government did not confine itself to measures to limit the number coming into Britain; for a while it once again took seriously the idea of repatriating unemployed seamen.[31] From late 1947 the Ministry of Labour and the Colonial Office became concerned with the number of unemployed seamen in all the large ports of which Liverpool, Cardiff and Manchester were the most affected. Local advisory committees, chaired by the Superintendent of the Mercantile Marine Office, were established on which the Establishment Administration, the Immigration Officer, the Colonial Office Seamen's Welfare Officer and the Union were represented. For those who had little hope of ever being employed at sea again, removal from the Seamen's Registers and registration for shore employment were recommended. Colonial Office Welfare Officers interviewed unemployed seamen in an attempt to persuade them to accept repatriation. Whilst many expressed an interest in the idea very few came forward when firm offers of transport were made.[32]

In 1949 through the regional offices of the Ministry of Labour, a survey (which became the first of very many) was conducted of the number of unemployed 'coloured' people, part of which was designed to determine how many were seamen registered for work at sea and how many had turned their attention to the land. The substantial levels of unemployment that the survey revealed (1,200 out of a total Asian and black population – including students – of between 20,000 and 30,000) were in significant part, as the government recognised, the result of overt discrimination against (mainly) African and Arab seamen. A more detailed survey of unemployed Somalis revealed that they had settled in Britain immediately after the war following service in either the Royal Navy, the Army or the merchant marine. After the end of the war the large majority found themselves, in the face of National Union of Seamen and Shipping Pool exclusion, quite unable to find seagoing employment. The number of unemployed Somali, Arab, West African and West Indian seamen was swelled by stowaways. Where they possessed technical qualifications these tended not to be recognised by the appropriate trade union. To increase their difficulties the largest concentrations of unemployed were found in areas like Liverpool, Stepney and Teesside where there was already a significant number of unskilled, white unemployed. As officials recognised, where employers had the choice, whites were generally employed first.

The results of the survey caused some despondency and, taken together with the violence that occurred in a labour hostel in Deptford in July 1949 (which involved West African stowaways and Poles) and a disturbance the following November at the Colonial Office itself brought about by demonstrating unemployed Somali seamen, it was decided to investigate the possibility of reducing the size of 'the problem' by encouraging repatriation. Somali seamen who faced severe discrimination and who were prepared to bring their troubles in person and in a vociferous manner to the very doors of the Colonial Office itself were a major target of the repatriation scheme. A great deal of official time and effort was expended on a scheme which appeared to achieve very limited results. Most considered for repatriation were between 20 and 25 years of age and had been resident in Britain for about two years. There had to be some good reason, such as mental or physical illness or instability of temperament, which would prevent them from working and from paying their own passage home. The National Assistance Board reported on the year September 1949 to August 1950 that only twenty colonials had actually been repatriated at a total cost of £800.[33] The two most significant barriers to the success of the scheme appear to have been the reluctance of the men to return home and the unwillingness of government departments, the National Assistance Board in particular, to use any significant sum of their own money to pay for the passages home.[34] The idea of repatriation, itself an echo of the policy of the inter-war years, was not revived as a serious proposition until 1959.

The government was determined to crack down on one-way seamen. In December 1949 Shipping Masters in the Dominions, Colonies, India and Ireland and all Consuls were reminded of the need to insert a repatriation clause in sailors' Articles of Agreement, to explain it fully and to emphasise the virtual impossibility of finding seagoing employment in the United Kingdom. Failure to include such a clause would contravene the

Ministry of Trade Circular 1810. The Shipping Federation made a similar approach to all registered shipowners. Another attempt to reduce the number of 'coloured people' seeking employment at British ports was the introduction in 1949 of the standard Seamen's Identity Certificate which was to be issued only to British and British protected subjects who were engaged in and had been accepted for sea-going employment. The measure was intended to exclude uncertified one-trip seamen from any prospect of gaining employment.[35]

Stowaways were more difficult to deal with. Under the existing legislation, the Merchant Shipping Act of 1894, a court had the power to fine a stowaway up to £20 or imprison with or without hard labour for up to four weeks. These were penalties unlikely to discourage the intending stowaway who, even if caught and fined, was at least £100 better off for having used this route. At the port of entry the stowaway would declare himself or be declared and, as long as he could prove his identity, could not be refused admission by an immigration officer. The British government showed that it was prepared to go to a great deal of expense and trouble to try to further limit the number of people entering Britain by this route. Colonial governments were instructed to tighten up access to ships visiting their ports and bound for Britain. In January 1950 the Colonial Office suggested to colonial governments a veritable battery of measures for application to harbours from which vessels sailed for Britain. They included controlling access to dock areas, registering dock workers, introducing gangway checks, licensing small boats and policing harbours. Shipping companies were also contacted and alerted to the problem. Through the Shipping Federation, companies and masters were reminded by 'strongly worded' circulars of the seriousness of the problem and of the need to take effective steps to prevent it. In 1949 the ship owners were asked to prosecute all stowaways, less for the deterrent effect than for the measure of control over stowaways that arrest and detention represented. At the request of the Ministry of Transport further 'even more strongly worded' circulars were issued in 1950 reminding masters of their ultimate responsibility for preventing embarkation. Approaches were also made to foreign governments whose reluctance to allow British vessels to unload their stowaways in their (intermediate) ports meant that stowaways, once boarded, were likely to end up in Britain. At a time when stowaways and one-trip seamen made up probably about half of all black and Asian immigrants coming into Britain these measures, taken together, were thought likely to have a significant effect on the level of entry.[36]

Immigration officials were ordered to tighten up the requirements for proof of identity and nationality for arrivals. Since 1942 it had been the practice of Immigration Officers to give the benefit of the doubt to persons claiming to be British or British-protected who arrived without a passport or other documentary evidence. After September 1949 even statutory affidavits and birth certificates were not acceptable unless supported by other evidence which established identity without doubt.[37] As the interpretation of what constituted acceptable evidence of identity was tightened so the number of 'colonial' stowaways refused entry increased. In the first nine months of 1950 a hundred were turned away. British Travel Certificates issued by West African governments primarily for local travel between British and French colonies were acceptable to immigration officers in Britain as proof of identity. In 1950 the Colonial Office requested the West African Council to accept certain changes in the Certificates designed to limit their use to travel between West African territories. In future they would omit all reference to the nationality of the holder and they would be valid only for travel to the countries specified in them.[38] These changes rendered them useless as proof of identity at a United Kingdom port of entry. Neither the Colonial Office nor the Commonwealth Relations Office was entirely happy with these changes but expressions of regret were limited to a comment by the Commonwealth Relations Office that it was 'anxious to preserve as far as possible the principle that all British subjects (Commonwealth citizens) are treated alike in this country'.[39] Further, the governments of the West African colonies agreed to refuse to issue Travel Certificates to those they suspected might use them as stowaways. All West African governments were asked to follow Nigeria's example in keeping a register of people who had been refused leave to enter the United Kingdom. No travel documents would be issued to people on those lists.[40]

The administrative arrangements and sets of instructions outlined here taken together comprised a consistent and clearly discriminatory set of practices specifically targeted at the restriction of Asian and black entry to the United Kingdom for the purposes of settlement. None of these measures affected white citizens of the Empire/Commonwealth whether they were Australian, Canadian or white British resident in India, Pakistan or the colonies. How effective they were is very difficult to assess, though it is perhaps worth noting how slow migration from India and Pakistan was to develop compared to that from the Caribbean. One of the significant differences between the two might well have been the refusal of the colonial government in Jamaica to countenance the type of restriction on the right to travel to the United Kingdom that the governments of Pakistan and India were prepared to enforce. It does seem likely that the restrictions had some effect. There is some convincing evidence from the late 1950s that when a vigorous attempt was made to restrict passport issue in both India and Pakistan, numbers of immigrants from those countries dropped appreciably. Officials in the Commonwealth Relations Office were certainly convinced of their effectiveness.[41] When the system broke down in 1959–60 the recourse to legislation was swift.

ASIAN AND BLACK LABOUR AND ECONOMIC RECOVERY, 1945–55

As this battery of obstructive practice reveals, the British government was keen to prevent entry to Britain of British subjects from the Indian sub-continent, the Caribbean and West Africa. It is difficult to see how the policies and attitudes illustrated here can be made consistent with the often repeated idea that the British Government was keen over the same period to attract members of this 'reserve army of labour' to the British economy.[42] After the war the economy suffered severe labour shortages; in 1946 a Cabinet Working Party estimated the shortage at between a million and a million and a half. The Cabinet established a Foreign Labour Committee with instructions to 'examine . . . the possibility of making increased use of foreign labour'. Indeed, in the late 1940s with emigration running at two and a half to three times the level of immigration and government sponsored programmes sucking in 180,000 European workers on various employment schemes between 1947 and 1949, there was good cause for the government to look towards the Empire/Commonwealth as a potential source of labour supply.[43] Not only, as we shall see, did the government consider and then reject the opportunity to import a 'reserve army of labour' from the Empire/Commonwealth, it also tried a variety of methods to restrict Asian and black entry to Britain and even attempted to reduce the small number who had managed to settle. Its first efforts were directed towards ensuring the departure of the relatively small number of skilled West Indians who had been directly recruited to the United Kingdom during the war to assist in key employment categories with the war effort.

There is evidence, from an examination of the treatment of Caribbean technicians and trainees recruited in Jamaica and Barbados to work in factories in the north-west of England during the war, that officials were keen to reduce rather than increase the sources of Empire/Commonwealth skilled labour in those immediate post-war years. Officials displayed a combination of determination and unseemly haste in attempting to secure passage back to the Caribbean for these men. Frustrated and delayed by the post-war shortage of shipping, by the reluctance of many of the West Indians to return home (a number of them had also married English women) and by the workers' insistence that promises about post-war training be kept, the Ministry of Labour nevertheless pursued the matter with great zeal. The pleas of some of the workers to be allowed to stay in Britain fell on unreceptive ears. Knowing that they were going home to face almost certain unemployment, in September 1945 sixty-five West Indian workers wrote to the Colonial Secretary asking to be considered for post-war work in Britain. But their fate was already settled. Noting the reluctance to return, an official had minuted in April that as they are British subjects 'we cannot force them to return' but it would be 'undesirable to encourage them to remain in this country. We should, therefore, take immediate advantage of every expression in favour of repatriation as the longer the men stay here, the less ready will they be to go.'[44] No suggestion appears at any stage that such a highly valued group of experienced and skilled workers should be encouraged to stay on and the Ministry of Labour succeeded in securing the repatriation of the majority by the middle of 1947.[45]

However, the Colonial Office took the view that because of the extensive use of European labour in post-war reconstruction, the government should look at the possibility of offering employment opportunities to British subjects from the Commonwealth/Empire. It had been pressed to do so by the Governors or Officers Administering in Barbados, British Guiana, Trinidad and Jamaica each of whom wrote to London in 1947 advertising the needs of their surplus, skilled and often ex-service labour. The demands of the Governors of Trinidad and Jamaica were provoked by – and they referred directly to – the use of labour imported from continental Europe in reconstruction in the United Kingdom. Huggins, the Jamaican Governor, even warned that publicity attempts to persuade Jamaicans that there was no work available in Britain would not be believed because of the wide publicity given in the island to the use of Polish and Italian labour.[46] In July 1947 A.B. Keith, the Head of the Welfare Department in the Colonial Office, was sent to the Caribbean to address issues raised by this correspondence. As well as discussing problems of unemployment in the West Indies and measures for the resettlement of ex-servicemen, Keith was to gauge the strength of the movement to the United Kingdom and to explain the difficulties of employment in Britain. Creech Jones expressed the hope that the visit did not give the impression that the intent was to arrange recruitment schemes. Nothing would have been further from the truth.[47]

In 1948, at the behest of the Colonial Office, an Interdepartmental Working Party on the employment in the United Kingdom of surplus colonial labour chaired by the Under-Secretary of State for the Colonies, was set up to enquire into the issues raised by the Caribbean authorities. The Treasury, the Foreign Office, the Home Office and the Ministries of Agriculture and Fisheries, Fuel and Power, Labour and National Service,

Health and National Insurance were all represented on it. Its first task was to determine whether there was a prima facie case for the use of colonial workers to assist reconstruction. The committee considered that there was no overall shortage of labour in the United Kingdom and that, of the sectors of the economy they discussed, only the health services experienced labour demands which could be satisfied from the colonies.[48] The minutes of the meetings contain a record of entirely negative attitudes to colonial labour. Doubts were expressed about the skills and endurance of West Indian workers, about the availability of 'suitable' accommodation and about the attitudes of workers and unions to the employment of colonial workers. One senior official at the Ministry of Labour expressed the view that the type of labour available from the empire was not suitable for use in Britain and that displaced persons from Europe were preferable because they could be selected for their specific skills and returned to their homes when no longer required. Colonial workers were, in his view, both difficult to control and likely to be the cause of social problems.[49]

A working paper on the possibilities of employing colonial labour, produced by the Ministry of Labour for the committee in 1949, did identify a number of areas of labour shortage – for females in the cotton, wool, silk and rayon, hosiery and pottery industries and in hospitals, and for males in tinplate and sheet steel, iron foundries, iron ore mines and general engineering. Considerable problems were anticipated from the unions. The National Union of Agricultural Workers and the National Union of Mineworkers were both sounded out by the Ministry and neither would 'in any circumstances acquiesce in any scheme of organised recruitment'. The Regional Controllers, the key Ministry of Labour officials in the provinces, were unanimous in their view that it would not be feasible to proceed with any version of the proposal to employ colonial workers in Britain.[50] A Ministry of Labour official who had visited the Caribbean in 1947 to investigate the possibility of officially backed schemes of migration had reported negatively. Another compared Polish ex-servicemen settlers who could be 'absorbed' with West Indian migrants who could not. Problems experienced during the war 'even under military discipline' with 10,000 RAF recruits from the Caribbean were noted and the feeling of the department was summed up by C.W. MacMullan: 'My personal view is that these people would be far more trouble than they are worth. If we agree to anything it is out of altruism and not out of self-interest.'[51] In July 1949 the committee recommended that, because employment opportunities in British industry were so limited, no organised large-scale immigration of colonial workers should be encouraged. Colonial workers would be likely to avoid undermanned industries which were unpopular ones (European Voluntary Workers on the other hand could be directed to them) and the 'inevitable drift to dependence on the National Assistance Board' could not be avoided. Small numbers of females might be encouraged to fill vacancies for domestic servants and hospital orderlies.[52]

As this suggestion indicates, one of the assumptions underlying the thinking of the members of the Working Party was that immigrants from the Caribbean would be unskilled additions to Britain's work-force. Applied to the male workers who arrived in the early years of the migration, this was an unwarranted assumption. Further, government departments had access to information about the early arrivals which made this point clearly. For example, the Government of Jamaica in June 1949 provided the Colonial Office with a detailed analysis of the 224 passengers on the MV *Georgic* who were sailing from Kingston to Liverpool for the purposes of employment and settlement.[53] Of the 128 males for whom details were available, sixty-four were skilled, sixty semiskilled and only four unskilled. The largest employment categories were carpenters (30), clerks (15), tailors (14), mechanics (11), welders (9), electricians, masons, shoemakers and agricultural workers (7 each) and machinists and cabinet makers (6 each). Of the twenty-eight women about whom data was available, eleven were skilled, sixteen semiskilled and only one unskilled. The survey also revealed that though only seven had made employment arrangements only fifty-five of the party did not have an address to go to. Almost all had to find employment quickly; the average cash holding was £12 and over 100 had £10 or less.[54]

Apart from their perceived lack of skills there were other major reasons why senior government officials believed immigrants from the Caribbean would not help rectify Britain's labour shortage. The Ministry of Labour took sufficiently seriously the problem of the 'placing of colonial negroes' to call a meeting of senior officials from all regions under the chairmanship of an Under-Secretary of State, Dame Mary Smieton. The clear feeling of the conference was that the major problem faced by 'coloured' workers was one of discrimination where white labour was available. Almost all regions reported that, with few exceptions, employers were reluctant to take on more than one or two 'coloured' workers at a time, particularly if the firms employed white women. The 'colour bar' was widespread, though BSA and Lucas in Birmingham and the textile industry in Bolton were mentioned as exceptions. However, though Dame Mary wondered aloud whether 'special steps should be taken to give them an equal opportunity with the white worker in finding employment', there was considerable opposition to the suggestion that a 'coloured' officer be appointed to deal with issues of 'coloured' employment and the meeting ended without any positive suggestion being made for change. But perceived West Indian frailties were not unconnected to their predicament. Though Jamaicans were 'usually of a good type' and 'intelligent at their work and easily managed', they were 'inclined to be childish' and had 'inflated ideas of their ability.'[55]

Even though a generally poor opinion was held of the possible contribution black immigrants could make to post-war recovery and while over a hundred thousand European workers were provided with jobs in Britain in the post-war years, it would be untrue to say that there were no officially backed schemes to import colonial labour. For the period 1945 to 1950 official papers contain references to two officially sponsored schemes, one for Barbadian women for domestic duties in hospitals and the other, more surprisingly, for men from St Helena for agricultural work. Both schemes contained repatriation clauses, for which the Barbadians were eligible after three years' service and the St Helenians after two. Both schemes were minute in scale compared to the recruitment programmes for Europeans. The Barbados Government agreed to pay the cost of the passages of thirty-three women who were to be paid at normal UK rates for work in National Health Service hospitals. The unique St Helena scheme, also of 1949, brought a hundred agricultural workers for employment by County Agricultural Executive Committees under the auspices of the Ministry of Agriculture and Fisheries. The scheme gave rise to a number of official concerns. A major fear was the possibility of unwelcome repercussions in other colonies with unemployment problems, especially in the West Indies. But this scheme could be justified because 'at one blow' it would solve St Helena's unemployment problem. Assimilation was not a fear. 'We are certain however that, since the St Helenians are said to be hard working and adaptable and are European in their outlook and way of life, they would be more acceptable in this country than West Indians.'[56]

'COLOURED' IMMIGRATION AND THE OFFICIAL MIND, 1945–55

Nothing occurred over the next couple of years to change the official mind on the inadvisability of encouraging the settlement of colonial workers. Indeed, by mid-1950 the position of industry had improved and there were reportedly fewer suitable vacancies. There were already, according to a specially commissioned survey conducted by the Ministry of Labour, 1,200 'coloured' – largely West Indian – unemployed workers in the country.[57] The official view remained that there was no need or requirement to encourage colonial settlement in Britain. In fact, the debate conducted within the ranks of the government and the senior civil service was only very rarely on the issue of whether to encourage but almost always on how to prevent further 'coloured' immigration. As we have seen, this debate predated – but was given a stimulus by – the widely publicised arrival in 1948 of the *Empire Windrush* and it continued, with several short interruptions, through to the introduction of the Commonwealth Immigrants Act of 1962 and beyond. The desire of officials and ministers to stop such immigration was widely evident even before the Asian and black population had reached a figure that was at all significant in national terms. As the next two chapters reveal, the question of the need to introduce immigration restrictions which would limit by law rather than by administrative practice the settlement of 'coloured' British subjects in Britain was the subject of lengthy debate in Cabinet and extensive study and discussion by both official interdepartmental and ministerial Cabinet committees.

In debate, ministers and high officials agreed that restrictions were essential if the problems which were thought to stem inevitably from the presence in Britain of a large 'coloured' population were to be avoided. It is clear that the key issue for the Cabinet throughout was that of numbers; not numbers of immigrants, but numbers of 'coloured' immigrants. They were resolved to limit the number of 'coloured' people settling in Britain to a number – never specified – that was 'assimilable'. 'Assimilation' and 'racial conflict' are two terms which frequently recur in official writings on the subject of 'coloured' immigration in this period. The limit of 'acceptable' numbers appeared to be set by the perceived ability of British society to assimilate immigrants who were different in appearance and culture from indigenous people. British subjects from the white Commonwealth and immigrants from Ireland, by contrast, could enter in unlimited numbers.[58] The assimilation of 'coloured' immigrants would be facilitated, it was believed, if concentrations of immigrants were avoided. This could be achieved by pursuing a policy of dispersal. In their many post-war files on the subject of colonial or 'coloured' labour the Ministry of Labour frequently referred to this ideal, though in practice efforts to achieve it appear neither co-ordinated nor successful. The minutes of the Home Office-led Interdepartmental Committee on colonial people in the United Kingdom at the end of the 1940s frequently cite examples of this strategy, which were usually unsuccessful either because of an alleged shortage of accommodation in areas where work was available or, more simply, because of the apparent reluctance of immigrants to move away from their fellows.

What officials plainly feared was the establishment of concentrations of 'coloured immigrants' substantial enough to claim recognition. In the official view such concentrations would lead inevitably to a clash of cultures, conflict and possibly race riots. Examples of violence which contained what were believed to be racial elements occurred in a number of cities – Liverpool and Cardiff, for example – immediately after the First World War. They were brought to mind by the more recent conflicts which broke out in Liverpool in August 1948, at labour hostels in Deptford and Birmingham the following year, and by the disturbance at the Colonial Office in 1949. Though sometimes reluctant to apportion blame for these disturbances, the simple logic developed by officials was that if the 'coloured' immigrants were not here the difficulties would not occur. The easiest way to avoid problems was to prevent the circumstances developing in which they would be likely to occur. The Home Office, which was the department of state responsible for both immigration policy and practice and the maintenance of law and order, was particularly prone to reflect on what it saw as the dangers of 'coloured' immigration.

These assumptions and attitudes are very clearly revealed in the decision to set up in 1949 an Interdepartmental Committee on colonial people in the United Kingdom drawing together representatives of all the departments of government that had an interest in 'the problem' – the Colonial Office, the Commonwealth Relations Office, the Treasury, the Ministries of Transport, Labour and National Service, Health, Civil Aviation, the Home Office and the National Assistance Board. The 'problem' was defined by the committee's first chair, William Murrie (who was Deputy Under-Secretary of State at the Home Office), as mainly one of new arrivals, of stowaways, one-way seamen and some fare-paying passengers from the West Indies and West Africa. Three sets of measures were to be considered by the committee: finding means of checking the traffic at source and on arrival; the employment and accommodation of arrivals; and the repatriation of the unsuitable. The rationale for setting up the committee was put by its first chair at its inaugural meeting in the following terms: whilst it was desirable to avoid giving 'these people' preferential treatment, it was necessary 'in the national interest to mitigate the difficulties under which coloureds lived'. There was no doubt that 'colour feeling' did exist, especially in areas where there was a shortage of work and accommodation. The problem was that 'this distaste' unless 'handled discreetly' and 'on the most realistic basis' might endanger law and order. 'It would be to our advantage to ensure that as a result of colour feeling people did not drift into small groups in bad areas where they constitute a threat to law and order; and with care and suitable placing they have already proved able and willing to settle down in the community.' On repatriation, it would clearly be 'cheaper in the case of misfits for the country to pack off the unemployable'.[59] There is no question that, in general, the new arrivals were seen as 'the problem'. Difficulties were to be expected as a consequence of their arrival and it was the function of government to ameliorate these by a policy of prevention, dispersal and repatriation. In the event, rather more official effort was put into prevention than cure.

Throughout this chapter official policy and attitudes have been treated as if they were the outcome of a single mind. It would, however, be fair to point out that though, in general, attitudes to colonial immigration were negative throughout the period under discussion, there were differing degrees of hostility. Fundamental assumptions about the difficulty of assimilating 'coloured' immigrants and the inevitability of conflict along racial lines were very widely shared but there were differences about how many non-white British subjects could be assimilated and about the seriousness of the dangers that continued 'coloured' immigration created. Approaches and policies were strongly affected by bureaucratic and departmental interests. The attitudes of officials from the Commonwealth Relations and Colonial Offices to the adoption of measures to prevent the settlement of 'coloured' people in the United Kingdom were conditioned, if not always commanded, by their interest in preserving cordial relations with Commonwealth and colonial governments and by an appreciation of the consequences for Britain of the adoption of openly or obviously discriminatory legislation.[60] The application of measures in Britain which could be seen as curbing the rights of British subjects resident in colonial territories could and did cause the governments of colonial territories to make strong representations to the Commonwealth Relations and Colonial Offices. After India and Pakistan gained their independence in 1947 the Commonwealth Relations Office became increasingly sensitive as the sub-continental governments became more assertive. During the 1950s West African and Caribbean governments began to enjoy increasing degrees of self-government and this was reflected in an increasing absence of timidity in their relationships with London. In particular, governments of the newly emergent black Commonwealth were quick to take offence at any measure which appeared to be directed against their citizens but not against the citizens of the established, largely white, members of the Commonwealth club.

Consequently, attitudes in those departments towards the introduction of controls ranged from equivocal to unenthusiastic. The unenthusiastic response may be illustrated by a Commonwealth Relations Office minute from the debate in 1950. It noted that the 'coloured' population of Britain was no more than 30,000 of whom only about 5,000 had arrived since the end of the war. The 'main difficulty' was with stowaways and one-trip seamen, but 'the problem' was too small to warrant the imposition of entry controls on all British and Irish citizens, which would be strongly disliked by Commonwealth and colonial governments and difficult and expensive to administer.[61] The assumption that 'the problem' was to be laid at the door of the Asian and black immigrants was shared by all. The equivocal aspect is exemplified by the reaction to a request for help from the New Zealand government to find a 'racially unobjectionable way' of excluding British subjects who were 'not readily assimilable'. 'Questions of considerable delicacy are involved in this, about which more than one view can be held'.[62] It was a Colonial Office initiative that created the Interdepartmental Working Party on the employment in the United Kingdom of surplus colonial labour and it was Colonial Office officials on the committee who persisted in trying to keep the issue alive against apparently unanimous opposition from other ministries.

At the other end of the spectrum the Home Office appeared to be singularly and unrestrainedly opposed to the permanent settlement of 'coloured' people from the Empire/Commonwealth, believing it to be likely to lead to social unrest in Britain and, at a time of Cold War tension, to the growth of communist influence in Britain.[63] Ministry of Labour officials opposed to suggestions to introduce planned immigration for surplus colonial labour significantly called for the addition of Home Office officials to a committee set up to consider the subject on the grounds that they 'would be likely to have definite views in the light of actual experience about increasing the coloured male population of this country'.[64] The assumption that all officials shared, irrespective of their ministry, was that the settlement of significant numbers of 'coloured' British subjects in Britain would lead to a range of social and economic difficulties, the severity of which would depend on the size and concentration of that population. Where they differed was in their assessment of the likely scale and balance of the costs and benefits of that immigration.

A POLICY OF OBSTRUCTION

While officially the illusion of the United Kingdom being freely open to all British subjects was carefully fostered, substantial and repeated efforts were being made to obstruct the migration to Britain for settlement of people from the Indian sub-continent, the Caribbean and West Africa. A panoply of measures was employed. One clearly identifiable set affected either directly or indirectly the issue and endorsement of travel documents that would be used by intending Asian and black emigrants to enter Britain. The British government's representatives in the Empire/Commonwealth used their discretion to decline to issue passports to those who were not closely identified by descent through both parents with the British

Isles. Commonwealth and colonial governments were induced to bring in, continue or tighten up procedures which limited the issue of passports valid for leaving their respective territories to settle in Britain. The measures were applied according to colour and perceived status. As far as the Caribbean was concerned, these efforts met with little success. Caribbean governments were reluctant to co-operate with Whitehall to control the flow of emigration. It is likely that migration from the Indian sub-continent was made much more difficult and the measures adopted jointly by the British, Indian and Pakistan governments may well account for the fact that, despite the door to Britain being theoretically 'open', immigrants from the sub-continent did not begin to arrive in any significant numbers until the very end of the 1950s and the beginning of the 1960s. The measures taken in West Africa appear virtually to have stopped the initial movement from Nigeria and the Gold Coast. The most effective measures were applied to the issue and endorsement of passports, but other rules applying to other travel documents were also changed.

Other measures were very diverse in character, ranging from changes in the rules about what proof was required from those entering the United Kingdom, to publicity in Jamaica about the difficult conditions that would greet immigrants, to attempts to manipulate the market in inexpensive passages from the Caribbean to the United Kingdom. Apparently alarmed by the build up of the 'coloured' population and the minor disturbances that broke out at the end of the 1940s, much of the government's effort over this period was directed at stemming and even reversing the flow of stowaways and one-way sailors into British ports. The battery of measures introduced in the period 1949 to 1951 appears to have had the required effect. It is clear that, taken together, all of these measures constituted a *de facto* immigration policy which had an impact on the pace of immigration to the United Kingdom but which was eventually ignored or circumvented.

Thus a policy which amounted to the obstruction of immigration from the Indian sub-continent, the Caribbean and Africa persisted over the first post-war decade, through an era of full employment. At no time during the decade did unemployment exceed 2 per cent of civilian employees and unfilled vacancies comfortably exceeded 1 per cent of the workforce through the decade and occasionally exceeded 2 per cent.[65] Whitehall did consider the possibility of encouraging colonial labour to come to Britain only to reject it firmly. Its discussions continued at great length on the subject of how to find ways of preventing the immigration of what it called 'coloured' people without stimulating overseas opposition and causing political and personal embarrassment. 'The outwards appearance of indifference' was indeed deceptive.[66] The official mind was either negative or hostile towards permanent 'coloured' immigration to Britain on any discernible scale. Given the prevailing hostility to 'coloured' settlement, the question the historian needs to answer is not why a restrictive immigration policy was introduced but why it took so long to introduce it and why Britain, despite the attitudes of its rulers, became a multi-racial society.

3 The making of policy, 1945–55

A MATTER OF CONSTANT CONCERN

During the period 1945 to 1955, spanning the two Labour governments of Clement Attlee of 1945–50 and 1950–1 and the Conservative government of Winston Churchill (taken over by Anthony Eden in 1955), legislative measures to restrict immigration were extensively discussed in Cabinet and in an interdepartmental committee of senior civil servants. The agreement between ministers to proceed with legislation in late 1954 and the drafting of a bill for Cabinet consideration in 1955 represented the high point of the first phase of discussion about the nature and timing of legislation intended to limit the growth of Asian and black communities. Disagreements about the nature of the measures required and their timing, and worries about their international consequences, resulted in a decision to postpone the proposed action in late 1955. But throughout the debates of the decade the undeclared objectives of the practice of immigration policy did not change; the nature and range of administrative methods outlined in the previous two chapters underwent some changes but their intentions were maintained and then extended. Administrative methods remained in favour for so long because they appeared to be broadly effective and, compared to their legislative alternative, they were thought much less likely to provoke political difficulties, either domestic and international.

The intensity of discussion about 'coloured' immigration varied widely through the decade. By far the most important single element contributing to its intensity was undoubtedly the perception of increasing numbers of Asian and black people entering Britain, related to fears about the effectiveness of the more traditional administrative measures to counter the increased inward movement. The questions for historians to ask are not about changing motivations and attitudes to 'coloured' immigration – they remained much the same throughout the century – but about why legislation as a means of control was eventually agreed to and why it took so long to reach agreement on it, particularly in view of what was perceived to be the very rapid growth in the number of Asian and black immigrants entering Britain.

Almost from the beginning of the decade 1945–55, the rate of increase by immigration of the Asian and black population was considered to be a cause for concern. Unlike the governments of India and Pakistan and the colonial governments of West Africa, Caribbean governments did not co-operate to any great extent with the restrictive measures proposed by London, and it was the rapid build up of the numbers of Caribbean migrants that precipitated the 'crisis' of 1954–5. As we have seen in the last chapter, before the flow of Caribbean migration began to achieve even modest numbers the government expressed strongly its concern about the growth in the number of 'coloured' seamen settling in Britain, usually arriving as 'one-way seamen' or stowaways, mainly from West Africa. Indeed, concern about the movement of 'coloured' people into Britain in the decade as a whole was dominated initially by movement from West Africa, overtaken in 1952–3 by concerns about fare-paying Caribbean immigration. The 'crisis' debate of 1954–5 provided a dress rehearsal for the decision of 1961. Of course, the number of Asian and black immigrants entering the country in 1955 was a fraction of that in 1961, just as the number of immigrants that caused such concern in the late 1940s was a fraction of the number entering in the mid-1950s.

The clearest indication that 'coloured' immigration was a matter of constant concern to the government was the large number of occasions during the period when the Cabinet discussed the level of immigration and settlement, variously described in the Cabinet Minutes as 'Coloured people from British Colonial territories' or more euphemistically as 'Colonial immigration' or 'Commonwealth immigrants', almost always linked to considerations of the possibility of introducing legal restrictions on the entry for settlement of British subjects. Between 1950 when the matter was first discussed in Cabinet (the arrival of the *Empire Windrush* had been greeted by a paper to the Cabinet by the Secretary of State for the Colonies but there was no minuted discussion) – and 1961, 'coloured' immigration was discussed on 37 separate occasions. Table 1 shows the chronological distribution of these discussions and provides a crude indication of the ebb and flow of government concern over these years. The 'coloured immigration' question never quite went away; in the 1950s, the longest period between Cabinet discussions was thirteen months (December 1952 to February 1954) during which period the interdepart-mental committee of senior officials was preparing an important report on the question. Two peaks of concern are clearly identifiable in the mid-

1950s, when a draft bill was discussed by Cabinet, and again in the early 1960s, both were clearly associated with a significant increase in the number of Asian and black immigrants entering Britain.

The Cabinet discussions provide a clue to the continuous work of officials who produced a mountain of papers on these questions. An Interdepartmental Committee composed of officals at senior (assistant under-secretary) level was originally suggested by the Colonial Office in 1948 as a means of involving a range of government departments in problems which it did not consider its own. The Colonial Office was keen to assert that it had no executive powers in the United Kingdom and that its responsibilities related to the supervision of colonial governments overseas. Issues about the settlement of colonial subjects in the United Kingdom were only indirectly its concern, in so far as they had an impact on the relationships between Britain and the colonial governments. At the initial meeting in February 1949 – called to discuss 'the problems of persons from the colonies and British Protectorates' – the chair was taken, and subsequently kept, by the Home Office. At first the committee was often referred to by the name of its first chairman, W.S. Murrie.[1] The committee was maintained in existence as a Working Party – for most of the period it was known as the Interdepartmental Working Party on the economic and social problems caused by the influx of colonial subjects – to provide a flow of ideas and advice first to the Home Secretary and then, after 1955, to the Cabinet Committee on Colonial Immigrants. It was fully involved in providing important discussion papers during the two periods of intense debate on immigration, 1954–5 and 1960–1.

THE *EMPIRE WINDRUSH*

The first time a memorandum was circulated to Cabinet members on the subject of 'coloured' immigration, it came from the Colonial Secretary Arthur Creech Jones and was a consequence of the public and parliamentary interest aroused by the arrival of the *Empire Windrush* in 1948. (The fact that this vessel was by no means the first in the post-war years to bring several hundred immigrants from the Caribbean escaped

Table 1 Number of occasions per year that the issue of 'coloured' immigration was discussed by the Cabinet, 1945–61

Year	1945–9	1950	1951	1952	1953	1954	1955	1956	1957	1958	1959	1960	1961
	0	2	2	1	0	5	11	2	1	4	1	2	6

Source: CAB 128, Public Record Office, Kew

attention then as it does now.) It also dealt with the wider and, at the time, more important issue of the growing number of stowaway and one-way seamen from West Africa, the Arabian peninsula, Somaliland and the Caribbean. The government's response to the news of the departure of the *Empire Windrush* had already been indicated by the Minister of Labour, George Isaacs, in the House of Commons in reply to questions from Tom Driberg. Though arrangements to meet and accommodate the party had been made it was thought unlikely that the movement would be repeated. It was bound to result in 'considerable difficulty' and no encouragement would be given to others to follow the example of the *Windrush*.[2]

The Colonial Secretary Creech Jones informed his colleagues of the arrangements made to deal with the arriving Caribbean workers, but in doing so indicated his department's and the Government's plain displeasure at the movement. He admitted that his department did not know who 'the ringleaders of this enterprise' were, but it had asked the Jamaican government to find out. He explained that 'every possible step has been taken . . . to discourage these influxes'. Adverse accounts of conditions in Britain had been published in the Jamaican press, all efforts had been made to keep the Jamaican Government informed of the difficulties in the United Kingdom and the Chief Welfare Officer of the Colonial Office had been sent out to the Caribbean in 1947 specifically 'to discourage people from coming over to this country to find work'. Due to transport shortages the Colonial Secretary reported that he thought it unlikely that more than a trickle would arrive in the future. Because of Jamaica's advance to self-government, the British authorities could not compel its government to legislate or take other action to prevent the movement, even if such legislation were to be acceptable in peacetime.[3] It is clear from Creech Jones' paper and the response to it that the government was concerned by – and opposed to – significant black immigration.

Publicly the government was far more positive. Attlee in his reply to the letter from the Labour MP J.D. Murray and ten others, who had called for the introduction of legislation to prevent what they saw as the impending flood of colonial immigrants, warned against regarding the Jamaican arrivals as 'undesirables or unemployables. . . . The majority of them are honest workers and can, I feel, make a genuine contribution to our labour difficulties at the present time.'[4] He moved to still fears of an influx, not by outlining the measures the government was taking or was about to adopt, but by referring to the 'peculiar combination of circumstances' that accounted for the 1948 influx which, in his view, were unlikely to be repeated. In particular, especially cheap passages were available on returning troopships and ex-servicemen recently in receipt of their gratuity were in a unique position to afford the crossing. Even so, it was observed, not all the cheap troop-deck passages were taken up.[5] Interestingly, the government did not reveal publicly its successful efforts to limit the supply of cheap passages available to intending immigrants from the Caribbean. Indeed, the private view of the migration was far less sanguine than the public view. The confidential Cabinet papers dwelt on the need for measures to prevent a recurrence. The dichotomy between the government's publicly expressed tolerance of black immigration and its private regret and hostility was established right at the start of the post-war debate.

THE BRITISH NATIONALITY ACT, 1948

At the very time the *Empire Windrush* arrived, the British Nationality Act of 1948 was passing through Parliament. In view of the widespread misunderstanding about the relationship of this Act to subsequent immigration from the Empire/Commonwealth it is worth pausing to reflect on its part in the debate about post-war immigration.[6] In no active sense did the Act contribute to the flow of British subjects into the United Kingdom, nor was it seen at the time as likely to do so. As far as immigration and emigration throughout the Empire/Commonwealth were concerned, the Act confirmed the situation that existed prior to 1948. It created no new rights or obligations. During the centuries of imperial growth and power Britain had never introduced or accepted a distinction either between the citizenship and nationality of the monarch's subjects resident in different parts of the Empire or between the monarch's citizens and the monarch's subjects. From the middle of the nineteenth century the economic imperatives of the free flow of goods, labour and services within the Empire enhanced the feeling that such distinctions were likely to be detrimental to broad imperial interests. The idea of Empire and later of Commonwealth was thought to draw strength from the notion of a common set of rights and obligations for all its inhabitants. As the white settled colonies gained self-rule in the mid- and late nineteenth century their residents remained British subjects. Those colonies, however, whilst recognising the concept of common citizenship, gained control of the make up of their own populations by taking responsibility for the control of immigration. From the turn of the century the rights of Indians to settle in many parts of the Empire were heavily circumscribed.

On the other hand, any and every British subject had the right to enter Britain, vote, stand for Parliament and join the armed forces. The Aliens Act of 1905 introduced the first set of peacetime British immigration controls and made the distinction between those who did not owe allegiance to the monarch – aliens (who became subject to control) – and those who did, who collectively remained free to enter Britain as and when they chose. The legal position was very clear. It was stated at the League of Nations by the British delegate in 1937: 'It is the practice of the United Kingdom not to make any distinction between different races in British colonies as regards civil and political rights, or the right of entry into and residence in the United Kingdom.'[7] He did not, of course, add that administrative practice in many colonies quite sharply limited the civil and political rights of non-white British subjects, just as the right of entry to the United Kingdom for certain classes and groups was circumscribed by the policies outlined in the previous chapter.

This state of affairs was disturbed by two sets of developments following the end of the Second World War. Canada in 1946 and India, Pakistan and Ceylon after gaining independence in 1947 all introduced their own citizenship laws, thus stimulating Britain to define for the first time by law its own citizenship. It did so by reaffirming its faith in the unity of Empire, by recognising all citizens of territories that made up the Empire/Commonwealth – Britain, the colonies and self-governing member states of the Commonwealth – as British subjects. Citizens of newly independent Commonwealth countries, whether they held passports from their own country or not, remained British subjects. Within this 'umbrella' status the Act created 'Citizenship of the United Kingdom and Colonies' which was available to all those who could not lay claim to citizenship of an independent Commonwealth country. Insofar as these aspects of the Bill were controversial they were so because to some Conservatives the bill was divisive. The Opposition accused the government of creating needless distinctions between different classes of British subject and threatened when back in office to revive the traditional concepts. Indeed, the Lords was convinced by a large majority that the new category of 'Citizenship of the United Kingdom and Colonies' was so potentially damaging to imperial unity that it passed an amendment abolishing it. Only one participant in the debate in the Lords, Tweedsmuir, found the prospect of being able to use the new distinctions to control entry inviting and he was rounded upon from all sides of the House.

The declaration of 1937 that the British Government made no distinction by race to the right of entry and settlement in the United Kingdom was loudly re-affirmed. In the Commons, spokesmen for the two major parties vied with each other for the title of the most imperially minded. Maxwell Fyfe spoke warmly of 'our great metropolitan tradition of hospitality' and expressed his pride in that fact that the United Kingdom imposed no colour bar restrictions.[8] He expressed the Conservative Party's fear that the new distinctions would be used as the basis for future discrimination and introduced – but did not press – an amendment which would explicitly have prevented this. Issues relating to the right of entry of British subjects did not form a significant part of the discussion in 1948 – the Bill had not intended to alter anything in that regard – nor were voices raised at the time to suggest that the new distinctions could or should be used to redefine the traditional freedom of access to Britain. The Conservatives, with Maxwell Fyfe and Salisbury to the fore – two significant figures in later debates – maintained their party's credentials as the party of empire, of imperial unity and commitment against what might have been seen as a Labour attempt to steal their clothes. But the Labour Government had also done well. As Nicholas Deakin put it:

> The solution they had recommended . . . chimed in well with the new concept of the Commonwealth which stemmed from the independence of India, Pakistan and Ceylon. By preserving the link in a less assertive form while underwriting the traditional right of free access through the new code of citizenship, the British Nationality Act helped to give practical expression to the new concept of Commonwealth to which Attlee as Prime Minister was a firm adherent.[9]

In retrospect, it is clear that neither party at the time of the Act thought there was any serious likelihood of large numbers of its Asian and black colonial subjects taking up their right to live and work in the United Kingdom. Viewed from the perspective of 1948, there was little evidence to suggest that this would now occur, or rather that the means of prevention would suddenly cease to be effective. From the perspective of the late twentieth century we can see that the small number of West Indians who were arriving at the time the Act was passed were the vanguard of a substantial inward movement. In 1948 there was very little reason to doubt the Prime Minister's assurance that the 'peculiar circumstances' which led to the arrival of the *Empire Windrush* were unlikely to be repeated. The government's vigorous actions behind the scenes were designed to ensure that this was so. Ironically, within two years of the extravaganza of imperial sentiment that flowed during the debate on the Nationality Act, its authors were discussing whether and how the right to emigrate to Britain as exercised by black British subjects could be *legally* curtailed.

LABOUR'S WAY, 1945–51

In its six years the Labour Cabinet discussed issues relating to Asian and black migration and settlement on only three occasions, all in the last year or so of office. The minutes and memoranda associated with these discussions reveal an attitude and approach to immigration little different in character from that of their Conservative successors. The views expressed by the Royal Commission on Population which reported in 1949 summed up the attitudes to immigration common to both parties. The Commissioners shared contemporary concerns about the impact of the future shortfall in the number of people of working age. The economy, it was predicted, would require an additional 140,000 workers a year which a carefully designed immigration policy could secure. Such a policy 'could only be welcomed without reserve if the migrants were of good human stock and were not prevented by their race or religion from intermarrying with the host population and becoming merged in it'.[10] In this statement the Commissioners neatly summarised both the widely held, if largely dormant, concern about the potential dangers of societies that contained racial divisions and the strong contemporary prejudice against miscegenation. Despite Attlee's public words of welcome to the black passengers aboard the *Empire Windrush* the British government, in a period of acute labour shortage, did not turn to its empire for additional labour. Government hostility to both Asian and black settlement, so apparent in the policy of the inter-war years, continued through the decade following the end of the war.

As Chapter 2 so clearly shows, government had already been active in devising measures to restrict the entry, and hasten the exit, of sea-related settlers. Evidently some of the concern about repatriation and the prevention of stowing away was brought on by disturbances at Deptford in July 1949 which involved, almost entirely, stowaway seamen. These incidents received widespead coverage in both the home and foreign press. The first Cabinet discussion in March 1950, though it appeared to flow out of a debate about the Seretse Khama affair, in fact reflected a growing concern about the 'serious difficulties which were thought would arise if immigration from British colonial possessions was allowed to continue or increase'. Associated with this movement was a growth in the incidence of racial discrimination and the related problem of finding employment for Asian and black workers. The Colonial Secretary was invited to join with his colleagues in the Home Office and Ministries of Labour and Health to submit to the Cabinet their ideas for dealing with the problems arising from such immigration.[11] In fact the interdepartmental committee of senior officials originally established in 1949 and now chaired by a Home Office official was already working on these very issues.

It is important to remember that when the resulting paper was taken at a Cabinet meeting three months later the 'coloured' population of the United Kingdom was officially estimated at between 20,000 and 30,000, of whom only some 3,000 to 4,000 had arrived since the end of the war. Problems of housing, employment, relief of distress and racial violence (incidents in Liverpool, 31 July–2 August 1948; Deptford, 18 July 1949;

and Birmingham, 6–8 August 1949) associated with the 'continuing influx' had led the interdepartmental committee of officials, whose first meeting had been held in February 1949, to recommend the adoption of new approaches to reduce the flow of immigrants. The Home Secretary indicated that measures relating to publicity in the colonies, the repatriation of colonial seamen, the use of British Travel Certificates and instructions to Immigration Officers regarding proof of identity had already been implemented or were in hand. The committee also recommended the setting up of a further Working Party to 'tackle the problem . . . by dispersal, by finding employment and accommodation and by arranging for voluntary repatriation of misfits'.[12] The Minister's report on the problems of housing and employment referred to both 'the undisciplined behaviour of the coloured colonials' and the 'certain amount of prejudice in this country against coloured people'. He concluded that so long as efforts could be stepped up to limit the influx 'the problem can be kept within bounds without resort to any drastic measures'.[13] In its discussion the Cabinet concentrated mainly on the issue of immigration – should not consideration be given to the question of whether the time had come to introduce restrictions on the rights of British subjects to enter the United Kingdom? A further review by the Prime Minister would establish whether the balance still lay against taking these steps.[14] Publicly there had been no question of even the possibility of restrictions on movement when the British Nationality Act had been passed two years previously.

The *ad hoc* committee of seven ministers, chaired by the Home Secretary Chuter Ede, considered three possible legislative methods of controlling the entry of coloured immigrants to the United Kingdom: the application to British subjects of the restrictions applying to aliens; the deportation of 'undesirable' immigrants; and the return of stowaways to their port of embarkation. The first approach, that of ensuring that no one entered Britain from the colonies or Commonwealth (other than students and genuine short-term visitors) unless they had work to come to, was seen as administratively possible but would involve significant increases in the staffing levels of the Ministry of Labour. The central problem with this approach was thought to be that it would be difficult to justify applying the controls to the Empire/Commonwealth without applying them to the Republic of Ireland. If that was done the additional administrative burden would be greatly increased, to the equivalent of almost the load created by the existing aliens restrictions. The most serious problem generated by this approach, however, was the fact that there was no desire to exclude the estimated thirty to forty thousand persons coming to Britain from the Republic every year. Deportation of Empire/Commonwealth residents of less than two years' standing who had applied for National Assistance, been convicted of a serious offence or had tried to stimulate industrial unrest was also thought to be administratively practicable despite anticipated problems with the National Assistance Board and with the identification of colonial territories of origin. Legislation to extend provisions for dealing with alien stowaways to British subject stowaways was the least problematic of the three approaches.

The committee concluded that 'in view of the small scale of immigration into this country of coloured people from British colonial territories and the important and controversial issues of policy involved in legislation to control it' no legislation should be introduced at present. The Cabinet endorsed their recommendation at a meeting in late February 1951. The ministers noted the relatively small size of both the permanent 'coloured' population and of the new immigrant groups. The committee put these figures at 30,000 and 5,000 respectively. Almost all of the post-war arrivals were West Africans and West Indians, of whom the former predominated. West Africans were entering Britain as a large percentage of the stowaways and one-way seamen at a rate estimated at about 400 a year; about 2,000 West Indians had so far arrived mainly as migrant workers. 'Coloured' unemployment, much of it temporary, was at just over 1,000; and under 600 were reliant on National Assistance when samples were taken in the middle of 1950.

The question of numbers was regarded by government as crucial from the very start of the debate. Though arguments against legislation to restrict entry of British subjects were persuasive – the additional staff and administration, the sacrifice of an aspect of the United Kingdom's special status within the Empire/Commonwealth, Commonwealth and colonial opposition and the difficulty of drafting legislation that kept out potential Asian and black immigrants without introducing a colour bar – the committee nonetheless concluded that a larger increase in colonial immigration in the future might make legislation essential. The Colonial Secretary was put on guard; he undertook to advise his colleagues of any large increase in the scale of immigration so that the question of introducing legislation might then again be considered.[15] In the meantime administrative measures for the control of stowaways and one-way seamen were to be reviewed with the idea that they should be 'applied vigorously' and made 'as effective as possible'.[16]

CHURCHILL'S WAY: THE BATTLE LINES DRAWN, 1951–4

The Labour governments of Clement Attlee set the broad tone and overall framework for the post-war discussion of the issue of immigration from the black and Asian Empire and Commonwealth. The tone in private was negative and the committee framework established in 1949 had, as its main objective, vigilance to ensure that the numbers did not grow more quickly than the government could tolerate. The approach was one which placed great emphasis on the 'problems' caused by the arrival of black British subjects; the size of the problems was assumed to be directly proportionate to the number of British subjects arriving from the Caribbean and Africa. The rationale for the establishment of the committee, provided by W.S. Murrie, the Deputy Under-Secretary of State at the Home Office and its first chairman, had stressed the danger to law and order that would be posed by allowing concentrations of 'coloured' people to develop in 'bad areas'.[17]

Winston Churchill did not need the advice of civil servants to alert him to the potential difficulties of continuing 'coloured' immigration. Few would deny that 'Churchill's racial assumptions occupied a prime place . . . in his political philosophy. . . . He was a convinced white . . . supremacist and thought in terms of race to a degree that was remarkable even by the standards of his own time'.[18] The Prime Minister's papers reveal a strong personal interest in the subject; indeed he was to tell the editor of the *Spectator* in 1954 that immigration 'is the most important subject facing this country, but I cannot get any of my ministers to take any notice'.[19] At the end of November 1952, a month in which he displayed great interest in questions related to colour, the Prime Minister asked in Cabinet whether the Post Office employed a large number of 'coloured workers' and if so whether difficult social problems were being created as a consequence.[20] The Postmaster-General was asked to report on the employment of colonial workers in the Post Office which he did three weeks later. Arguing that as the largest government employer, the Post Office was likely to have the largest number of coloured workers, he pointed out that his Department was no different from others in this respect and could not be expected to introduce a colour bar as a matter of departmental policy, though it would be prepared to accept one if it became government policy. From the issue of the employment of black workers in the Post Office it was a short step to the discussion of immigration. For the time being, the government confirmed the policy of free entry 'despite the risks involved' but agreed that there was a case for reviewing the situation to establish the facts. It was agreed that the Home Secretary would ask the interdepartmental committee to examine the possibility of preventing further increases in the number of coloured people seeking employment in Britain. At the same time the Chancellor was to examine the possibility of restricting the entry of coloured people into the Civil Service.[21]

It can reasonably be inferred – from the length of time it took the Home Office-chaired interdepartmental committee, reconvened in January 1953, to make its report – that immigration and settlement was not an issue of priority for either of the ministers tasked by the Cabinet meeting of December 1952. However, when the commmittee finally delivered its findings in December 1953 it produced evidence which had clearly been based on a major effort involving the Ministries of Labour and National Service, the National Assistance Board, the Colonial Office and the Chief Constables of areas of Britain in which Asian and black minorities had settled. The Working Party report provided the best researched picture of Britain's ethnic minority group that had yet been available to government. It included estimates of the number in each minority group and the rate of arrival, an account of the conditions of life of 'coloured people', including details of employment and unemployment, dependence on national assistance and relationship with crime.

In making its enquiries about the size and distribution of the 'coloured' population the Working Party implicitly rejected figures, based only – and often misleadingly – on place of birth, which could have been derived from the Census of 1951. In April 1953 it found that the total permanently resident Asian and black population of the United Kingdom was approximately 36,000. It had apparently been growing at an average rate of about 2,400 per year since the war – in 1939 it was estimated to have been about 7,000. The Caribbean derived population was still only 8,600, compared to 9,300 Indians and Pakistanis and 15,000 West Africans. Possibly well over half of the Indian/Pakistani population had arrived as deserting seamen – 6,304 Indian and Pakistani seamen deserters were reported to the police between 1944 and 1953 and less than a thousand had been either returned to their vessels under the Merchant Shipping Act powers or had voluntarily sought repatriation.[22] However, the balance between the communities was changing. West African migration, much of which had occurred since the war through stowaways and one-way seamen, often to join the well established communities of West African origin in the seaports of Cardiff, Swansea, Glasgow, Liverpool and London, was now growing only very slowly following the successful government crackdown against those forms of entry. By far the largest number of arrivals (almost three-quarters of the total) were from the Caribbean; for the first time in 1952 fare-paying passengers had established themselves as the largest group among the immigrants. The age of the seaman and stowaway had finally given way to the age of the suitcase and trunk. Linked with this was the fact that though the large majority were men, some married women with children and also single women were beginning to arrive from the Caribbean to provide the migration with an aspect of 'permanency altogether different from the conditions of the pre-war seafaring settlement'.[23] As the report clearly indicated, the Asian and black population of Britain was still very small in 1953, its membership was largely transient in character and its pattern of settlement was still confined to a few towns.[24]

The overall picture the report painted was almost entirely negative, though it admitted to a lack of evidence to connect its subjects to crime and it did occasionally give modest voice to the view that the position of the minorities might in some cases not be entirely unconnected with the discrimination they suffered. In general, the report was a remarkable case of blaming the victim. Such positive thoughts as it contained were confined to its discussions of the various ways in which 'coloured people' could be kept out of Britain. It warned that any method that was not openly discriminatory – and it accepted that no approach to this question could be – was going to be very expensive because it would have to apply to all people entering the country from the Empire/Commonwealth and possibly to the Irish as well. Extra manpower, without adding any element for other costs, for the Home Office and the Ministry of Labour would be about £130,000 – and if the Irish were included in the controls the estimate was at least £260,000. The report noted that there was no desire to limit the number of Irish coming to Britain, estimated at 60,000 per year or twenty times the rate of arrival of 'coloured immigrants'. They were economically useful and in no sense 'difficult to assimilate'.[25]

It was probably on the Prime Minister's initiative that the matter was raised again in Cabinet, provoked by a report in the *Daily Telegraph* of 29 January 1954 of an 'influx of West Indians'.[26] The explanation for the ministers' tardiness may be found in the figures presented by the Home Secretary to the Cabinet. Once again, the question of numbers was central to Cabinet concerns and Cabinet decisions. The 'coloured' population of Britain, the Home Secretary reported, stood at about 40,000 (or less than 0.1 per cent of the total population) and was increasing at the rate of about 3,000 each year. Presumably to give credence to the notion that the 'coloured' population already posed a threat to British society, he claimed that it was disproportionately dependent on the welfare system and disproportionately involved in crime. Over 3,300 'coloured people' were unemployed and 1,870 were receiving National Assistance, and of the sixty-two men convicted in London of living on immoral earnings during the previous year twenty-four were coloured.

The Home Secretary identified two possible courses of action to prevent coloured immigration. Britain could extend immigration control to cover all British subjects, but that would affect white and black alike and would call for considerable increases in staff at the Home Office and Ministry of Labour. Alternatively, powers of deportation could be taken to 'remove the riffraff amongst British subjects from overseas' who had committed a serious criminal offence or who were a charge on public funds. Although there was already evidence of some racial feeling in areas where 'coloured people' congregated, on balance he did not believe that 'the problem' had yet reached sufficient proportions to justify reversing the traditional position on immigration and antagonising liberal opinion. The Government would stand accused of introducing a 'colour bar'. Though there was some support for taking deportation powers, the consensus in the Cabinet appeared to be opposed to immediate action. The Prime Minister warned that easier transport, rising standards of living in the colonies and the attractiveness of welfare provisions in Britain were likely to lead to increasing 'coloured' immigration which would be resented by large sections of the British people. In the light of changing conditions traditional practices might have to be modified. The Cabinet charged the Commonwealth and Colonial Secretaries with the task of reporting back to Cabinet on the present powers of other Empire and Commonwealth governments to deport British subjects.[27] Three years previously the Labour Cabinet had received precisely these details from the Home Secretary. The pattern of prevarication and repetition had already begun.[28]

The arrival on ministers' desks of the response of the Colonial and Commonwealth Relations Secretaries to the demands of the Cabinet coincided with a parliamentary question on the immigration of 'overseas British subjects' by Thomas Reid, the Labour MP for Swindon. He wanted the government to set up a committee to report on the matter. Reid's question, and the evident concern of the Home Secretary to get the response to it right, reflected an increasing level of public debate on the question. This was evidenced in at least two ways: first, in the increasing attention given by newspapers to the subject and second, in the increased number of questions being put to MPs by their constituents and by the MPs to relevant government departments. Several junior ministers had been approached by MPs. Manchester and London constituencies had recorded complaints claiming that disproportionate numbers of 'coloured' men were living off either National Assistance or the immoral earnings of white women. Special objection was also taken to 'coloured' landlords acquiring old property, driving out white residents and turning the houses over to tenancy by much larger numbers of black lodgers.[29] In turn these were almost certainly responses to the justified belief that the number of black immigrants entering the United Kingdom from the Caribbean had increased dramatically over the previous couple of years.

In mid-March 1954, therefore, the Cabinet again considered the whole question of colonial or 'coloured' immigration. This time it decided that though there were substantial political disadvantages to introducing legislation to restrict entry – damage to the unity of the Commonwealth and possible reprisals against British business interests by India and Pakistan were cited – nonetheless, the Home and Commonwealth Secretaries should be asked to consider whether powers of deportation over 'undesirables' was a sufficient response to the growing numbers of immigrants.[30] Some ministers evidently felt that this would not be enough, that the rising tide of black immigration would increase the population to 'unmanageable proportions' in ten to fifteen years' time. In their view legislation of a more far-reaching kind was essential to prevent this from occurring. It was decided to reject the suggestion of a committee of inquiry, but Reid was assured that the matter was receiving 'continuous thought and study'.[31]

In a divided Cabinet the member who took the strongest line in favour of the introduction of legislative controls was Lord Salisbury, who was Lord President of the Council (1952–7), Leader of the House of Lords and a very powerful influence in the Conservative Party. In the 1950s he was on terms of the closest friendship with the Churchills, the Edens and the Royal Family. He sought to reflect in Cabinet the view that 'the problem' would become 'unmanageable' unless it was tackled.[32] 'Coloured' immigrants were a threat to the very fabric of British society and he would have their entry stopped. Unless measures were taken the flow of immigrants, attracted by welfare benefits, would simply increase and would be unlikely to turn down as employment opportunities declined.[33] An appreciation of his views on 'coloured' immigration and its effects on British society can be gained through an examination of an address he received in March 1954 from the Conservative Commonwealth Association (Liverpool Group) which he described to a colleague in government as 'extremely moderate and sensible'. He personally agreed with almost everything in it.[34]

In this three-page document 'coloured immigrants' are characterised as being a charge on public funds, likely to be associated with – if not the cause of – a range of 'grave social problems' and posed a threat to Britain's relationship with its colonies. In Liverpool a 'new Harlem' was being created where

> Rooms in large and dilapidated houses are sub-let at high rentals to coloured immigrants who exist in conditions of the utmost squalor. Vice and crime are rampant and social responsibilities are largely ignored. Hundreds of children of negroid or mixed parentage eventually find their way to the various homes maintained by the Corporation, to be reared to unhappy maturity at great public expense. Large numbers of the adults are in receipt of unemployment benefit or National Assistance and many are engaged in the drug traffic or supplement their incomes by running illicit drinking dens or by prostitution.

Trying to improve the conditions of immigrants would only encourage others to come, attracted by 'the benefits of a welfare state which will ensure them a better standard of living than they have been accustomed to work for'. Further, this 'canker' threatened to poison the good relationship between Britain and its colonies. The discrimination that 'coloured workers' suffered – 'it might be considered not unreasonable for employers to favour white men with roots and traditional rights in this country to coloured men lacking such claims' – was enlarged upon and 'often provoked them to unsocial activities'. Those who returned to their country of origin 'often do so as enemies of this country and constitute an unfortunate element in the present stage of political evolution in the dependent territories'.[35]

Salisbury did not think it adequate to introduce legislation which would permit deportation. 'It is for me not merely a question of whether criminal negroes should be allowed in or not; it is a question whether great quantities of negroes, criminal or not, should be allowed to come.' He wanted legislation on the same lines as that already adopted by New Zealand, Canada and Australia to prevent a situation developing in Britain similar to that 'now causing such great difficulties for the United States'. In apocalyptic language he referred to the issue becoming 'a fundamental problem for us all'. Though now only 'just beginning to push its ugly head above the surface of politics', he thought it may 'easily come to fill the whole political horizon'. Arguments against legislation were of a different and lower order. 'I feel that we should recognise that this coloured problem is potentially of a fundamental nature for the future of our Country.'[36]

When the battle-lines formed, Salisbury found himself supported by Oliver Lyttleton, the Colonial Secretary, against an alliance of Lord Swinton (Commonwealth Relations Office) and David Maxwell Fyfe (Home Office) who were both happy with deportation provisions. The arguments marshalled against Salisbury's position were based on political expediency rather than on principle. Swinton was quite clear. Other white-dominated 'old' Commonwealth countries – South Africa, Canada, New Zealand and Australia – all employed either discriminatory legislation or practices to prevent the entry for settlement of significant numbers of non-Europeans:

> If we legislate on immigration, though we can draft it in non-discriminatory terms, we cannot conceal the obvious fact that the object is to keep out coloured people. Unless there is really a strong case for this, it would surely be an unwise moment to raise the issue when we are preaching, and trying to practise, partnership and the abolition of the colour bar.[37]

Swinton had no liking for immigration from the new Commonwealth. Indeed, he had opposed India's membership of the Commonwealth as a republic on the grounds that it would weaken ties with the old dominions which were, in his view, of a different and higher order. On questions of policy objectives Swinton's position was identical to Salisbury's. They both wanted to see the immigration from the non-white Empire/Commonwealth stopped. They differed on the question of the most appropriate and effective means.[38] As the minister responsible for Commonwealth Relations, Swinton was closely aware of the possible international repercussions of introducing immigration legislation which, in either appearance or effect, was discriminatory.

THE INTERNATIONAL DIMENSION

As Oliver Franks, until 1952 the British Ambassador in Washington, expressed it in the Reith Lectures of 1954, the conventional wisdom about Britain's place in the world in 1954 was that without the Commonwealth 'we cannot continue as a Great Power. Little argument is needed to show the necessity of the Commonwealth to Britain's continuing greatness. It is a truth which the British people have intuitively perceived: they do not require a demonstration.'[39] In the mid-1950s Britain was at a crucial stage of its decolonisation process. The colonies and protectorates of South Asia had, from the British point of view, passed successfully from dependence to membership of the British Commonwealth of Nations. In turn the Commonwealth was in the process of being transformed from a close-knit club of European settler-dominated dominions to a multi-racial association of states with a common history of British Empire membership. Up until the mid-1950s only Burma had refused to go along with the idea of a continuing close association with Britain, and it was anticipated that as other colonies and protectorates moved to independence so they too would join the Commonwealth.

The Commonwealth was more than either a sentimental notion or a spot of moral morphia designed to kill the pain of transition from Empire to European offshore island. Until the rude shocks administered by the Suez crisis in 1956 the Commonwealth appeared to sustain an impression of a common approach in foreign policy; India in particular played a crucial role here, and Nehru was yet to assert his complete independence of the Raj. Leaders met about every two years. The meetings of 1951 and 1953 had been particularly successful in reaching agreement on communiqués which, in coded terms, urged restraint on the USA and sought to encourage China and the Soviet Union to join a dialogue with the West. Co-operation of a military kind was no longer very significant, but it did survive. A Commonwealth Division, including an Indian Field Ambulance, had been part of the UN forces in Korea. With its range of more intimate, more close-knit political and diplomatic contacts Britain could pretend to others that its position at the top table was still merited. Others no doubt saw Britain's decline more clearly than her own leaders did.[40]

But it was also more than an illusion of international power and influence. Relations with colonies and ex-colonies in general mattered more to Britain because almost all members of the Commonwealth were also members of the sterling area. In the early and mid-1950s Britain's international economic position was still closely bound to that of the sterling area. A very large debt overhang survived from the war, and with many colonies moving to independence there was considerable sensitivity still about the position of sterling and the sterling balances. The practice of wartime and post-war discrimination against the dollar area was still very much alive; to conserve the common pool of gold and dollars, controlled by the Bank of England, Commonwealth countries traded more with each other and with Britain than would otherwise have been the case. Trade and investment patterns, strongly stimulated (in almost all cases) by common membership of the sterling area, were still closely linked to the Empire/Commonwealth. At the time of the debate in the Cabinet 56 per cent of Britain's overseas investment was located there; the Indian sub-continent had over twice as many pounds invested in it as any European country. Almost half of Britain's overseas trade was with the Empire/Commonwealth.

In the mid-1950s the Commonwealth was still an important dimension of Britain's international role, position and character. Relations with the 'old' dominions were still important out of all proportion to the size of the latter's population; relations with the new members were crucial too because their success would demonstrate the utility and attractiveness of the association for territories in the process of decolonisation. With the old white dominions the relationship was founded not just on interlocking economic interests, but also on very considerable ties of sentiment and affection based on an extensive network of family connections built up over many generations of British emigration. Overall, their immigration policies still very strongly favoured British immigrants, New Zealand's entirely so, Australia's very substantially and South Africa's and Canada's quite considerably. The recent experience of two world wars in which dominion troops had fought with great distinction and very large losses of life added to Britain's sense of commitment. The Commonwealth relationships formed since the war with newly decolonised states would, on the other hand, be more solidly based on the 'new' Commonwealth's ideas of freedom, self-determination and racial equality.[41]

If the new conception of the Commonwealth was to succeed, the soon-to-be independent colonies in Asia and Africa had to be persuaded to join. Decolonisation had reached a crucial phase; Sudan (which gained its independence in 1956) and the Gold Coast (which as Ghana became independent in 1957) were both close to taking important decisions about their international future. Those decisions would, in turn, influence the behaviour of the third wave of colonies to become independent. It was clearly not the time for a decision on a major issue of public policy which could readily be characterised as racially discriminatory. In an era when the Cold War was intense, international critics would not be slow to point out the obvious hypocrisy to a largely anti-colonial Afro-Asian world busily collecting ammunition, actual and intellectual, to undermine the old colonial empires.

Salisbury's proposal, in effect, to discriminate openly against Commonwealth subjects who were citizens of the emergent Asian, African and Caribbean territories was unacceptable to Swinton and Maxwell Fyfe. If the restrictions were not discriminatory they would limit the entry to Britain of subjects from the 'old' white Commonwealth. Swinton summed up the problem:

> The essential difficulty which I see about any proposal for restricting the entry of British subjects into the United Kingdom . . . is that they force us into the dilemma of either admitting into our legislation and administrative practice the more or less open discrimination practised by the 'old' Commonwealth countries; or they will have to be applied against all British subjects of European race seeking to enter this country. . . . There is, in fact, a continuous stream of persons from the old Dominions to the United Kingdom who come here, with no clear plans, in order to try their luck; and it would be a great pity to interfere with this freedom of movement. I see great objection to applying restrictions to Commonwealth European citizens, which the Commonwealth countries do not apply to United Kingdom citizens.[42]

Family ties with the white dominions were still very close. Though all except New Zealand increasingly looked to other European countries to provide migrants, Britain was still the major provider and still supported state-sponsored emigration schemes to the old dominions. Close ties with the 'mother country' had manifested themselves through full dominion participation in two world wars. These ties would be undermined, it was thought, if the freedom or right of emigrants to return 'home' was taken away. In the case of British communities outside the Empire, for example in Argentina, the effect would obviously be even more severe. The impact of the development of a large 'coloured' community in Britain would weaken ties still further: 'such a community is certainly no part of the concept of England or Britain to which people of British stock throughout the Commonwealth are attached'.[43] Swinton held the view strongly that immigration legislation which adversely affected the rights of British subjects should be avoided 'if humanly possible' and if it did become inevitable it was better for the legislation to be overtly discriminatory than to stand in the way of all Commonwealth citizens who wished to come to Britain.[44]

THE FIRST GREAT DEBATE, 1954–5

So concerned was Swinton at this 'big and controversial issue' that he argued for a bipartisan approach with Labour. 'Nothing could be worse', as he expressed it, 'than to put half the Commonwealth and all the Labour Party against us on a difficult issue.'[45] In April a meeting was arranged between party spokesmen on colonial affairs in the Lords at which Lord Listowel, previously a Labour Secretary of State for India, indicated his support both for restrictive legislation and for the bipartisan approach. 'Everything should be done', he agreed, 'to prevent the matter becoming party politics'.[46] Before the Opposition could be approached formally, Government ministers had to sort out their own differences. To this end a meeting of Maxwell Fyfe, Salisbury, Swinton and Lyttleton was held in mid-April to try to map out an agreed approach. The ministers were agreed that powers of deportation for undesirable persons or persons becoming a public charge were necessary; what divided them was the question of how much further they should go. They agreed to ask the Interdepartmental Working Party to look at the suggestion that anyone entering the country for settlement from the Commonwealth/Empire who could not show that they had a job to come to should make a deposit of £25. The Working Party should also consider whether £25 was 'sufficient deterrent' and whether the power to restrict entry should be confined to citizens of the United Kingdom and colonies who were not resident in the United Kingdom.[47]

The Working Party report failed to make the unequivocal recommendation ministers clearly hoped for. Salisbury labelled it 'unnecessarily negative'. It set out once again the difficulties and possible consequences of each of the suggested approaches to the problem of trying to limit the number of Asian and black immigrants to Britain. The only effective way was to introduce checks at border points. These would involve all of those entering Britain, including returning residents, in possibly lengthy delays and would be costly to administer. Its discussion of how the checks should be applied threw up some clear suggestions but the discussion of whom they should be applied to left ministers with a set of unresolved and painful dilemmas. The Working Party threw out the ministerial suggestion of a deposit, arguing that £25 would not be effective at all, whereas a higher sum, say £100, would 'operate against British subjects from overseas of a type we should not wish to exclude'. Control could only be effectively and properly exercised if every arrival for settlement had to obtain leave to land which could only be granted by an immigration officer. The terms on which leave could be granted would include proof of a job or the ability of the immigrant to prove the possession of sufficient means to ensure maintenance. The criminal, the ill and insane and stowaways and deserters would be turned away.

The ministers' suggestion that the checks be applied to those citizens of the United Kingdom and colonies who lived outside the United Kingdom was considered very problematical. It would involve a definition, initially, of who 'belonged to the United Kingdom' and who did not and that would lead to the suspicion 'offensive to liberal opinion in this country and throughout the Commonwealth' that the measure was 'directed against coloured people'. Those not subject to exclusion would include those born (or naturalised) in the United Kingdom, those resident for at least seven years, their wives and any of their children who were still minors. Paradoxically, the Working Party considered that this was problematical because it would not include United Kingdom citizens of 'British stock' living abroad, yet citizens of Commonwealth countries, including India and Pakistan would have every right to enter without hindrance. To extend the control to all Commonwealth citizens would weaken Commonwealth ties, upset India and Pakistan who would probably retaliate and still leave the difficult issue of the Irish. Failure to include the Irish would lead to objections from the Commonwealth, yet to include them would be to undertake a huge administrative burden and limit a supply of labour that was still much needed in the United Kingdom. Perhaps the Anglo-Irish origins of the Working Party's chairman shone through in the assertion that the Irish issue was the most difficult of the dilemmas and that the only way to resolve it was by declaring that – on grounds of common sense and expediency (for which read administrative expense and labour demand) – the British Isles, for the purposes of population movement, were essentially a single entity.[48]

Salisbury was determined not to be deflected. He believed that the Working Party's report was unbalanced in failing to 'recognise the dangers of the immigration of coloured people into this country' and in emphasising and underlining 'some possibly mechanical difficulty'.[49] Through the autumn months both Salisbury and Churchill kept the matter under review; both picked up numerous newspaper reports of increased numbers of West Indians arriving in Britain for settlement and both requested clarification and further detail from their staffs. *The Times* in September carried a report that 'according to a reliable estimate' close to 7,000 West Indians had arrived in Britain to settle in the first nine months of 1954, more than double the figure for the whole of the previous year.[50] Colourful reports in the *Empire News* on 3 October ('Colour Bar War is Threatened in London') and on 6 October in the *Evening Standard* ('Mr. Petrie finds an £11 Job in London's "Little Harlem"') found their way on to ministers' desks. The *Daily Herald* and the *Daily Sketch* both ran major features on West Indian immigration in October.

Both ministers attempted to collect 'ammunition' to use in the impending discussion. Neither had very much success. Salisbury's attempt to obtain figures of immigration from 'coloured' areas from the Board of Trade met with a reply from an official who insisted that such figures as she supplied were very unreliable because they included both students and a large number of UK subjects returning from a period of residence abroad, and they excluded people arriving by air or via Europe across the Channel. (From January 1955 the Board of Trade's statistics would include reference to where the passport was issued, thus allowing that component to be identified.)[51] Following the 'Colour Bar War' article Churchill asked the Home Office to provide him with 'an assessment of the feeling in London on the increasing number of coloured people arriving from the colonies'. He must have been disappointed with the resulting note which referred to the report as 'greatly exaggerated'. Whilst the police thought there was no basis for the prediction that widespread violence against coloured people was to be expected, they did report some feeling developing, ranging from mild apprehension generally to strong resentment in Paddington where many of the West Indian immigrants had concentrated.[52] In mid-October the Home Secretary was reminded rather sharply by Cabinet of his responsibility to bring proposals forward: the matter was both urgent and serious.[53] Perhaps it was not coincidental that on the day in October when the matter was raised in Cabinet *The Times* carried a three-column report and a large photograph headed 'West Indians in Britain – "Planned" Migration Increasing – Work and Housing Difficulties', which Salisbury asked to be sent to Churchill.[54] Churchill's reshuffle of 10 October 1954, which saw Major Gwilym Lloyd George replace David Maxwell Fyfe at the Home Office, caused a further delay and it was not until late November that the matter was discussed again in Cabinet.

In the meantime, the Working Party found that the task set it by ministers, to make proposals for a deportation bill to cover 'colonial immigrants' was not without its difficulties. The most awkward problem was to decide which British subjects the bill should apply to and who should remain outside its jurisdiction or, to put it another way, which British subjects 'belonged to Britain' and which did not. Deportees by definition had to have somewhere to be deported to. The civil servants determined that individuals who would not be liable to deportation were those who were either born in the United Kingdom or whose parents were normally resident in the United Kingdom at the time of birth. Those ordinarily resident for at least seven continuous years and those naturalised in Britain were also exempt. Grounds for deportation were less problematical. The grounds would be criminality – specifically, conviction of an offence for which the court had the power to imprison and for offences connected with prostitution – or dependence on public funds – defined as being substantially dependent on state benefits for a period of twelve months. Undesirability as a ground for deportation was a concept capable of so broad a definition that the Working Party was clearly reluctant to see it used. The Working Party reported to its ministerial masters on 22 October 1954.[55] Salisbury was advised by his private secretary on the basis of the report that deportation was 'a tricky subject' and 'really only marginal to the main issue of restriction of immigration'. Further he advised that 'if anything is to be done about this problem, it must be done by restricting immigration'. Such controls would be 'deliberately designed to hit impecunious "blacks"', and it would be impossible to conceal that intention.[56] For those in Lord Salisbury's office the device was not sharp enough. The 'most doubtful element' of the recommendations was that no one resident in Britain for more than seven years could be deported. 'This means that coloured people could only be deported within the first seven years of their residence here; thereafter they would account as belonging to the United Kingdom and therefore would not be eligible for deportation.'[57]

Nonetheless, when the Lord President met the Commonwealth Relations, Home and Colonial Office ministers on 1 November they agreed to proceed by asking officials to produce a more detailed set of proposals for a deportation bill. Pressure for further and more far-reaching action increased when the question of colonial immigration was raised three times in the House of Commons within the space of a fortnight in early November. James Johnson and Albert Evans, both Labour MPs, asked questions and John Hynd, Labour MP for Sheffield Attercliffe, initiated the first Commons debate on colonial immigration on adjournment on 5 November. Johnson and Hynd both called for the establishment of a committee of inquiry, though in the debate speakers from both sides of the House called upon the government to take urgent action. Replying for the government Henry Hopkinson, the Minister of State at the Colonial

Office, admitted that he had received a number of letters from MPs on the subject, spoke of the urgency and of the deep concern the problem was causing and assured the House that the matter was receiving very careful attention.[58] Evidently as a result of the strong feeling expressed in that debate Lloyd George appears to have swung around to become an ally of Lord Salisbury. Determined upon 'a wider approach to the question' he now believed that it was no longer possible to 'continue to look with equanimity on a large, increasing and uncontrolled flow of immigrants into the United Kingdom of a kind which does not readily assimilate itself to the native population of this country'. This must be done without giving 'any impression of being influenced by any desire to impose any colour ban'. The power to deport was no longer enough; it would incur great displeasure by breaching the principle of free entry for Commonwealth citizens but would yield a small return.[59] The Home Secretary sought the support of his colleagues for a departmental Committee of Inquiry to consider whether any changes were required to laws covering the right of entry to the United Kingdom and if so what those changes were. With Churchill clearly impatient for the matter to be raised again in Cabinet, Lloyd George was evidently hopeful of reaching an agreement quickly with his colleagues.[60]

His hopes were quickly disappointed. Swinton wanted to rush forward with a deportation bill which, he argued, did not require the government to consult with other governments. He believed its deterrent effect would be considerable on 'immigrants of the kind which is troubling us'. Although in favour of a simultaneous announcement setting up a committee to look into the need for further immigration restrictions he expressed very strong reservations about any solution which would either affect the right of free entry of all Commonwealth citizens or which gave citizens of the Irish Republic more favoured treatment than Commonwealth citizens. The first would subject the government to strong political criticism both internally and externally and the second would be resented by Commonwealth countries and be politically indefensible. He was not convinced that the legislation which was needed 'in order to deal with an unwanted influx of Jamaicans' needed to be non-discriminatory. In order to conceal the real purpose of the legislation the country would have to resort to 'a degree of administrative discrimination' which was 'alien to our practices in this country'.[61] He wanted the terms of reference for any committee to enable it to report in favour of restrictions designed to affect 'only the particular class of immigrant we have in mind'. Swinton's views caused a rapid and angry reaction from Lennox-Boyd, the Colonial Secretary. He 'profoundly disagreed' with the notion that the inquiry could be limited in the way suggested by Swinton, a matter about which he felt 'very strongly'. Any attempt to discriminate openly would have 'widespread repercussions'.[62] Nonetheless he fully supported the need for legislation to control immigration from the Commonwealth.

When the matter finally came to Cabinet for discussion at the end of November, Lloyd George and Swinton submitted separate memoranda, the Commonwealth Relation Secretary's paper outlining his misgivings about Lloyd George's approach. It was agreed that the matter was urgent and that the Home Secretary should be asked to submit proposals to Cabinet as soon as possible for a Departmental Committee to report within a few months. The rate of West Indian immigration was now running at 10,000 per year and within three or four years the 'coloured' population of the United Kingdom would reach the magic figure of 100,000.[63] The issue was of such national concern that the Home Secretary suggested that the Prime Minister approach the Leader of the Opposition to achieve agreement before any announcement was made.[64] Two weeks later the Home Secretary's proposals for a committee were rejected in favour of a requirement placed upon both the Home and Colonial Secretaries to submit draft legislation to Cabinet which would place 'suitable restrictions on the admission of British subjects from overseas'. Though it would be necessary to drop legislation already proposed in order to make way for an immigration bill the Cabinet felt that it ought to examine a draft bill before it could decide whether early legislation on the subject should be attempted.[65]

At this point it seemed likely that the response to the first major post-war increase in black colonial immigration was to be legislation to amend the traditional right of British subjects to enter the United Kingdom. Ministers had apparently agreed on the need for a law covering the deportation of undesirables as a minimum and agreement had then emerged on the need for wider powers. However, almost exactly a year later, in November 1955 Prime Minister Anthony Eden appeared to rule out action by the government on the matter. A split in Cabinet allied to the pressure of other business, particularly the general election of 1955 meant that, by the end of the following year, legislation had still not been agreed, let alone put to Parliament. It is worth looking in some detail at why the Cabinet, apparently in agreement on the need for restrictive legislation in December 1954 – after thirteen separate discussions on the question in just under a year, including the consideration of a draft bill to limit entry from the Commonwealth – decided to shelve the matter in November 1955. The debate in 1954–5 about the need for, and the content of, restrictive legislation on 'coloured' Commonwealth immigration is particularly revealing about the range and balance of views on questions of race and immigration represented in the country, in the ruling Conservative Party and in the Cabinet. It was a full dress rehearsal for the debate in 1961, similarly provoked by a rapid rise in the number of immigrants from the black and Asian Empire/Commonwealth. The Cabinet meeting of 3 November 1955 brought to a climax, or rather an anti-climax, the first period of debate about the legislation to keep out 'coloured' immigrants. The decision of November 1955 was, in retrospect, of the greatest possible importance to the making of multi-racial Britain. Given the rates of immigration then prevailing, it is highly unlikely that, had the Cabinet finally agreed to legislation in 1955, multi-racial Britain would ever have come about.

THE REASONS WHY NOT

Press and public interest in the new levels of immigration was strong and somewhat hostile in the last quarter of 1954 and, judging by the Prime Minister's papers, one of the causes of his concern. Press interest fell away quite sharply in 1955 as the novelty of black settlement wore off. The coverage in the *Daily Herald* was an exception to the generally unsympathetic tone in that it emphasised the difficulties faced by the immigrants, especially the colour bar, rather than the alleged inadequacy and poverty of the arrivals. 'Can they be happy here?' was folowed by 'No Colour Bar? Then why does this happen in Britain?' Even so, the *Herald* thought 'coloured people' were misguided if they complained about discrimination and did not believe that the situation could be improved by legislation.[66] Likewise, the *Star* expressed sympathy for those facing colour prejudice but warned that 'race problems' were among the most difficult to solve and urged caution on the Government 'lest we get them in this country too'.[67] The *New Statesman* was unequivocal in its opposition to immigration controls on colonial subjects. In its view restrictions would be morally indefensible, equivalent to imposing the burdens and responsibilities of citizenship without granting the rewards and privileges. Britain was responsible for the plight of the colonies, which was the root cause of the exodus, and it was Britain's obligation to remedy the deficiencies or else set the colonies free.[68]

Not unexpectedly the *Sunday Times* took the view that in light of the inevitability and intractability of colour prejudice and the problems that arise from it, the government should reconsider the entire question of the right of British subjects to enter and work in Britain. Perhaps it was also time to consider whether it was not too difficult to bring in an Italian housemaid to a guaranteed job and a good home.[69] The *Daily Sketch* ran a series of three articles in early January 1955 which it labelled a 'special investigation'. The reporter in Genoa, Italy recorded for readers the plight of a party of West Indian migrants who were en route for Britain, a long twenty-four hour journey away from 'paradise'.[70] The novelty of black immigration was, however, short lived. From January 1955 press interest declined even though the number of migrants probably increased during the year. The Home Secretary informed the Cabinet in May that the degree of public interest in immigration had fallen.[71] Certainly press cuttings about immigration are notable by their absence from the Prime Ministers' papers for 1955, in sharp contrast to late 1954. By the middle of 1955 some members of the Cabinet were so uncertain about the state of public opinion that they thought an independent Committee of Inquiry would help to make the country aware of the 'nature and extent of the problem' prior to the introduction of restrictive legislation.[72]

The divisions on the issues of whether or not legislation should be introduced and what type of legislation was appropriate were apparent in the press as they were in Parliament and in the Cabinet. As we have seen, Alan Lennox-Boyd, the Colonial Secretary, took strong exception in November 1954 to two aspects of the approach of his Home and Commonwealth Relations colleagues. He made it clear, however, that he was disputing the framework of the legislation rather than the need for it. During the course of 1955 opposition to legislation in Cabinet appeared to harden and Lennox-Boyd moved away from his position of support for the proposed legislation. The Colonial Secretary's closeness to the Prime Minister, his popularity in the party and the strong possibility that he would have resigned had discriminatory legislation been approved by Cabinet altered the balance within the Cabinet in a significant way.[73] Likewise Lord Home, from April 1955 Swinton's replacement at the Commonwealth Relations Office, was prepared to defend his corner vigorously. Like Lennox-Boyd, but unlike his predecessor, he was strongly opposed to discriminatory legislation if it affected the rights of people from India and Pakistan to enter Britain. He believed that the governments of India and Pakistan would probably retaliate if Britain imposed controls and that would damage the already troubled British business communities in the sub-continent. Though they were not very large Home described them as 'of vital economic importance to us'. He regarded increasing Indian working-class immigration as likely to become 'a menace' but was prepared to trust the Indian and Pakistani governments to do all in their power to keep such emigration to Britain down to a low level. Nor was he prepared to support legislation which adversely affected the rights of citizens of the white dominions to enter the United Kingdom.[74] Home and Lennox-Boyd were the crucial figures in the Cabinet balancing the pressure of Salisbury and Lloyd George for legislation.

One of the key elements behind the shift in the balance of opinion was the change of prime minister that occurred in early April 1955. During Churchill's last year of office, the prospect of immigration legislation was reduced by the general inertia and lack of direction that affected the final phase of his administration. The attention of the leading figures in the government was diverted from affairs of state to the long drawn out business of the succession. More than a year before he retired, the Prime Minister told Butler: 'I feel like an aeroplane at the end of its flight, in the dusk, with the petrol running out, in search of a safe landing.'[75] Nonetheless, the change of leadership made the prospect of legislation more remote. Unlike Churchill, Eden appeared to possess no strong views about immigration, tending to view it in the light of his preoccupation with external affairs and therefore to weigh more heavily than his predecessor the impact of the negative international consequences of a decision to legislate. As a deep believer in the New Commonwealth he was particularly sensitive to arguments that immigration legislation would have a damaging impact.[76] Again unlike Churchill he was reactive rather than proactive on the question of immigration. Churchill kept up with the press coverage of the subject and personally brought the matter to Cabinet on several occasions. Eden was anxious to be regarded as a moderate in domestic affairs and disliked even the prospect of controversial legislation which would divert his energy and attention away from the international arena.[77] But the explanation for the swing in the balance of opinion in Cabinet is more complex than a change of leadership and a softer media focus on immigration questions. Closer examinations of the costs and benefits, both international and domestic, of introducing a ban were undertaken and offered somewhat different results from the rough-and-ready arguments of 1954.

The scale of the likely political costs and difficulties of introducing legislation were illustrated clearly when the Conservative MP for Louth, Cyril Osborne, attempted to introduce a bill to control immigration under the ten-minute rule into the House. The Cabinet had already speculated on the range and scale of the political difficulties that an anti-immigration bill would provoke in the House of Commons. At the Cabinet meeting on 13 January 1955 Lloyd George set out the type of legislation he believed would be necessary to stem the immigrant flow from the Caribbean. He sought to empower immigration officers to prohibit the landing in Britain of any British subject 'not belonging' to the United Kingdom. Opinion in Cabinet held that such a bill would not obtain the full support of the Conservative Party and would be opposed in the House by the Labour opposition and outside the House by the Trades Union Congress.[78] Party support was a particularly sensitive question as the government's Commons majority was only fifteen.

Osborne's attempt to introduce a bill broadly similar to that proposed by Lloyd George confirmed these fears. Before it reached the House, Osborne's bill was discussed by the Commonwealth Affairs Committee of the Party. Fourteen of seventeen members present spoke, all but one of them against the bill. To an extent Osborne's failure to carry the Committee was the result of tactical considerations. He was obviously not the right man to carry forward the bill: his extreme views were well known, as was his tendency to lose his temper and 'put his foot right in it'. Relations with the new government in Jamaica, the timing of the bill to coincide with the 300th anniversary of Jamaica under British rule, the problem with the Irish and the damage legislation would do to Britain's position in the Commonwealth were further important considerations which turned the committee away from Osborne's proposal. After his experience before the Committee, the Whips would not have had to exert themselves to persuade Osborne to desist.[79] The divisions in the party on the question of immigration controls were confirmed at the meeting of the Central Council of Conservative Associations two months later.[80] The Election Business Committee of the Cabinet evidently regarded immigration as an issue of some sensitivity and sought the advice of the Cabinet on it. It was not an issue that received any attention in the manifesto.[81]

During 1955, in an attempt to strengthen the case for legislation, its supporters in the Cabinet urged two investigations both of which eventually only added to the difficulties of proceeding further. By the first, the result of a decision in January 1955, the Commonwealth Relations and Colonial secretaries were instructed to bring to Cabinet in the form of a draft white paper details of the approaches used by other Commonwealth governments on the entry of colonial subjects. It was felt that public opinion could be more readily brought round to support legislation if it could be shown that other Commonwealth governments were already limiting the entry of other Commonwealth citizens. At the same time objections from those Commonwealth governments would be silenced by the publication of details of their practices.[82] When, as might have been anticipated, the research revealed a veritable litany of discriminatory practice both overt and 'administrative' the Secretary of the Cabinet, Norman Brook, advised the Prime Minister that some Commonwealth governments 'might prefer that the attention of the Parliament at Westminster should not be directed in this way to the extent to which they discriminate against British subjects not of European race'. From the point of view of the Commonwealth as a whole Brook was 'not sure that it is wise to give unnecessary advertisement to this'.[83] Cabinet shared Brook's concerns, particularly as they felt that some of the administrative methods did not have the support of any statutory authority.

The two ministers were instructed to begin the necessarily lengthy process of checking the accuracy of their research.[84]

The second investigation resulted from the long-term determination of the Home Secretary, Gwilym Lloyd George, to set up a departmental Committee of Inquiry to look into the whole issue of colonial immigration. He saw it initially as an exercise to educate and prepare public opinion for legislation. He was opposed by members of the Cabinet who felt that such an inquiry would probably highlight disagreements on the question, result in a majority as well as a minority report and act as a spur to potential migrants to come to Britain.[85] In memoranda to Cabinet in May and June 1955, six months after his initial proposal, he urged his colleagues to agree both to a declaration that it intended to legislate and to a Committee of Inquiry principally for fact-finding purposes. Finally in June the Cabinet rejected the proposal once more and gave to the interdepartmental committee of officials the task of drawing up an authoritative statement on the increasing volume of immigration and 'the social and economic problems to which it gave rise'. In the view of the Cabinet, this would be likely to provide a more satisfactory basis for action than a rather unpredictable Committee of Inquiry report.[86]

It failed to do so. When the draft statement was published for circulation to the Cabinet in August it provoked some interest, particularly from Lord Home, but it certainly did not provide the expected spur to action. The preamble to the draft statement adopted an apologetic tone; the officials were clearly aware that they were failing to deliver the goods. As the document was intended for publication the officials indicated that they had included only statements that were capable of being verified by evidence and had omitted reference to problems that were 'potential rather than actual'. They clearly regretted that 'the statement may . . . give the impression that the position is less serious than it is likely to become'. One of the examples used by the author of the report to illustrate this dilemma was the 'suggestion' that there was a high incidence of venereal disease among West Indians. No statement to that effect could be included because it could not be supported by figures. Indeed it was possible to read the report, as opposed to its preamble, in a way that reflected quite positively on colonial immigration. Although 'coloured' immigration was running at the rate of about 30,000 a year it was apparent that even those arriving most recently had found jobs easily and were making 'a useful contribution to our manpower resources'. Unemployment – at under 2,900, almost all of a short-term nature – could not be regarded as a problem, nor could undue demands on either National Assistance or the National Health Service. A London County Council centre for recently arrived destitute coloured men, established in Stepney in 1952, had been closed down as it had outlived its usefulness. The immigrants were for the most part law-abiding except for problems with Indian hemp (cannabis) and living off the immoral earnings of women. Though the immigrants had not been 'assimilated' there was no evidence of racial tension and it was apparent than some 'coloured' workers in the transport industry had made a favourable impression. The only serious problem provoked by the new arrivals was in the overcrowding of poor areas of inner city housing.

The authors of the report were driven to speculation about the future in order to darken the picture. While the 'coloured' population remained at its present levels and in a period of prosperity the present situation might be expected to continue, but the arrival of families, the increasing geographical concentration of the coloured population and a possible economic downturn could all, in the committee's view, contribute to a rise in racial tension.[87] The Home Secretary was forced to conclude that the statement, if published, would not lead to a demand for legislation to restrict Colonial immigration and that, 'generally speaking, Colonial immigration was not an acute problem at the moment'.[88] The Cabinet decided not to publish the report of either investigation; neither had advanced the cause of the restrictionists. Nonetheless, at the insistence of the Lord President, the Cabinet moved finally to a discussion of the draft bill to restrict Commonwealth immigration drawn up by the Home Office at the request of the Cabinet in December of the previous year. At the Cabinet meeting of 3 November 1955 this extended phase of intense high-level discussion about the need for immigration controls reached its denouement. At that meeting the Cabinet decided to put the matter to one side for the time being and set up a Cabinet Committee to keep a watch on the developing situation.

Two questions might be asked about the discussions of the previous year. Why had they been so long drawn out, and why did they result in what was, in effect, the reversal of an intention to legislate? Two particular circumstances contributed to the delay in coming to a decision. The last months of Churchill's government were not characterised by speed of decision and action; it was a government without effective leadership. The succession, which finally occurred on 6 April 1955, was the central and preoccupying issue in the minds of senior Cabinet members in the months leading up to Churchill's resignation. Eden's succession was quickly followed by a general election held on 26 May. Not many weeks after the Conservatives were returned with an increased majority, the long summer recess began. However, the most central and important aspect of both the delay and the shift of position was the division that emerged in Cabinet as soon as the question of how controls were to be enforced was discussed. In November 1954 there had appeared to be unanimous support in Cabinet for the idea of legislation to limit the entry of immigrants from the Caribbean but as soon as specific issues, about who was to be affected and how the controls were to be administered, were introduced into the discussion disagreements of an important, and apparently unbridgeable, kind emerged.

The suggestion of the Home Secretary that the legislation should identify a class or classes of migrants – that it should be openly discriminatory as between British subjects – was quite unacceptable to the Colonial Secretary, while the Commonwealth Relations Secretary objected strongly to legislation that made it more difficult for people from self-governing parts of the Commonwealth to enter Britain. Behind those positions lay fears about the anticipated effect the legislation would have on the coherence of the Commonwealth, on the strength of Britain's position as its leader as well as on Britain's bilateral relations with individual countries within the Commonwealth whose citizens would be adversely affected by the changes.[89] There was a major, unresolved dilemma over the position of the Irish. To exclude them from the legislation was objectionable to both the Commonwealth Relations and Colonial Offices because it would mean that citizens of a foreign country, moreover one that had actually left the Commonwealth, would be more advantageously treated than people who were British subjects. To include the Irish in the proposed restrictions would involve huge expense, the erection of border posts between Eire and Northern Ireland and the acceptance of a limitation on the flow of needed and assimilable labour. To these difficulties would have to be added short-term political difficulties caused by a crowded legislative programme and the divisions in the Party revealed by the Osborne affair. Through 1955 public and press interest in the question appeared to decline and ministers' attempts to revive it via the publication of a report on the social and economic impact of immigration misfired when the committee of deputy under-secretaries failed to paint the bleak and dangerous picture anticipated by ministers.

While there is some justice in the view that the government was indecisive – thirteen Cabinet discussions in the course of a single year without a clear-cut decision is surely an extravagant use of Cabinet time – there is no sense at all in the widely publicised, recent judgement that the indecision was inexcusable in the face of [*sic*] a 'post-imperial population implosion'. Such a judgement reflects a serious misunderstanding of the chronology of growth of Britain's black and Asian population as well as a failure to appreciate the sharpness of the political dilemmas that the government faced in 1954–5.[90] Asian and black immigration had hardly begun. The black population of Britain did not exceed 100,000 by the end of 1955. Multi-racial Britain was a long way off: Britain was still 99.8 per cent white. Caribbean and West African communities made up small parts of a handful of British towns and migration from the Indian sub-continent was not yet significant. The effect of a decision in favour of legislation in 1955 would have been damaging to their prospects of future growth and would have prevented the South Asian derived communities from establishing themselves in any significant fashion.

The interdepartmental committee had, no doubt, made every effort to define the social and economic problems that ministers believed derived from that immigration but had failed to write a convincing case. There was even a report by the Home Secretary's Parliamentary Private Secretary, made following a summer-time visit to the Caribbean and circulated to leading Cabinet members, which suggested that Caribbean immigrants were both skilled and enterprising.[91] The government in its discussion of the issues and in its administrative policy very clearly expressed a strong and almost unanimous prejudice against colonial or 'coloured' immigration, but it decided it could not stop it without paying a very considerable political price. At the prevailing levels of immigration the price was regarded as simply not worth it.

4 Policy and practice under strain, 1955–62

'TOO MANY DIFFICULTIES TO PROCEED NOW'

Many considerations counted against the adoption of legislative restrictions on 'coloured' immigration in November 1955. The issue as perceived by the Cabinet was not one of the need to restrict immigration in general – far larger migrations of Europeans from Eire and the Old Commonwealth arrived without comment – but of the desire to place limits on the arrival of increasing numbers of black immigrants from the Caribbean. By late 1955 immigration levels from the Caribbean had risen to an unprecedented annual rate of 20,000. The most important barrier to legislation was the difficulty of squaring the openly discriminatory measures that would be necessary to keep out Britain's Caribbean subjects with Britain's position of leadership in the British Commonwealth of Nations, a multi-racial institution designed to retain ex-colonies within a web of British influence. Though the newly independent members of the Commonwealth – and the colonies set on the path to self-government that Britain hoped to attract to the organisation – were aware that the other members of the 'Old' Commonwealth already imposed restrictions on the entry of non-white British subjects, British leaders believed that those governments would find it difficult to accept publicly the adoption of racially discriminatory legislation by the founder and central member of the Commonwealth. Its introduction would be likely to lead to retaliation against British businessmen and British economic interests in India and Pakistan and such people would become subject to parallel legislation. Openly discriminatory legislation, it was thought, would be likely to have a disastrous effect on Britain's relationship with many territories in the West Indies and would jeopardise the future association of the proposed Federation of the West Indies with the Commonwealth.

The alternative was legislation that applied to either the colonies or the whole Empire/Commonwealth without distinction. That course appeared to be open to objections almost as weighty. All such legislation would have to draw a clear distinction between those who were subject to it and those who were not, who 'belonged to the United Kingdom' and who did not. That distinction was anathema to the supporters of the idea that at the heart of the concept of the New Commonwealth was a sense of common citizenship. The definition of who belonged and who did not would create an invidious hierarchy of British subjects. Beyond that argument the logic of applying the proposed restrictions only to the colonies was denied by those who argued that, though such an approach would allow in welcome visitors from the Old Commonwealth, it would not address the growing 'menace' of immigration from the Indian sub-continent. It would also lose its effect as colonies gained their independence. The obvious objection to the application of legislation to the entire Empire/Commonwealth was that it made all, welcome and unwelcome, subject to the same rules.

Further difficulties lay with the Irish; if they were not exempted from the provisions that applied to all parts of the Empire/Commonwealth, British citizens from Northern Ireland would either become subject to immigration controls on entering the mainland or border controls would have to be established between Eire and Northern Ireland. Both approaches were politically difficult and costly. No one in government wished to exclude the ample supply of 'assimilable' labour from Eire which was entering Britain at two or three times the rate of entry from the Caribbean.[1] The alternative was to exempt the Irish from the provisions of the new legislation. If it took this path the government would have to be able to justify treating Fenians more generously than Australian or New Zealand veterans of two world wars. More practically, unless the Irish adopted similar legislation, the Republic could become a conduit for illegal immigration.

A further objection to the proposal for legislation affecting the whole of the Empire/Commonwealth was that the intention behind it would be guessed and that Britain would forgo the benefits and retain the costs of the broad approach. Norman Brook minuted Eden just prior to the crucial Cabinet meeting in November 1955 that although the bill proposed might be non-discriminatory in form, 'it would be clear against whom the Bill was directed and the Government would not be able to avoid disclosing its real objects'.[2] Accusations of racial discrimination in domestic legislation would have been very damaging at a time when the government was preaching the virtues of multi-racialism and racial partnership to others, most sensitively in the mid-1950s to East and Central Africa. The very essence of the still-emerging Commonwealth of Nations was its multi-racial, multi-cultural and multi-lingual character. The ideal of racial equality, powerful enough to bring about the expulsion of one its oldest members, South Africa, in 1961, was widely regarded as a core value of the organisation. Ministers clearly recognised that immigration legislation which could be seen to offend this principle, either directly or indirectly, would be damaging to Britain's position of leadership, both moral and political, within the Commonwealth.

Further, the government felt itself uncertain of commanding consensus on immigration legislation of this type, and did not wish to face the potential political difficulties that might result from an open debate on the subject. The coalition of forces that would combine against either type of legislation would be formidable: it would include a substantial part of the Commonwealth, the Labour Party and, most seriously of all, influential members of the Conservative Party itself. The debate on Osborne's proposals and the vigorous discussions within Cabinet were clear indications of the strength of feeling of those within the Conservative Party who opposed legislating against 'coloured' immigration. In addition to all of these political difficulties there were administrative and financial objections to consider as well. Government had great difficulty deciding just how it could impose restrictions on entry. Whatever method was suggested seemed fraught with difficulties relating to possible evasion and all of them were expected to lead to a considerable increase in staff and impose a substantial additional financial and administrative burden. Taken together the objections were too numerous and too weighty. It was also clear that increasing numbers of immigrants would, at some unspecified point in the future, be likely to make legislation necessary. The centrality of numbers is absolutely clear from the minutes of the Cabinet meeting of 3 November, as it was in the crucial Working Party Report of October 1955. At its present level 'the problem of Colonial immigration had not yet aroused public anxiety'. Clearly it would if immigration was 'allowed to continue unchecked'.[3] 'Should any large-scale influx of families take place . . . the situation . . . might quickly become critical.'[4]

If, as will be argued here, the key determinant of the Cabinet decision on whether or not to legislate was the question of numbers, there is an important underlying question to be asked and answered. The issue the Cabinet kept returning to was not the issue of the number of immigrants in general but the question of the number of Colonial or 'coloured' immigrants. All agreed that in an era of full employment the economy needed more labour. The 750,000 Irish who had entered Britain since 1945 were welcome. Yet government-assisted emigration schemes continued to take significant numbers of scarce British workers and their families to the white Commonwealth countries at the height of post-war labour shortages. The issue the Cabinet was concerned with was not fundamentally one of labour supply, or of immigration and emigration in general, but one of 'coloured' immigration and its consequence, the growth of 'coloured' communities in Britain. Small numbers were acceptable, though what constituted small was subject to redefinition, but large numbers were seen as giving rise to problems significant enough to warrant legislation even at substantial political cost, both domestic and international. Given the evident strength of feeling about the issue – and as we have seen ministers had become gravely concerned about the 'influx' well before the 'coloured' population of Britain reached a total of 50,000 – why was it that the minority ethnic communities exceeded half a million before legislation was finally enacted?

THE WATCHING BRIEF, NOVEMBER 1955–JULY 1958

The Cabinet meeting of 3 November 1955 left the future consideration of the question of colonial immigration in the hands of the Prime Minister. He soon had at hand an answer to the question of how to proceed, from the pen of the Secretary of the Cabinet, Norman Brook. The centrepiece of Brook's proposal was a six-member Cabinet committee 'to consider what form the legislation should take if it were decided to take powers to control this immigration'. It could also draw up a case to justify legislative action. It is clear from Brook's proposal that the key difference in the Cabinet was the question of timing, which related directly to a judgement about numbers. The main question on which the Cabinet was divided, as Brook expressed it, was 'whether the time is ripe to deal with the matter by legislation'. As numbers were expected to increase it was appropriate that the issue should be dealt with by a Cabinet committee until such time as it became critical again.[5] The inaptly named Cabinet Committee of Colonial Immigrants remained in being until 1962, supported by and receiving reports from a committee of officials, the precisely named 'Interdepartmental Working Party on the social and economic problems arising from the growing influx into the United Kingdom of coloured workers from other Commonwealth countries'. The title of the Working Party openly reflected the assumption that Asian and black immigration gave rise to social and economic problems and its purpose was to measure their scale.

At its first meetings the minority of the ministerial committee, led by Lord Salisbury, continued to press for action to be taken as soon as possible. The majority, however, agreed to a report to Cabinet in July 1956 which argued that 'the problem' had not yet become acute and that it was sufficient to keep it under review. All members of the committee were agreed, however, that if the present projected growth in 'coloured immigration' continued, 'action to bring it under control would probably be inescapable eventually'. That it might not do so, that the immigration might be self-regulating, was also suggested in the report. Rising unemployment would discourage coloured workers from coming and remove the need for regulation.[6] After a lengthy Cabinet discussion in July 1956, during which Salisbury clearly put his point of view across effectively, the Ministers decided that the recommendation for another review after twelve months was too complacent and called for the committee to report on the need for legislation in the autumn and to give more thought to the problem of how to deal with the Irish when and if the need for legislation arose. Meanwhile the Colonial Secretary was to discuss the issue of immigration with the visiting Chief Ministers of Jamaica and Barbados.[7]

When the committee's next report was discussed in November 1956, the prospect of legislation had apparently somewhat receded. The previously accelerating rate of increase of immigration had been checked and it was now clear that the number coming in 1956 would be no greater than that in 1955. It was thought that – as economic conditions were now less favourable – the number of 'primary' immigrants had fallen, a higher proportion of the total number being made up by women and children. What to do about the Irish was still a matter of sharp disagreement. The Cabinet, no doubt preoccupied by the political and economic conse-quences of the Suez débâcle, decided to shelve the issue until the decision to legislate had been taken and a resolution of it was, therefore, necessary.[8] On the same day in the House of Lords, Mancroft – the Home Office Parliamentary Under-Secretary – publicly reassured some worried lords, led by Elton, that 'reasonably effective' legislative and administrative measures could be put into operation at short notice if they were deemed to be necessary.[9]

Though in November 1956 it had been agreed to raise the matter again the following spring, it was not until July 1957 that the Cabinet, now reconstituted under the chairmanship of Harold Macmillan, discussed the question again. Perhaps, in view of the changes that had occurred in the Cabinet in the meantime, it is not surprising that each period before the next discussion of the issue was longer than the last. The outlook of Cabinet had changed: Lloyd George had given way to Butler at the Home Office and Lord Salisbury had resigned over Cyprus. Harold Macmillan, as a recent biographer put it, 'devoted ten times as much attention to the problems of the Central African Federation as he did to the problems of Commonwealth immigration'. Macmillan's eyes were firmly fixed on the international stage; domestic matters were left to the liberally inclined Rab Butler. Macmillan did not interfere and, in ten years of chairing the Cabinet Home Affairs Committee, Butler never had need of the Prime Minister's help. In his assessment of the relative importance of the different circles of British influence in international affairs Macmillan undoubtedly rated Europe and the USA more highly than the Commonwealth, though he was aware of 'the emotional spark that the Commonwealth concept could still kindle when suitably invoked in domestic politics'.[10]

These shifts in Cabinet attitudes as well as Cabinet membership coincided with a fall in the number of immigrants from the Caribbean. Compared to 1956 when the figure for Asian and black immigration in the first five months was 12,700, the equivalent level for the same period of 1957 was 5,500. Movement of people from the Indian sub-continent, however, though still on a smaller scale than that from the Caribbean, was showing a steady increase. The Cabinet agreed with the committee recommendation that public opinion was not yet ready for legislation despite the 'transformation of particular areas of certain cities into exclusively coloured districts'. The committee would report again at the end of the year.[11] In fact it was not until July 1958 that colonial immigration was considered again by the Cabinet and by then the situation had changed considerably. In 1958 the debate about immigration legislation, activated by the surge in immigrant numbers from South Asia and by the riots in Nottingham and London, began its second intensive phase which this time was to culminate in the decision to legislate.

CALCULATING THE RATE OF ASIAN AND BLACK IMMIGRATION, 1955–62

The period of almost four years from the beginning of 1958 through to October 1961 when the decision to legislate was finally made is an interesting, important and complex one during which the rate of Asian and black immigration fluctuated considerably. The overall picture was of a substantial fall in Asian and black immigration from a peak of 46,050 in 1956 to a trough of 21,600 in 1959 followed by a dramatic rise to a figure of 136,400 in 1961, which was three times the previous peak (1956). Within that overall picture, however, there were some important developments, not least of which was the quite dramatic change in the ratio of Caribbean to South Asian immigrants. At the beginning of this period the number of immigrants from the Indian sub-continent was continuing to rise overall though it was still very small in comparison to West Indian numbers. It began to fall quite sharply in (April) 1958 and the fall continued through to (April) 1960 when it began to rise again quickly to reach a figure four times greater than any previous level by the beginning of 1961. It continued to rise through to the application of the Act in July 1962. West Indian figures followed a different pattern, falling until early 1959 and then beginning an increase which peaked in 1961 before falling slightly prior to the Act.

The decline and then rise of South Asian figures in relation to West Indian over this period is dramatic and highlights the different responses of migration flows from different parts of the Empire/Commonwealth to government policy. The application of administrative measures to limit immigration clearly had a marked effect on the level of South Asian immigration in 1958–9 and the slower response to the signals that government was about to introduce legislation is almost certainly a function of the greater distance and more substantial barriers, both political and economic, to immigration from South Asia. The steep rise in numbers from South Asia between 1959 and 1961 also points to the particular importance of the increases in migration from South Asia as an influence on the government decision to introduce the Commonwealth Immigrants Act of 1962. A study of the figures in relation to the making of government decisions about legislation once again indicates the overriding importance of numbers.

As numbers were to play such an important part in the decisions that were made about immigration policy, and as numbers provide the basic data for the discussion about when Britain became a multi-racial society, it is perhaps worth pausing briefly to look at the question of the origin and accuracy of the immigration figures used by officials and ministers. There is a watershed in 1962 when the introduction of the Commonwealth Immigrants Act obliged the Home Office to carefully collect and collate data from all ports of entry, though their accuracy is disputed by those who insist that illegal immigration was very substantial. Indeed the anti-immigration lobby argued that immigration statistics always under-estimated the level of Asian and black immigration into Britain.[12] Until 1955 it appears that immigration estimates were based on Board of Trade statistics collected from the manifests of ships arriving in Britain via the long sea routes. Because of the growing use of air travel and the arrival of immigrants via Italy and the Channel ports it is unlikely that these figures accurately reflected the rising numbers. From 1955 these figures were superseded by a head count allied to some passport inspection by Home Office Immigration Officers at all ports of entry. This produced a net monthly figure of arrivals and departures including workers, dependants, students and visitors.[13] Given the reliance on a visual check, the often-voiced suspicions that the figures may have been less than entirely accurate is probably well founded. On the other hand, it is likely that they were very broadly accurate. Ministers and their officials thought the figures important and were generally critical of any suspected major inaccuracy in data they were using.

Various rough-and-ready checks were available to them which, in broad terms, confirmed the Home Office figures. For example, the Ministry of Labour ran regular checks on the number of 'coloured workers' who were unemployed and drawing benefits. Providing a much more accurate check for the Home Office figures were the data on new entrants from overseas into the National Insurance system, drawn up from 1956 by the Ministry of Pensions and National Insurance. These figures obviously include only those who actually registered for work. They, therefore, excluded relatively small numbers of children from the Caribbean and even smaller numbers of females from the Indian sub-continent, as well as those who failed to comply with the requirement to register. Most women from the Caribbean registered for employment soon after arrival. There appears to be quite a strong correlation between entry figures produced by the Ministry of Pensions (for National Insurance registration) and those produced by the Home Office.[14]

The Jamaican Welfare Officer at the Colonial Office kept a record of Caribbean immigration based on the manifests of ships, a task which was taken over in 1956 by the British Caribbean Welfare Service. The BCWS figures, which are not reduced to allow for returnees, are slightly lower than the official estimates.[15] The most remarkable, if not entirely typical, testament to the accuracy of Home Office figures came in 1960 when communication by the Colonial Office with the Jamaican Government revealed that the latter's estimate of emigration to Britain for the first nine months of the year was 23,760; the Home Office estimate of the excess of arrivals over departures from Jamaica for the same period was 23,763.[16] It is, of course, impossible to estimate with confidence the accuracy of the Home Office figures and given the fallibility of the data against which they can be checked, they can be accepted only as very broadly accurate.

Table 2 Annual immigration taken from National Insurance and Home Office figures: West Indies, India and Pakistan, 1956–8

Origin	Year	National Insurance	Home Office
West Indies	1956	29,113	29,812
	1957	18,518	23,016
	1958	16,205	15,023
India	1957	6,154	6,620
	1958	4,876	6,200
Pakistan	1957	5,273	5,170
	1958	6,148	4,690

Source: Toogood (Min. of Labour) to Greig (CO), 26 Jan. 1959, in CO1031/2946

Table 3 Annual immigration taken from Welfare Officer and Home Office figures: West Indies, 1951–8

Year	Welfare Officer*	Home Office
1951	1,500	–
1952	2,000	–
1953	2,000	–
1954	10,000	–
1955	24,000	27,550
1956	26,000	29,800
1957	22,000	23,000
1958	13,000 (*to Aug.*)	15,020

* The Jamaican Welfare Officer at the Colonial Office, 1951–5; the British Caribbean Welfare Service, 1956–8

Source: J. Wickenden, 'Colour in Britain', London, IRR, 1958

Table 4 Home Office estimates of the net inward movement of persons from the tropical Empire/Commonwealth, 1955–62

Year	1955	1956	1957	1958	1959	1960	1961	1962 (first half)
West Indies	27,550	29,800	23,000	15,020	16,390	49,670	66,290	31,800
India	5,800	5,600	6,620	6,200	2,930	5,920	23,750	19,050
Pakistan	1,850	2,050	5,170	4,690	1,860	2,500	25,080	25,090
E. & W. Africa	2,200	2,660	2,830	1,380	1,880	–240	18,110	8,940
Ratio:WI to I&P	4.55	3.79	1.95	1.38	4.11	5.90	1.36	0.70
Other	0	6,740	4,780	2,610	–1,460	–150	3,170	9,210
Totals	37,400	46,850	42,400	29,900	21,600	57,700	136,400	94,890

Source: Home Office figures reproduced in R.B. Davison, *Black British: Immigrants to England*, London: Oxford University Press for IRR, 1966, p. 3 (1962 figures go up to the point when the Commonwealth Immigrants Act took effect)

The figures of new entrants into the National Insurance system from abroad are a relatively reliable set of figures which allow a comparison on the same statistical basis between immigration from the Indian sub-continent, the Caribbean and Africa and immigration from other sources. The term 'immigration' in common usage in Britain in the 1950s and 1960s came to mean 'coloured' immigration, as that was the only category of arrivals that attracted any attention. The Ministry of Pensions figures (Table 3) show very clearly that arrivals from the Indian sub-continent, the Caribbean and Africa were only a quarter of the immigration total over the years for which figures are available. Of course, it is possible that some who came from Europe and the 'white' dominions did so for a limited period of time, for example, as seasonal workers, student employees or entertainers. However, to allow for returning expatriates, the significant number of re-entrants has been excluded from the figures reproduced here. For all of the years except 1960 (when they were approximately equal), the number of immigrants from Eire considerably exceeded the number from the Indian sub-continent, the Caribbean and Africa combined.

1958: THE SOUTH ASIAN SURGE

That the timing of debates in government about immigration policy was a matter of numbers is proved as much by the absence of debate in times of falling Asian and black immigration as by the frequency of debates when the number of those immigrants was rising. After slumbering quietly for a couple of years the issue of 'coloured' immigration suddenly came alive in the early months of 1958. The development that caused alarm bells to ring in the Home Office and Commonwealth Relations Office was a very sudden and 'alarming' increase in the number of immigrants arriving from Pakistan and India. In the single month of February 1958 a number equivalent to thirty per cent of the previous year's entire inflow arrived. Immigration officers from London Airport observed Pakistanis, 'chiefly of

Table 5 Number of new entrants into the National Insurance Scheme, 1956–60

Year	1956	1957	1958	1959	1960	Totals
West Indies	30,442	19,576	17,084	17,895	44,825	129,822
Pakistan	2,828	5,000	5,892	5,387	5,272	24,379
India	6,764	5,933	4,571	5,031	7,088	29,387
East Africa	1,289	1,251	1,510	1,731	2,543	8,324
West Africa	2,837	2,843	3,369	3,467	4,401	16,917
Eire	57,304	58,672	47,869	51,139	57,798	272,782
Europe	40,723	52,784	39,394	39,296	44,734	216,931
Australia	5,923	4,546	4,306	4,795	5,956	25,526
New Zealand	2,097	1,652	1,594	1,808	2,278	9,429
Canada	2,469	2,070	2,273	2,276	2,833	11,921
South Africa	3,250	3,008	3,199	2,986	4,006	16,449
% from New Commonwealth	26.1	20.5	23.3	23.3	33.2	25.7
Other	13,300	11,128	8,121	7,712	11,186	51,441
Totals	169,226	168,463	139,182	143,523	192,914	813,308

Source: CAB13/1005 'New Commonwealth' includes Pakistan

the labouring class and with little, if any, knowledge of English' arriving in organised batches of up to thirty a day.[17] Once again the question of the number of 'coloured' immigrants was the key determinant in raising the issue of immigration on to the government's political agenda. A growing amount of interest was being shown by the press and in Parliament, a steady trickle of Parliamentary questions began and the matter was debated in the Commons on 3 April 1958 on an adjournment motion initiated by Henry Hynd.

It was immediately clear to ministers that if the movement stayed at this level there would be little alternative but to proceed directly to legislation. It was not just the number but the perceived quality of the new arrivals that had the ministers reaching for the panic button. Indeed, the total of new arrivals in the first five months of 1958 was not exceptional by the standards of recent years; 15,356 West Indians, Indians and Pakistanis was below the figure of 16,151 registered for the same months of 1956.[18] For ministers the problem was that arrivals from Pakistan and India now equalled those from the Caribbean and were compared very unfavourably to them. The new arrivals were 'not as readily employable as West Indians' and were 'handicapped by their inability to speak English, by illiteracy and by poor physique, which makes it impossible for them to take normal labouring jobs'. In the opinion of Lord Home, the Secretary of State for Commonwealth Relations, 'Not to put too fine a point upon the matter, most of the Indians and Pakistanis now arriving here are quite unsuitable and cannot be absorbed'. He had no reason to believe that 'the public at large will extend to them the degree of tolerance which has been shown on the whole to the English-speaking, literate, Christian, able-bodied and reasonably capable West Indians'.[19]

One of the Commonwealth Relations Office's resident South Asian experts described the new type of immigrant as 'usually a villager, either a small land-owner or tenant, or perhaps owns a small shop'. Nearly all were married but came alone usually from Azad Kashmir and the adjoining districts of West Pakistan, or the Sylhet District of East Pakistan, or they were Sikhs from the Punjab or the Delhi area. They had generally sold or mortgaged their property in the expectation that they would gain employment and be able to remit substantial sums of money.[20] Ministers and their officials saw this inflow as quite unprecedented, a new element in the situation and one that almost certainly resulted from careful planning at the other end. No widely agreed explanation for the sudden movement emerged, though various ideas connected with 'organised rackets' and foreign exchange fiddles were mooted. The use of forged or stolen passports was also thought to be a factor in the situation.[21] The consequences were likely to prove politically very difficult to handle because so many of the new arrivals moved immediately to areas where there were significant settled 'coloured' populations – Coventry, Sheffield, Bradford and Birmingham were the locations favoured by Pakistanis – and added to the already difficult situation locally in housing and employment.

The recent recession in some industries, notably textiles (which was one of the largest employers of Pakistanis in Yorkshire), exacerbated the social problems. Against a background of rising unemployment, figures were produced to indicate that a large proportion of the new arrivals failed to gain employment and became immediately dependent on National Assistance. In the six months prior to April 1958 Indian and Pakistani unemployment had increased from 1,500 to 5,800; and of the 1,600 unemployed Pakistanis in Yorkshire, 1,300 had never had jobs in the United Kingdom. Dependence of Indians and Pakistanis on National Assistance had grown from 500 in September 1957 to 4,100 by the end of March 1958. It was repeatedly said that the new arrivals were illiterate except for the correct words ('P.1') necessary to request the appropriate National Assistance application form. A disproportionately large number of Indians and Pakistanis were to be found among pulmonary tuberculosis sufferers in sanatoria and chest hospitals.[22] These were the type of figures that the critically important Working Party Report of October 1955 had failed to produce, with damaging results for the advocates of controls.

Immediate action was taken. The first step was for the Commonwealth Relations Office to send a confidential dispatch to New Delhi and Karachi setting out their anxieties and stressing the need for the governments in those countries to act to stem the flow. Officials were 'seriously disturbed . . . by the evidence . . . of the serious social and other problems to which this sudden influx is giving rise' and the High Commissioners were instructed to point out to the Indian and Pakistani governments that the United Kingdom regarded this as a new phenomenon and one that it could not allow to continue unchecked. They would prefer that the checks be put in place by the South Asian governments but wished the High Commissioners to find out what the local reaction would be if London was forced to legislate.[23] Further immediate measures included the secondment of a Principal in the Commonwealth Relations Office to work full-time on the question, the employment of Urdu-speaking interpreters at Heathrow and in Bradford to try to develop a better understanding of the movement, and rapid action to place in the vernacular press in India and Pakistan materials designed to discourage migrants from coming.

The motivation for this spurt did not derive entirely from a distaste for the new immigrants. What the Commonwealth Relations Office appeared to fear most was the potential for damage to Commonwealth relations that the new migration posed. Centrally, Commonwealth Relations Office officials predicted that continued high levels of migration would lead to demands for controls which, taking into account past decisions, would probably be imposed on the whole Commonwealth with effects which the Commonwealth Relations Office believed would be certain to be damaging. They were extremely keen to stem the flow, if possible before such demands were voiced. As Snelling, the Assistant Under-Secretary of State, put it:

> My hope in all this is that we shall be able to curb this traffic without the necessity for passing legislation to control the entry of all British subjects into this country. I fear such legislation would not only be highly controversial here but would cause the utmost disappointment to our closest friends in the Commonwealth and I can see at any rate Messrs. Diefenbaker, Menzies and Nash pleading earnestly with us not to take any steps that would put obstacles in the way of the free flow of people from their countries here.[24]

By mid-April ministers ordered the 1955 draft bill to be taken out of mothballs, reprinted and distributed to the six members of the Cabinet committee. It was given a place in the list of contingent bills in the future legislative programme. Both the Commonwealth Relations Office and the Colonial Office were strongly opposed to it: the Commonwealth Relations Office regarded it as 'a last resort' and the Colonial Secretary would reportedly 'not have it at any price'.[25] To strengthen their defences further against the bill the Commonwealth Relations Office sought the opinion of its High Commissioners, clearly hoping that they would provide strong evidence of the seriousness of the likely repercussions.[26] The draft bill sent out to the Commonwealth capitals empowered the British government to control entry for settlement to Britain of British subjects who did not belong to the United Kingdom (by birth or by holding a United Kingdom issued passport) unless they were coming to a job or were able to support themselves. Even if they could satisfy one of these requirements arrivals could still be excluded if they were unable to prove that they had suitable accommodation available in Britain. The Irish were excluded from the terms of the bill. The Commonwealth Relations Office wanted it 'put back in its pigeonhole' until they had time to show that they could deal with the influx by administrative means.[27]

The Commonwealth Relations Office's opposition to legislation deepened when it had absorbed the replies from the High Commissions to its questions about the likely impact of legislation. The general sense of the replies from the old dominions was that their governments and still more their public opinion would 'deplore' measures that would disturb the traditional right of unrestricted entry exercised by between a quarter and half a million of their citizens every year.[28] For example, Canberra pointed out that the Australian government had just introduced legislation requiring the issue of entry permits to all persons, except people from Great Britain, coming to Australia. His view was that there would be 'a great outcry and indignation' if Australians were required to secure an entry permit before beginning their journey to Britain.[29] The Irish Ambassador added to the consensus that legislation would bring fearful political difficulties in its train. He pointed out that the recent levels of emigration from Eire to Britain were around 60,000 per year which was about the same level as the total of hard-core unemployed in the Republic. A reduction in emigration would have 'a disastrous effect on the already somewhat precarious economy' causing an increase in unemployment, a reduction of remittances (an important feature of the country's invisible exports) and a marked fall in spending power.[30]

Replies from Pakistan, India and Ceylon were even more strongly worded. Fowler in Karachi wrote of the likelihood of 'severe press and public criticism' and of the 'great strain' such legislation would impose on Pakistan's links with the Commonwealth and the associated regional defence pacts. 'Serious damage' to Britain's relationship with Pakistan would result from the passage of legislation which differentiated between the rights of Pakistanis and the rights of other Commonwealth citizens to enter Britain. In India such legislation 'would inevitably arouse high emotions' and lead to public questioning of the benefit of the Commonwealth link. Press and public opinion could not be expected to be 'entirely reasonable' in this matter and there would be a probably 'irresistible demand' for reciprocal measures against the British business community, which the Indian government could undertake without the need for further legislation of its own.[31] The reply from Colombo advised that from time to time a 'certain price' might have to be paid to maintain the cohesion of the Commonwealth and Britain's place in it. In the judgement of the High Commissioner in Ceylon, the open-door policy was 'a very considerable factor in holding the Commonwealth together'.[32] Not surprisingly the clear conclusion was that there would be little or no chance of persuading governments in the sub-continent to accept legislation that was either plainly or implicitly discriminatory. Just as the Colonial Office had led the fight in 1955, so now the baton was taken up by the Commonwealth Relations Office.

The administrative means that the Commonwealth Relations Office promised to employ to combat the increase in immigration flows from the Indian sub-continent showed encouraging early signs of effectiveness. At the meeting of the ministerial committee on 19 May 1958 it was reported that the governments of both India and Pakistan had co-operated fully and agreed to institute a number of additional practices which, they believed, would significantly reduce the flow of emigrants. In both countries, before the new restrictions were applied it was already difficult to obtain a passport valid for travel to the United Kingdom. In 1954 the Indian government had centralised the issue of passports in order that it could be more carefully controlled. The Indian Ministry of External Affairs in 1955 issued a directive which had the immediate effect of preventing the migration to Britain of Indians with low educational and financial qualifications. The Indian government required an applicant for a passport to state the reason for the application and the countries the applicant wished to visit. It tried to enforce the rule that those leaving India for Britain had to obtain an appropriate stamp or endorsement.[33] If the applicant appeared to be borderline – with an educational qualification of less than a graduate and of limited financial means – the Indian government still operated the old pedlar checks which involved reference to London, though increasingly applications from 'illiterates and other undesirables' were being refused out of hand. In addition the Indian government now required a substantial financial guarantee or bond (which ranged from Rs.5,000 to Rs.10,000) from applicants for passports to travel to the United Kingdom unless they could prove that they had adequate resources. If an applicant claimed to be travelling to Britain to become a student, evidence of admission to a recognised and bona fide educational institution as well as proof of adequate financial resources for travel and maintenance were now required. Doubtful cases were referred to the Indian High Commission for an on-the-spot check.

The airport police in India had been strengthened and there had been a general crackdown, including arrests, of persons involved in assisting illegal immigration. The old style of passport which had been relatively easy to forge or pass on to another bearer had been replaced by one which was far more difficult to reproduce or modify. Procedures in the passport issuing offices had been tightened up considerably and a crackdown had started against families, mainly Sikh, whose members had been involved in illegal travel. Care was now taken in endorsing passports for travel to countries from which it was easy to reach the United Kingdom, and Indian missions abroad had been ordered not to endorse passports for travel to the United Kingdom without referring the application to Delhi. According to a Regional Passport Officer the Indian authorities had to satisfy themselves that the applicant would reflect credit on India when abroad and that the applicant did not need protection from his own ambition to travel abroad. An example was provided of the refusal of passport facilities to a Bengali landowner who proposed to sell all his land to pay his family's passage to Britain.

So effective were the measures that the bearer of a high-ranking High Commission employee was refused facilities despite the support of his employer, and great difficulties were experienced and reported by an Indian journalist who had been invited on a tour of Britain by the Central Office of Information. Even more harshly, when a person of Indian origin applied for the renewal of a passport at the High Commission in London and the passport was found to be forged, the applicant's wife and children were refused permission to join him irrespective of the fact that the applicant was well established in the United Kingdom. If the passport of the applicant did not have the proper endorsement, facilities were generally refused for the wife and children. From the Commonwealth Relations Office's point of view the only clearly unsatisfactory revelation about the control of passport issuing in India was the treatment of Anglo-Indians, who were expected merely to provide a note from the Anglo-Indian Association proving they were Anglo-Indian and who were not expected to provide a financial deposit or any other assurances.[34] In summary, the Indian government assured London that passports for travel to Britain were only issued after educational and financial qualifications had been scrupulously examined and only to those who, unquestionably, had proof of employment 'in well-established business concerns, in certain liberal professions or in other fields which are remote from peddling, hawking and very petty jobs'. In the judgement of the Indian Government's Chief Passport Officer his government's policy was now 'severe to the point of being unjust'.[35]

The most significant part of the recent increase in Asian and black immigration was that from Pakistan rather than India. In the face of this increased flow Pakistan's measures appeared to be even more successful than India's. A system of cash deposits had almost completely replaced the old pedlar system of referring the applications for passports for the United Kingdom from 'low class' citizens to the Home Office. The deposit had initially been set at Rs.1,100, had been increased to Rs.1,800 and now was being further increased to Rs.2,500 (£187). Passport offices in Pakistan would in future conduct all interviews for people applying to come to the United Kingdom in English and would reject applicants who were unable to demonstrate a working knowledge of the language. Further, a passport would not be issued unless the applicant could prove either that there was a job waiting in Britain or that admission had been obtained to a recognised educational establishment. Publicity was being given to the plight of those who had already arrived without a job, language or skills. The High Commission staffs and their local employees took on a range of monitoring functions to check up on the effectiveness of these measures. Evidently, the practice at local passport offices was checked periodically and 'security officers' stationed at the major international airports reported to the High Commissions on visual sightings of working-class migrants.[36]

The Cabinet committee appeared convinced that the measures were already enjoying some success and its report to the Cabinet met the immediate anxieties of the Commonwealth Relations Office and Colonial Office. The committee concluded that legislation was not needed at the moment, but everything possible had to be done to ensure the continuing effectiveness of the measures taken against Indian and Pakistani migration. Where possible they should be extended to include the West Indies. The government must, however, be ready with legislation should present trends stop or be reversed. Conservative members in the House of Commons should be informed of the difficulties and their views sounded. In order that the appropriate bill could be readied the Cabinet was asked to decide which territories the legislation should apply to should it prove necessary.[37]

The advice to Harold Macmillan from his private office supported the committee recommendation that the time was not yet ripe for legislation. However, it was still a matter of when and how rather than whether. The Prime Minister was advised that the monthly influx of 3,000 coloured immigrants 'can hardly be continued indefinitely without potentially serious social consequences' yet at about 200,000 the 'coloured' population of the United Kingdom is 'still not a very large figure in itself'. Public opinion was not yet ready for legislation and the British government should continue to seek to discourage excessive immigration by administrative measures and by appropriate publicity in the countries of origin.[38] There was optimism that measures that did not require legislation could be made to work rather more effectively. Governors in the Caribbean had recently been sent a draft telegram for comment which suggested to Caribbean governments that for a period of six months they stop issuing passports to West Indians seeking to come to Britain for work.[39] In early July 1958 the Cabinet decided to take no action and to keep the matter 'under close review'. It was to be raised again in early autumn.[40]

1958: THE RIOTS

The anticipated timetable was disrupted by the outbreak of rioting from 23 August to 2 September 1958, first in Nottingham and then in Notting Hill, London. The significance of the riots of 1958 has been emphasised in a great deal of the literature on post-war race and immigration, but it is apparent that the direct impact of the riots was, if anything, to restrain the inclination of ministers to legislate against 'coloured' immigration.[41] Ministers did not wish to be seen to be responding to violent conduct, particularly if such action was likely to be seen as directed at the minority communities. It has been suggested that the riots may have contributed indirectly to the legislation in that they helped to restore the race question from the obscurity into which it had declined after the flurry of interest in 1955 to a subject of media and public interest. This may well be so, particularly as the riots occurred at a time when Asian and black immigration was in decline and the government had very recently concluded that legislation was not yet necessary. Indeed, the period between spring of 1958 and spring of 1960 is one during which old-fashioned administrative controls apparently enjoyed an Indian summer of success.

There is no doubt that initially the riots were seen by the government first and foremost as a source of strong additional pressure for immigration legislation. The assumption was made that the riots would be used by groups who favoured immigration controls as evidence of the social problems that would inevitably arise from black and white living together and, therefore, of the need to strictly limit further 'coloured' immigration. The Commonwealth Relations Office immediately telegraphed its High Commissions to warn them of these likely repercussions and to ask for a summary of overseas press reaction.[42] In Britain press and public reaction to the riots did not bring as much pressure on government to legislate as it had at first feared. An in-house analysis of editorial comment divided the press into three groups: those who were against immigration control; those proposing some form of control short of exclusion, such as deportation; and those who advocated full legislative control. The list of those in the latter group contained only two national dailies: the *Daily Mirror*, the *News Chronicle* (the control must not be discriminatory and should be considered with great caution), the *Birmingham Post* (but no concessions to hooliganism), the *Western Mail* (via a Royal Commission) and the *Spectator* (which called for a detailed investigation of the issue) were the only publications to come out in favour of control. The balance on the other side was more substantial both in quality and quantity: the *Manchester Guardian*, the *Daily Mail*, the *Daily Herald*, the *Daily Worker*, the *Evening Standard*, the *Glasgow Herald*, the *Scotsman*, the *Observer*, *The Economist* and the *New Statesman* made up a strong alliance of varied political hue. An influential group of newspapers including *The Times*, the *Daily Telegraph* and the *Daily Mail* argued that the government should modify its stand, at least by the introduction of a law which allowed the deportation of mischievous elements.[43]

The link between the riots and the need to discuss the immigration question was made immediately in Britain and throughout the Commonwealth. Before the riots had finished the Federal Government of the West

Indies signalled its desire to send its Deputy Prime Minister, Dr Carl Lacorbiniere, to London immediately for ministerial level talks. Norman Manley, Prime Minister of Jamaica, also flew to London on 5 September to be joined two days later by Dr Hugh Cummings, the Premier of Barbados. While the dust was still settling Macmillan wrote to Butler, the Home Secretary, to ask him to bring forward the next Cabinet discussion of the 'immigration question' from the previously agreed date in early autumn, and Butler asked the Ministerial Committee under Lord Perth to reconvene and examine what steps might be taken to deal with immigration.[44] The two Cabinet discussions of 'Racial Disturbances' on 8 and 11 September were, if the minutes are an accurate reflection of them, almost entirely discussions about the need for immigration control.

The underlying analysis was startlingly simple. According to the minutes of 8 September the riots arose out of competition for housing and employment, aggravated in some cases by disputes about women. It was, therefore, necessary with the co-operation of the appropriate governments to restrict the number of emigrants leaving for Britain from India, Pakistan and the Caribbean and to take powers to deport such undesirable immigrants from the Commonwealth as were already here. Yet the Cabinet, with apparent neglect of all logic, committed itself 'to continue to deal with the problem empirically' and to 'base our action on the practical considerations of the availability of housing and the capacity of the labour market'. Once again there was a divorce between private and public behaviour. While vigorously pursuing the cause of emigration restrictions (other people's, that is) the Cabinet noted 'the need to avoid any pronouncement of policy about the principle of Commonwealth immigration'.[45] Yet strangely, the government's almost complete public silence about the riots was interrupted by a press statement on 4 September which drew attention to the connection between the disturbances and immigration legislation. It referred to the 'long-term importance' of the racial disturbances in terms of the continuing need to examine 'the result of this country's time honoured practice to allow free entry of immigrants from Commonwealth and Colonial Countries'. The Government did not think it right to take long-term decisions except after 'careful consideration of the problem as a whole'. The implication was clear enough: the victims of the riots were to be punished eventually for the attacks made upon them.[46]

It is a widely held belief among many who have written on the subject of race and ethnicity in post-war Britain that the 1958 race riots had a direct and marked effect on the decision to legislate against 'coloured' immigrants.[47] The relationship between the riots of 1958 and the legislation of 1962 was much less direct than has often been supposed. In the four-year period between the riots and the legislation, Asian and black immigration actually fell (before it rose again) and as it did so the argument for legislation was seen to lose much of its force. As we have seen in the last chapter the support for legislation did not build up incrementally; it was very much a function of how serious 'the problem' was perceived to be, which in turn was directly related to the number of Asian and black immigrants arriving in Britain. Of course, the riots provided another confirmation, albeit a rather dramatic one, for those many officials and ministers who already believed, or rather assumed, that 'coloured' immigration in substantial numbers was likely to lead to a range of serious social and economic problems.

But it was not as if ministers and their officials had decided before the riots not to legislate. It was for most of them, given that numbers continued to increase, a matter of time and method – of when and how rather than whether. In general, officials assumed that large-scale immigration, allied to the residential concentration of racially distinct immigrants, would lead directly to public order problems.[48] It has been argued that the riots did contribute to the decision in the sense that they raised public awareness of an issue which had, hitherto, been of only occasional public and media concern. After the riots, it was said, race and immigration remained closer to the political surface in Britain.[49] More convincingly, the evidence shows that the pattern of both public and government concern about 'coloured' immigration was sporadic – periods of intense interest interspersed with periods when no interest was shown in the matter at all – rather than incremental. It could still ebb away into the backwaters of public life. Immigration had been an issue in April and May 1958 following the swift increase in movement from Pakistan and India yet was seldom mentioned during the general election campaign fought in 1959. In the two years between February 1959 and February 1961 the subject of 'Commonwealth' immigration was discussed by the Cabinet on only two occasions.

In a more convincing sense the riots made it more difficult for the government to enact legislation in the short term. Among ministers and officials there was a substantial body of opinion which argued that legislation was not now possible because it could be seen as giving in to the bully boys who had stimulated the riots. The Home Secretary was keen to avoid any impression of being 'panicked' into action and resisted suggestions for a Commission of Inquiry because he believed that by doing so he would contribute to the already marked tendency to 'over-emphasise the seriousness of the disturbances'.[50] Indeed, ministers did all they could to play down the importance of the riots by, for example, limiting the number of public statements on the issue and by confining the discussion at the annual Conservative Party Conference in October to a mere sixteen minutes. Domestic and international imperatives pointed in this same direction. Given the wide national and international media attention the riots attracted, the introduction of immigration controls at this time would have been seen as representing an admission of failure by Britain, the head of a multi-racial Commonwealth, to manage race relations in its own capital.

Sir Henry Lintott, the Deputy Under-Secretary of State at the Commonwealth Relations Office expressed the point clearly in a minute for Lord Home:

> Although I suppose that these incidents may well lead to an increase in the political pressure for legislation to control coloured immigration, it is to my mind more difficult for this Office to contemplate such legislation after the riots than it was before. We have always thought that to depart from the traditional and inspiring policy of free entry for all Commonwealth citizens would be a very grave step, and we know that it would be resented and criticised in many quarters. But we might perhaps have got away with it without too much difficulty if it had been clear that we were taking powers only to deal with certain specific difficulties, such as the immigration of diseased or unemployable persons, and if the measures had been introduced in a calm atmosphere. If after these incidents we take such powers of control over immigration, it will appear – and be said – that we are doing so because the British people are unable to live with coloured people on tolerable terms. This could be immensely damaging to our whole position as leaders of the Commonwealth which, in its modern form, largely draws its strength from its multi-racial character. If, therefore, strong pressure develops for the introduction of legislation to control immigration, I would hope that some way can be found to delay action and to permit passions to cool.[51]

The Colonial Secretary and the Home Secretary both shared the view that Britain's moral leadership of the Commonwealth would be threatened if the demand for legislation was accepted.[52]

ADMINISTRATIVE MEASURES AND DEPORTATION, 1958–9

In fact the riots provided a stick with which to beat the High Commissions in India and Pakistan and the government in Jamaica. For the reasons set out by Lintott they were now increasingly seen as the front line in the battle against increasing immigration. The riots were linked to gloomy employment prospects to provide two elements that were together likely to lead to strengthened calls for legislation. The High Commissions and the Jamaican government were encouraged and expected to redouble their efforts so that legislation, so potentially damaging to Britain's Commonwealth relationships, would not be necessary. The High Commissioners were asked to bring to the attention of their government a very gloomy note about employment prospects in Britain. Total United Kingdom unemployment – at 244,000 in July 1957 – had risen to 412,000 by July 1958. Britain already had many thousands more unskilled workers than it needed and could not reasonably be expected to absorb further immigration.[53]

But it was apparently only potential immigrants from the Caribbean and the Indian sub-continent who could positively affect the unemployment figures. No thought appears to have been given to stemming the more substantial flow of unskilled labour from other quarters, such as Eire. The British government was trying vigorously to solve what it saw as its immigration problem – or rather its 'coloured' immigration problem – by exporting the obligation to staunch the flow of immigrants to the governments of the countries from which they originated. The Colonial Office was the focus of attention. Indeed, senior Commonwealth Relations Office officials were harsh in their criticism of Colonial Office ineffectiveness in an area in which they had already succeeded. Further, it was West Indians rather than Indians, Pakistanis or Ghanaians who were seen to be involved in the disturbances. There was concern that continuing West Indian immigration was threatening the rights of all Commonwealth citizens to come to Britain. The Colonial Secretary should 'urge forcibly' the visiting Prime Ministers of Jamaica and Barbados and Deputy Prime Minister of the West Indies Federation to do all in their power to halt the flow from the islands.[54]

Accompanied by Lennox-Boyd, the Home Secretary put proposals – for limiting the flow of emigrants leaving the Caribbean and for the adoption of a deportation law covering the Empire/Commonwealth – to a senior-level delegation of Caribbean politicians. The visitors, Manley, Cummings and Lacorbiniere made it clear that they did not object to deportation legislation if well defined and sparingly used, but they were unwilling to do anything publicly to affect the flow of emigrants from the Caribbean. They expressed sympathy with the British government's position and undertook to do what they could 'unobtrusively to restrict the flow'.[55] As both the British ministers were no doubt aware, it would have been politically suicidal and economically costly for the Jamaican, or any Caribbean, government to attempt to interfere with the flow of migration. The following day, at a meeting with Lennox-Boyd, the visitors were prepared to go a stage further. They promised to intensify at once a publicity campaign designed to bring home to people in the West Indies the present grave unemployment situation facing West Indians coming to

Britain and they agreed to take administrative action to slow down, and regulate more strictly than before, the issue of passports. A five-day wait for a passport could be extended to a six-month delay.

However, they reiterated that it would be politically impossible to stop the issue of passports even for a limited period. Such a move would lead to 'a serious loss of faith in the United Kingdom'. They agreed to recommend 'such administrative action as is practicable to be taken to regulate the pace of issue of passports'.[56] Publicly, Norman Manley maintained a stance strongly opposed to any limitations on emigration from Jamaica. On departure from Britain on 12 September he said:

> We do not consider it right or practicable to limit emigration in any way – and we do not propose to do it. If emigration is to be limited by law then England must, on her own responsibility, decide to do that in England, due regard being paid to what will happen in the Commonwealth if England's traditional policy of 'open door' is closed . . . But that is England's business, not mine.[57]

Colonial Office efforts were not entirely wasted. In accordance with their suggestions all Caribbean governments from September 1958 began to refuse passports to applicants known to have been convicted of a serious offence, particularly one involving violence. Jamaica also began to impose restrictions on the issue of passports for unaccompanied juveniles and for the old and the infirm.[58]

While the Colonial Secretary was putting pressure on the Caribbean governments the Commonwealth Relations Office was still active in the sub-continent. Noting small increases in the number of 'labouring immigrants' arriving in August (as a high proportion of 191 net arrivals from Pakistan and 377 from India) it wrote immediately to New Delhi and Karachi demanding an explanation and asking whether more could not be done.[59] In effect the letter placed on the New Delhi and Karachi High Commissions the duty of averting the introduction of immigration controls. The riots, London explained, had reawakened public interest in the question of Commonwealth immigration and pressure for measures would become irresistible unless the flow was checked. The Indian government appears to have been genuinely perplexed at the continuing high levels of movement into Britain. The number of arrivals in the United Kingdom was far in excess of the number of passports issued and renewed in India. The only possible conclusion was that the immigrants were leaving India either with papers for a country other than Britain or with forged passports.

To officials it seemed likely that significant numbers of Punjabis (the main group from which migration came) were crossing the border into

Pakistan, either legally or illegally, and moving on from there to Britain with passports supplied by local agents. Indian police action against gangs of forgers had resulted in arrests and prosecutions in Delhi, Bombay and Jullundur. A case tried in Bombay in September 1958 involved immigrants from Punjab applying for a special Indo-Pakistan passport which allowed travel only to Pakistan, where they picked up forged or recycled Indian passports at Karachi airport before boarding French, Swiss or Scandinavian aircraft for London. The system involved bribing airline officials and police in Bombay and Pakistani officials at Karachi airport. Other immigrants from India were re-using passports posted back to India after the initial user had arrived in Britain.[60] A further indication that Punjabi migrants were using forged or non-endorsed passports came from the official Indian government figures for the issue of passports for travel to the United Kingdom which showed that between 1955 and 1958 almost as many passports for settlement were issued at Calcutta as at New Delhi.[61] One of the main concerns of the newly formed Indian Workers Association in Britain in the late 1950s was the problem of forged passports. When Jawaharlal Nehru visited London in 1957 the IWA represented to him the interests of the large number of Indians in Britain whose passports could not be renewed and which could not be used to visit India. Nehru was lobbied to order the Indian High Commission in London to exchange invalid and forged passports for new ones.[62]

From Pakistan came more reassuring sounds. There was confirmation of the likely effectiveness of the changes already introduced. The increased deposit and the new restrictions which had come into effect on 1 July 1958 would take a little time to take effect because of the backlog of passports already issued under the old regime. Karachi had experienced a fall in those applying for passports and Lahore now insisted that all applicants for passports who cited a friend or a relative as a future employer were checked out by the London High Commission. London was assured that the flow of unskilled workers had ceased – no applicant for a passport had yet agreed to pay a deposit. Additionally people were now much more reluctant following the introduction of martial law to put their signature on an affidavit.[63] The reassurances from the High Commissions in Delhi and Karachi did not inspire the fullest confidence in Whitehall. 'Experience has shown that the orders of the Government of Pakistan . . . are not always enforced, particularly by the Dacca Passport Office'. Some passports issued since August had already been seen, the holders had been unemployed and not all had been required to make the enhanced deposit. 'Dealers' had sprung up in response to the new restrictions, capable either of forging endorsements or passports, or arranging travel to the United Kingdom via an intermediate destination. Nonetheless, so effective did the new measures appear to be that from the peak levels of February 1958 immigration from India and Pakistan fell to such a level that the annual totals for 1958 were eventually 1,000 less than those for 1957. By the end of 1958 the South Asian population of the United Kingdom was, at an estimated 54,000, only 0.1 per cent of the population of the country.[64]

As well as beefed up administrative arrangements the government decided, in the aftermath of the riots, to look again at the issue of the deportation of undesirable immigrants from the Empire/Commonwealth. The whole question of deportation had been examined in great detail in 1955 when, briefly, ministers had agreed on the necessity for this type of legislation. The practices of other Commonwealth and Colonial governments had been interrogated and a paper produced for Cabinet perusal. At the Conservative Party conference in October 1958 both the Colonial Secretary and the Home Secretary had indicated that this type of legislation was being considered and came close to giving an undertaking that it would be introduced. Restricted to criminality such a measure was predicted to lead to the deportation of only twenty to forty a year, but the measure was thought to be politically important as a clear indication of the government's concern and preparedness to act about immigration.[65]

The government was concerned that it would be faced with pressure to introduce more far-reaching controls and, though these had very limited support in the Conservative Party, there was a suspicion that, unless appeased, anti-immigration sentiment might grow. Norman Pannell, Cyril Osborne and Lord Salisbury, as the leading advocates of controls, commanded little active but perhaps rather more tacit support in the Party.[66] The Conservative Party Conference in October provided a platform for the issue to be aired, an opportunity that Pannell took to win approval for a motion calling for controls on the basis of reciprocity and for the deportation of criminals. Later the same month Osborne raised the issue in the debate on the Queen's Speech. It was introduced again in the Lords by Lord Pakenham in November and by the persistent Osborne in a private member's motion in December. Osborne quoted a recent poll in the *Daily Express* which indicated that close to 80 per cent of the electorate favoured the introduction of immigration controls.[67]

Osborne's private member's motion was an episode that apparently caused the government once again to consider its attitude towards legislation. The Home Secretary at the Conservative Party conference and later Lords Perth and Chesham in debates in the House of Lords had all emphasised the government's strong reluctance to legislate against Commonwealth immigration, even if the legislation was non-discriminatory.[68] Reconsideration of a deportation bill was, therefore, particularly timely in the light of possible electoral considerations. Though Macmillan was not required to go to the country until June 1960, the advice he was receiving from his Party Chairman favoured May or October 1959.[69] If public interest in race and immigration should develop, and there were some signs that it would, there was still time for the government to show its concern and responsiveness through its support of a deportation bill. This would have the effect of heading off or deflecting demands for full immigration controls, the introduction of which would run the serious risk of a major political controversy, something all governments sought to avoid in the period prior to a general election.

At its first meeting in 1959 the Cabinet Committee on Colonial Immigrants discussed a draft deportation bill which, at its last meeting, it had decided to have prepared in order that the disagreements evident on the committee could be defined more clearly. The draft bill discussed was very limited in scope. The Home Secretary only had the power to deport following the recommendation of a court and those excluded from its provisions included not just those born in the United Kingdom and those holding a United Kingdom issued British passport but also those who had been resident for five years or more and those whose father had been born in the United Kingdom. The meaning of 'belonging to the United Kingdom' had been considerably extended since deportation of Commonwealth citizens was last discussed in 1955. Despite the modest nature of the proposed measure and the strong political arguments in favour of the idea of moving forward with deportation legislation, the Cabinet Committee failed to agree on the need to act. The argument against the legislation, almost certainly put forcibly by Iain Macleod and supported by the Lord Chancellor, Kilmuir, was significantly based on numbers. The number of West Indian immigrants in the last quarter of 1958 had been less than 20 per cent of the figure for the same period of 1957. During the same quarter the arrivals of Indians fell by 40 per cent and there was a net outflow of Pakistanis. Apart from being restrictive, discriminatory and a departure from the principle that British subjects from the Commonwealth and Empire had the same rights as British born and resident citizens, 'the problem was no longer sufficiently great to justify legislation of the kind proposed'. The arguments for and against the draft legislation were to be put to Cabinet.[70] At its meeting on 19 February 1959 the Cabinet discussed 'coloured' immigration for the last time for almost a year and a half. At the prompting of the Lord Chancellor the argument based on numbers was accepted, though Cabinet also agreed that further enquiry and consultation was necessary as legislation might be necessary at some point in the future.[71]

Members of the Cabinet committee continued to disagree on the question of the need to legislate against 'coloured' immigration at the last meeting before the general election of October 1959. Though a majority of ministers thought the time was 'fast approaching', that is certainly during the next parliament, when legislation would be necessary, the Colonial Secretary was still 'strongly opposed.' However, the committee found that immigration levels were down and the key indicators showed a distinct improvement in the situation. The committee found itself in a dilemma about giving support to projects which would either improve the conditions in which Asian and black immigrants lived or assist in their integration. For example, at this and other meetings the committee spent a considerable time discussing the possibility of setting up a housing association whose primary objective would be to provide improved housing for West Indian immigrants. Though it could clearly identify the need for such a project the commitee's negative decision was determined principally by the consideration that, in the absence of a policy to limit immigration from the Caribbean, action of this type would only make emigration from the Caribbean more attractive.[72] The Working Party on behalf of the Cabinet committee was examining the conditions in which immigrants lived, in an attempt to find justifications for introducing immigration restrictions. Projects designed to improve those living conditions could not be supported because they would attract more immigrants. The lesson to those who opposed immigration restrictions was obvious. If they wished to see programmes designed to improve the conditions of immigrant communities, they should support legislation to limit entry.

Against a background of steadily falling numbers of Asian and black immigrants entering the United Kingdom, the arguments of the advocates of restrictions were difficult to press successfully. The decline was quite sharp. In the first half of 1959 immigrant numbers were the lowest for five years (5,300 entered from the Caribbean, India and Pakistan in the first five months of the year) and, though they picked up in the latter half of 1959, they stayed flat for the first half of 1960. (The figures were 12,500 from the three areas for August to November 1959 and 16,500 for January to May 1960). The annual rate remained well below that for 1955 – when the government had last come close to legislative action on immigration – until well into 1960.

THE OFFICIAL MIND AND THE SEARCH FOR A JUSTIFICATION, 1959–61

From the standpoint of 1959, to most ministers and officials involved in the subject of immigration, the introduction of control by legislation seemed a likely development, but one for which there was no urgency. The role of the two key committees, one an interdepartmental Working Party of officials and the other comprised of ministers, was to watch the indicators of both movement and unrest: the Working Party was to report to the Cabinet committee and the ministerial committee to report to the Cabinet at the first sign of change. Over the period from the beginning of 1959 to the time the decision was taken to legislate in 1961, the committee of officials produced a report every four to six months. The format of the report stayed the same throughout the period until July 1961. Its table of contents tells us a good deal about the concerns which senior government officials and their ministers shared about 'coloured' immigration.

The report's first heading was always 'numbers'. The usual sequence thereafter was: 'relations with white people and public order', 'relations between coloured residents and police', 'crime', 'housing', 'employment', 'unemployment and race friction', 'health', 'welfare arrangements for coloured people in the United Kingdom' and 'future outlook'. The approach was consistently pathological; the report always attempted to measure the responsibility of 'coloured' immigrants for public disorder, criminal activity, overcrowded housing conditions, unemployment, inter-racial tension, unemployment and the spread of contagious diseases. The reports of the Working Party were considered at meetings of the Cabinet committee, the Committee on Colonial Immigrants as it was known until 1959 when it was renamed the Commonwealth Immigrants Committee. Its terms of reference were 'to consider and keep under review the problems caused by the uncontrolled entry into the United Kingdom of British subjects from overseas'.[73] Formed after the Cabinet decision against legislation in November 1955, the Cabinet Committee appears not to have met between July 1959 and February 1961 during which period the Working Party reports appear to have gone directly to the Home Secretary.

A point of very considerable interest about the Working Party reports between the beginning of 1959 and the end of 1961 is their almost total failure to uncover evidence of the kind that government clearly thought was necessary in order to justify the introduction of legislation to restrict immigration to Britain. Throughout the period almost all of the indicators, except the key one of numbers of Asian and black immigrants, pointed to inaction. It will be instructive to look at these Working Party reports for the two years leading up to the decision to legislate, in order to gain an understanding of the approach and attitudes of the official mind to the issue of 'coloured' immigration. The officials' task was clear: it was to construct a case which could be used to justify a recommendation for immigration controls. The Working Party was not only expected to provide the evidential basis on which Cabinet could take a final decision to legislate, it was also asked to provide recommendations and advice on the operation of immigration controls. The expectation was that the grounds for imposing limitations would also suggest the means by which it could be done. Housing, health and employment were the three candidates. The draft bill of 1955 had suggested a combination of housing certificates and labour permits.

In the area of 'relations with white people and public order' the report of 3 July 1959 discussed the murder of Kelso Cochrane, the friction caused by 'frequent long and noisy parties held by coloured residents' and 'unpleasantness caused when coloured landlords acquire property occupied by white tenants'.[74] However, the murder of Kelso Cochrane on 16 May – 'misrepresented elsewhere as a racial murder' – was portrayed as an 'unfortunate episode that was exploited by ill-disposed factions and misguided persons to try to make political capital out of the situation'. Despite the lurid treatment of the murder by the tabloid press and the provocation caused by Sir Oswald Mosley's decision to stand as a parliamentary candidate in North Kensington, there was apparently no indication of any desire to resort to violence. Behaviour in all circumstances was described as 'restrained'. The number of incidents involving the police and 'coloured people' was not regarded as being in any way abnormal or unexpected.[75]

No major incidents occurred subsequently. The demonstrations that followed the Sharpeville shootings and incidents associated with the expression of opposition to apartheid and the trade boycott of South Africa were not regarded by the Metropolitan Police as indicators of an increase in racial tension.[76] Nonetheless, in its summary of the case for legislation drawn up in July 1961, the Working Party concluded that there was 'little evidence that the coloured communities have really been assimilated' and that they were tending to become identified with the lowest class, a situation which had 'inherently explosive possibilities'. It noted that the disturbances of 1958 gave 'grounds for anxiety' but that incidents on this scale 'have not so far been repeated'. What it called 'the dangers of social tension inherent in the existence of large unassimilated coloured communities' was one of the two clear grounds the Working Party identified for recommending restrictive legislation.[77]

Crime was another area that failed to produce much substantial evidence. Working Party reporting concentrated on a number of narrow areas in which it was evidently thought by the Home Office that Caribbean involvement was disproportionately high. Offences related to the possession of Indian hemp or cannabis were one constant in the reports which charted the growth of convictions of West Indians in overall numbers and as a proportion of the total. Some alarm was expressed when the number of offences of this type threatened to exceed a hundred in one year but in general the reports' authors found it unsurprising that the number of West Indian cannabis possession cases should increase with the rapid increase in the West Indian population of the United Kingdom. The other area of consistent concern was the offence of living off the immoral earnings of women. Here there were disappointments when it became evident that Maltese men were very much more frequently convicted as pimps than West Indians.[78]

With dissenting views expressed by the Chief Constables of Liverpool and Sheffield, the provincial police forces found that the 'coloured' population was a law-abiding one, 'no more prone to crime and violence than the white population'.[79] The Metropolitan Police believed that 'coloured people' were more likely to commit offences against the person than white but, given that the incidence of crime was greater among young males and that young males made up the bulk of the coloured population, it was admitted that the picture was 'far less disturbing'. Also, since official records in London did not distinguish between white and coloured offenders, any figures had to be regarded with the greatest caution.[80] Overall, the Home Office failed to offer any convincing evidence to the Working Party that, aside from an association with cannabis, Asian and black immigration was likely to lead to an upsurge of criminal activity. The Working Party fairly concluded that restrictions on immigration would make no significant contribution to the reduction of crime.[81]

Like the crime section of these reports, the investigation into the impact of 'coloured immigration' on the nation's health also failed to produce any significant evidence worthy of publication, or even concern. As Enoch Powell was the Minister of Health at the time (he was also a member of the Cabinet committee), it is unlikely that many stones were left undisturbed in the search for evidence that would damage the reputation of Asian and black immigrants. Asian and black immigrants were allegedly associated with the spread of leprosy, tuberculosis and gonorrhoea. The British Medical Association at their annual conference in 1959 had passed a resolution expressing their anxiety about uncontrolled immigration of people from the Commonwealth without adequate medical examinations.[82] The Standing Tuberculosis Advisory Committee of the Central Health Services Council was of the view that immigrants from the Indian sub-continent were associated with an increase in the incidence of tuberculosis in Britain and urged the Minister of Health to insist on immigrants undergoing a chest X-ray examination before being allowed to enter the United Kingdom. Given the limited access to advanced medical technology in the sub-continent the committee accepted that this was clearly not a practical suggestion.

Closer investigation of reports often revealed evidence of scaremongering and exaggeration. The Town Clerk of Bedford, for example, had drawn the Minister of Health's attention to the incidence of tuberculosis among Pakistani arrivals in his town. An analysis of the chest clinic records at Bedford General Hospital revealed 14 cases of infection over 3 years, of which at least a half were reckoned to have been contracted in the United Kingdom. The problem of tuberculosis among immigrants from the sub-continent was held to be too small to justify the introduction of expensive screening procedures.[83] Though no venereal disease clinics recorded the country of origin or ethnicity of its patients, it was a 'known fact' that 'coloured men are adding to the increase . . . in the number of cases of gonorrhoea'. An increase in the number of cases of leprosy was again attributed to recent immigration, though once more the regulations under which cases were reported did not require the country of origin of the patient to be reported.[84] Allegations, insinuations and suggestions abound in the reports, but evidence of an association between the spread of serious diseases and the increase in the number of 'coloured' settlers was, as the reports finally admitted, in short supply. The Ministry of Health's view that there was 'little cause for concern' over the health of immigrants was also the inescapable conclusion of the Working Party.[85]

If there was one area which, more than any other, appeared to produce tangible evidence of difficulty directly related to the growth of immigrant numbers, and which was to have an effect on Ministers' decisions, it was housing.[86] The Working Party consistently described unsatisfactory conditions of overcrowding in areas of immigrant settlement, often related to single men congregating in private lodging houses. These houses were usually obsolete but not unfit for habitation. Rehousing would take a considerable time as there was already great pressure on local authorities involved in slum clearance and urban renewal schemes. It was suggested that the continuation of large-scale immigration added considerably to the already onerous housing burdens borne by local authorities. Indeed, even with the additional powers granted by the 1961 Housing Act, the Cabinet Committee thought it would be impossible to deal with the problem effectively without immigration controls. Dispersal of immigrants, for so long the hope of governments, was now seen as impractical because suitable employment was only available in major cities.[87] The problem of tackling the housing shortage was related directly to the need to introduce immigration controls.

The argument was advanced that successful attempts to improve housing conditions would only act as a magnet to attract more immigrants, something the government clearly wished to avoid. It was a short step from this argument to its extension that nothing could be done to help settled immigrants unless controls were introduced.[88] This view and variants of it became very familiar in the 1960s and 1970s as a justification for the introduction of further controls. At one point it was even thought that a type of housing permit could be used to limit the inflow. Under the 1955 draft bill an immigrant could be refused entry if they could not satisfy the Immigration Officer that suitable accommodation was available for them in the United Kingdom. It was quickly appreciated that this approach to control was impractical. It was thought that the measure might be too effective if local authorities, as government expected, issued few or no housing certificates, that it would hamper immigration from the Old Commonwealth and that the effectiveness of the housing certificates would be difficult to ensure.[89] The effect of immigration on housing joined public order as one of the two arguments advanced by the Working Party to ministers to justify the introduction of legislative controls in July 1961.[90]

Concern about levels of unemployment among Asian and black settlers had been a constant refrain in correspondence between the British government and its agencies overseas. Dispatches from the Colonial Office to the Caribbean and from the Commonwealth Relations Office to Pakistan and India frequently stressed the poor prospects of the new arrivals in the United Kingdom. New notes of warning were struck when a Ministry of Labour argument was repeated to them that employment prospects in the United Kingdom for unskilled labour were likely to deteriorate sharply in the medium term with the onset of industrial automation, the ending of National Service and the entry of the post-war population bulge into the job market. Prospects were dire. Colonial governors were told that the Ministry of Labour considered it 'extremely disquieting' that the substantial influx of Commonwealth and colonial immigrants should have coincided with the onset of these structural changes in the employment market.[91]

It is clear from the Working Party reports that there was an expectation that growing unemployment among 'coloured' immigrants would provide both a justification for introducing legislation and a mechanism by which limitations on entry could be regulated. From the start the means of control envisaged was through a job voucher scheme; entry to Britain would be controlled by the availability of jobs. It was assumed that unemployment figures among 'coloured workers' – which, despite public denials, had been collected via special irregular counts at local Labour Offices from 1949 and at regular quarterly intervals since 1958 – would rise sharply if the number of immigrants arriving increased sharply.[92] From July 1958 through to February 1959 the total of registered unemployed 'coloured workers' stood at over 17,000, representing about 8.5 per cent of the total Asian and black population of the United Kingdom. The Working Party report of July 1959 argued that the absorptive capacity of the economy had already been reached and that further immigrants could not be taken in 'without some risk of friction'.[93]

As the Working Party reports reveal, the pre-election boom of 1959 – which continued through 1960 and 1961 – initially sharply reduced unemployment in general and, therefore, the number of 'coloured workers' who were registered as unemployed. More surprisingly to members of the Working Party, as the rate at which Asian and black immigrants entering Britain for settlement through the period 1959 to 1961 accelerated from 21,000 a year to 136,000 a year, the number of unemployed resolutely refused to rise at anything like the same rate. As Table 6 indicates (and it is reproduced from the Working Party Report appendices) immigrants were absorbed with amazing speed into the job market; the percentage of the Asian and black population unemployed during the years 1959 to 1961 never rose above 5 per cent. Indeed, when the Working Party moved to a position of recommending the introduction of controls based on a job voucher system, first the Colonial Office and then, with considerably more weight, the Treasury, were moved to point out the difficulties of this approach.

M.Z. Terry, the Colonial Office member of the Working Party, minuted in January 1961 her disagreement with the Ministry of Labour view that labour from the West Indies was no longer needed. She became convinced that the message being sent to the West Indies about the very poor prospects for Caribbean labour in the United Kingdom was simply incorrect.[94] In September 1961 the West Indian Department of the Colonial Office produced a paper which showed that, while net immigration from the Caribbean in the year between August 1960 and July 1961 had been 61,246 the increase in West Indian unemployed was only 3,635.[95] The thesis that 'coloured' immigrants were not needed by the United Kingdom economy and were likely to be unemployed in large numbers and, therefore, disproportionately dependent on National Assistance and a burden to the state was, according to these analyses, deeply flawed. The sections of the Working Party reports covering the issue of employment display frustration and even petulance after the firm predictions of large-scale Asian and black unemployment, which had been used to justify the extension of administrative measures to block immigration, failed to come true. Despite the evidence to the contrary which it collected and presumably examined every quarter, the Ministry of Labour remained convinced that controls were necessary.[96]

Though the authors of the Working Party reports undoubtedly knew that Asian and black immigration represented only a small proportion of those entering the United Kingdom labour force each year, nowhere were arguments deployed which indicated that – from the perspective of those concerned with unemployment levels – there might have been alternatives to placing limits on Asian and black immigration. In 1960, for example, in the last 'normal' year before the large increase stimulated by the prospect of legislation, it was noted that with emigration at a low level for the third consecutive year and immigration running at a high level for the fifth consecutive year, the net inflow of labour – measured by the number of new entrants from overseas into the National Insurance Scheme – was just under 200,000 for the year. The fact that of that total around 50,000 or about 25 per cent were from the Caribbean, Africa and the Indian sub-continent appears to have gone unremarked.[97] The officials on the Working Party indicated that they believed the 'coloured' immigrants were particularly disadvantaged in the labour market because most of them were thought to be unskilled. However, when the number of unemployed 'coloured' workers resolutely refused to rise, officials fell back either on more dire predictions about the future or on the technique of identifying particular small groups who were proving especially difficult to employ – West Indian women and Pakistani and Adenese Arabs who spoke little or no English were generally mentioned – or to suggest that there was a growing number of long-term unemployed among the 'coloured' unemployed.[98] These points failed to survive closer investigation.

When the Treasury finally made its views known on the key issue of whether or not Asian and black immigration benefited the economy its clear advice was that on economic grounds there was no justification for introducing immigration restrictions. The Treasury assessed, in its customarily rigorous fashion, the economic costs and benefits for the existing inhabitants of Britain of 'coloured' immigration. Its clear conclusions were that the influx was economically beneficial in that the immigrants added more to the value of the gross national product than they consumed or remitted abroad. The large bulk of the immigrants found employment without creating unemployment for the natives and, especially by easing labour bottlenecks, contributed to the productive capacity of the economy. Only those immigrants with large families (of whom there were very few in 1961) were likely to impose any net cost upon the economy, and that only represented the cost of sustaining and training a future generation of workers, which would have to be met in any case. The Treasury also judged the more rapid growth of population encouraged by immigration to be economically beneficial. The costs of limiting immigration would be seen in the considerable rise in wages. Unable to resist the strength and logic of these arguments the Working Party Report of July 1961, which summarised the case for controls, placed the economic benefits of unrestricted immigration in the balance as an argument against the introduction of controls.[99]

In recommending the introduction of a system of control based on employment the Working Party admitted that the 'curtailment of immigration ostensibly on employment grounds would not be easy to justify' because the great majority of immigrants found and kept work 'without undue difficulty'. The work that immigrants did was admitted to be of 'real importance' to the country and therefore a system which severely curtailed numbers based upon a labour permit system (similar to that operating for aliens) was not, as the Treasury insisted, desirable on economic grounds. Nonetheless, the Working Party went ahead with its recommendation to base the controls on a labour voucher system, one with a three-fold classification. It is worth quoting from the justification advanced by the Working Party:

> While it would apply equally to all parts of the Commonwealth, without distinction on grounds of race and colour, in practice it would interfere to the minimum extent with the entry of persons from the 'old' Commonwealth countries. . . . The control over the entry of the unskilled would be of the most flexible character. Decisions reached in London could at any time increase or decrease the flow by the simple process of sending out more or fewer permits. While any scheme which effectively limits free entry is bound to run into political criticism, the flexibility of operation of this scheme should keep such criticism down to a minimum.[100]

The Working Party was quite clear. Most of those coming under the permits available for skilled workers – the definition would be 'a broad one' – and for people coming to a specific job with a named employer would be white immigrants from the Old Commonwealth. The 'essence of the whole problem' – as the Working Party put it – was to control the numbers coming in the third, or unskilled category. The formulation was a triumph of invention inspired by prejudice. It provided a system that appeared to treat all applicants alike, and which could be defended against criticism that it was discriminatory, yet which in its application could be used to regulate the numbers of Asian and black immigrants without significantly affecting the movement of kith and kin from the white Commonwealth. Once it had been decided to exclude the Irish from the provisions of the bill, the problem of securing a sufficient supply of labour, both skilled and unskilled, while keeping 'coloured' immigrants out, had at last been solved. It is absolutely clear from the papers of the Working Party that it was the government's intention to devise legislation in a politically acceptable form whose result would be a sharp reduction of Asian and black immigration into Britain.[101] Openly discriminatory systems, such as the application of quotas to particular parts of the

Commonwealth, were considered but rejected on the grounds that 'the advocacy of exclusion of stocks deemed to be inferior is presentationally impossible'.[102]

Thus the Working Party eventually provided both the means and the justification for the imposition of controls on 'coloured immigrants'. Underlying its arguments was the issue of numbers. In July 1961 when it made its unequivocal recommendation for the introduction of controls it did so at a time when numbers were rising rapidly and it could suggest that the Asian and black population of the United Kingdom would reach one million in the near future unless steps were taken to control movement. The justification was quite clear. The recommendation was made not on

Table 6 Numbers and percentage of 'coloured workers' registered unemployed by visual count at regional Labour Offices, 1953–61[103]

Date of count	Number unemployed	Est. 'coloured' popn	% regd unemployed
Jun. 53	3,366	35,000	9.62
Jun. 54	2,462	45,000	5.47
Jan. 55	3,337	50,000	6.67
Jul. 55	2,853	72,000	3.96
Jun. 56	5,203	117,000	4.45
Sep. 56	6,722	128,000	5.25
Mar. 57	7,085	150,000	4.72
Sep. 57	7,566	170,000	4.45
Mar. 58	15,056	190,000	7.92
Jul. 58	17,101	198,000	8.64
Nov. 58	17,276	210,000	8.23
Feb. 59	17,283	215,000	8.04
May 59	13,144	222,000	5.92
Aug. 59	9,656	226,000	4.27
Nov. 59	10,156	234,000	4.34
Feb. 60	9,601	236,000	4.07
May 60	8,537	250,000	3.41
Aug. 60	8,355	270,000	3.09
Nov. 60	11,712	280,000	4.18
Feb. 61	14,281	300,000	4.76
May 61	15,082	350,000	4.31
Aug. 61	13,926	385,000	3.62

Source: Numbers of unemployed come from the Interdepartmental Working Party Progress Reports; numbers of the black and Asian population are the author's estimates based on various sources

the grounds of health, crime or employment but on the 'strains imposed by coloured immigrants on the housing resources of certain local authorities and the dangers of social tensions inherent in the existence of large unassimilated coloured communities'. Against those two elements had to be weighed the economic costs and the danger to Commonwealth sentiment.[104]

'Assimilibility' – that is, of numbers and colour – was the criterion that mattered in the end. The Working Party received Home Office reports of very large increases in the number of people coming to Britain for the purpose of settlement from the Caribbean and from India and Pakistan. Indeed, immigration from many non-Anglo-Saxon parts of the Commonwealth and British territories overseas was increasing at an unprecedented rate. The first signs came in the first half of 1960 when the figures for Caribbean immigration began to show a clear increase, the figure for May 1960 being the highest monthly aggregate on record. The annual level for the first half of 1960 was, however, still below the previous highest year (1956) and only slightly higher than for the equivalent period in 1958. Indian sub-continental figures were still low but the report of June 1960 recorded that there were indications that fresh ways had been found to circumvent the recently applied restrictions.[105] Not until the first half of 1961 did immigration from the Indian sub-continent show a similar movement. The increase from the Caribbean peaked in 1961; the increase from the Indian sub-continent continued to rise, swiftly from the beginning of 1961 through to July 1962, the point of enforcement of the Commonwealth Immigrants Act.

When the increases came they were far in excess of anything previously experienced. The Working Party Report of June 1960 described the West Indian figures as 'sensational' and asked the General Register Office to provide an actuarial estimate of what the coloured population of Britain would be in five, ten, fifteen and twenty years' time.[106] The report of February 1961 found the West Indian figure for 1960 to be 'startling' and concluded that nothing further could be done by other governments of the Empire and Commonwealth to restrict emigration to the United Kingdom.[107] The substantial increases in 1961 in net immigration from the Indian sub-continent were found by the Working Party to be 'particularly disturbing, since many of these people do not speak English, and they are among the more difficult groups to assimilate into the community'.[108] It was a remarkable surge. In June 1960, only two years before the first legislation began to apply, the Asian and black population of the United Kingdom was approximately a quarter of a million, one in two hundred of the population as a whole. Within two years the size of these communities had doubled. It had taken three hundred years for the Asian and black

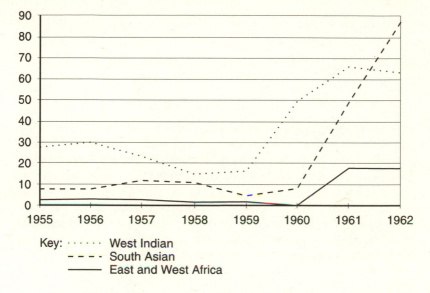

Key: ······ West Indian
     - - - - South Asian
     ———— East and West Africa

Figure 1 Net inward movement from the Caribbean, Africa and South Asia, 1955–62 (in thousands)

Source: Davison, *Black British*, p. 3.

population to reach ten thousand, a further fifteen years to reach a quarter of a million and only two more years to achieve a half million. West Indians still dominated: they comprised three-fifths of the quarter million and just over a half of the half million.[109]

Viewed objectively, the reports of the Working Party consistently failed to fulfil the purpose defined in its title – to identify 'the social and economic problems arising from the growing influx of coloured workers'. In the areas of public order, crime, employment and health there was little noteworthy to report to their political masters. Where the officials could find little or nothing by way of existing problems they compensated by identifying problems which they though would be bound to arise if Asian and black immigration was allowed to continue at its present level. Thus in February 1961, whilst it was admitted that black immigrants were being readily absorbed into the economy, 'it is likely to be increasingly difficult for them to find jobs during the next few years'. Further, it was doubtful if the 'tolerance of the white people for the coloured would survive the test of competition for employment'. The report's conclusion was prophetic, if almost wholly wrong:

For the next few years unemployment among them [West Indian immigrants] may be expected to rise, and acute overcrowding is certain, with obvious attendant risks to social relations. . . . In default of some action by this country to impose a legislative curb on this immigration, there can be no escape from social problems which promise to become increasingly serious with the passage of time.[110]

In the end the officials were prepared to admit that the case for restriction could not 'at present' rest on health, crime, public order or employment grounds. The case was not economic but social: 'The immigrants are not being assimilated and tend to become identified with the lowest class of the population. Social tension is likely to increase as the number of immigrants increases.'[111] In the end the official mind made recommendations based on predictions about the likelihood of future difficulties which were founded on prejudice rather than on evidence derived from the history of the Asian and black presence in Britain.

POLITICAL AND POPULAR PRESSURES FOR CHANGE, OCTOBER 1959–OCTOBER 1961

In the general election of October 1959 race and immigration were not issues of any importance. Sir Oswald Mosley's attempts to campaign on the issue in North Kensington led to him losing his deposit for the first time in his long career. The small steering committee that drafted the Conservative election manifesto, comprising Macmillan, Butler, Home, Macleod, Heath and Hailsham, evidently had no difficulty in excluding any references to deportation or immigration control.[112] A confident Conservative Party did not think it would be a vote-winner, and immigration was an issue that would divide rather than unite the party. If not of the first order of political importance, race and immigration had been live issues in the country in the first half of 1959, stimulated by the actions of individuals on the extreme right, with Colin Jordan and Oswald Mosley to the fore, and by the murder of Kelso Cochrane. Government was content to confirm that they were watching the situation closely and let it be known that they were still considering the possibility of deportation legislation.[113] This was quite sufficient to enable the Home Secretary to maintain his position without difficulty. As Asian and black unemployment declined and West Indian immigration suffered a fall, the race issue almost disappeared from the national political scene, notwithstanding Oswald Mosley's feeble and unsuccessful attempts to keep it alive in North Kensington.[114]

Despite the somewhat increased level of public attention which issues of race and immigration received after the election, partly due to the presence in the House of Commons of a set of newly elected Midlands-based Conservative MP's with strong views on the question, the Government did not think the issue of sufficient importance to give it close attention. Cabinet discussed the matter twice in 1960 and on both occasions thought it sufficient to request its committee to continue its monitoring exercise. In fact the Cabinet committee appears not to have met again until the pressure of Cyril Osborne's Private Member's Bill forced it into action in February 1961, a break of eighteen months since its last meeting. By then there had already been some significant developments, among which were the admissions in the House of Commons by Iain Macleod in May 1960 that he had asked West Indian governments to strengthen their efforts to reduce emigration to the United Kingdom and then in December 1960 that administrative measures were no longer considered sufficient to stem the growing tide of immigration.[115] More importantly, by February 1961 the Home Secretary was prepared to admit to colleagues that 'there is a strong feeling among our own supporters that something should be done'. The previous July he had told his fellow ministers that there was 'little support' for legislation.[116]

Whereas in November 1960 the Cabinet had agreed that the present situation was 'disquieting' and that it needed to keep a close watch on it, by February 1961 a lengthy discussion concluded that, in the imminent debate on Cyril Osborne's private member's motion on the Order Paper, the government would neither accept nor deny the need for legislation. Its members would abstain on the vote. The sensitive position of the negotiations over Central Africa, the West Indies bases agreement and the West Indies Federation provided strong reasons for further delay in announcing a decision. The Cabinet committee was instructed to look into possible methods of control and to bring its recommendations to Cabinet. There appeared to be no sense of urgency.[117] Potential difficulties at the Commonwealth Prime Ministers' meeting in London in March 1961 were successfully sidestepped by keeping the matter off the agenda, though Eric Williams of Trinidad in a private conversation with Harold Macmillan warned the British Prime Minister that British withdrawal of help allied to the cessation of Caribbean migration to the United Kingdom would cause 'a social revolution and a Castro-like situation' in the Caribbean.[118]

The Cabinet committee moved strongly towards a decision to recommend legislation to restrict the entry of Asian and black British subjects at its meeting in May 1961. Butler noted that government supporters now recognised that in view of the rapidly escalating numbers of 'coloured' immigrants – his prediction for 1961 was for a net 'coloured' immigration of between 150,000 and 200,000 compared to 58,000 in 1960 – legislation was unavoidable 'if we were not to have a colour problem in this country on a similar scale to that in the USA'[119] The figures were being swelled by movement from East Africa where political apprehensions related to the transfer of power into African hands were stimulating outward movement, but the highest rate of increase was now from India and Pakistan. Butler made it clear that the passport control system which had kept down the rate of migration from the Indian sub-continent had now broken down completely. Before it reached agreement the Cabinet committee surveyed other negative aspects of the continuing high level of immigration of workers of 'deteriorating quality' from the Indian sub-continent and the Caribbean. The continuation of the movement at its present level would 'gravely impede' the government's current proposals in the Housing Bill, aggravate the problems of the hospital service in certain areas and, most curiously, inhibit the development of automation. In the political cost–benefit analysis the benefits of legislation now clearly outweighed the costs.

Even so, at its May 1961 meeting the Cabinet committee accepted arguments for further delay. The Colonial Secretary, Iain Macleod, argued strongly against any announcement until after the critically important referendum on the Federation proposals to be held in Jamaica in September. The Federation's chances of success hinged upon Jamaica's consent, and that would be seriously endangered if immigration restrictions were to be announced before Jamaica's people were able to vote on the Federation proposals.[120] The committee's decision to accept Macleod's advice proved to be of very considerable importance in determining the size of Asian and black Britain. In particular, the delay of six months, at a time when the government's intention to introduce legislation had already been widely signalled, gave perhaps a hundred thousand Asian and black immigrants the chance to 'beat-the-ban'.[121]

This Cabinet committee also took vital decisions about who was to be subject to control and on what grounds control would be exercised. It was agreed that the legislation would apply to all British subjects who could not claim citizenship by right of birth or residence in the United Kingdom. Those subject to controls would be divided into three categories: skilled workers, those with a job to come to and others. People in the first two categories would be allowed to enter with restriction but those in the third category would be subject to control on the basis of a 'first come, first served' allocation of entry permits, the need for which would be determined annually. The great merits of this system, according to John Hare, the Minister of Labour, were its flexibility – the government could vary the level of immigration according to economic, social and political considerations – and the fact that it could be operated to the benefit of immigrants from the 'old' Commonwealth without overt discrimination on grounds of race or colour.[122]

This particular form of control had been recommended by the interdepartmental Working Party whose chairman, K.B. Paice, put it forward to the Cabinet Committee as 'the only workable method of controlling immigration from the Commonwealth without either bringing such immigration to a virtual standstill or ostensibly discriminating against immigrants on the basis of colour'. Two weeks later the Cabinet generally endorsed the committee's recommendations but put off a final decision until the implications of different forms of control could be investigated and further study could be given to the questions of who should continue to be admitted to the United Kingdom without restriction, how the Irish should be treated, what effect the possibility of entry to the European Economic Community would have on the possible arrangements, whether deportation rules should be included in the legislation and whether there could be some selection of unskilled immigrants according to country of origin. Again no sense of urgency appeared to inform the Cabinet's discussion. No announcement was to be made and the Cabinet committee, acting on the advice of the Working Party, was to report to Cabinet in the autumn.[123]

The Cabinet Committee required two further meetings on 31 July and 29 September to work out details and to consider the first draft of a bill which was discussed and approved by Cabinet on 10 October. Already, by late July 1961 it was clear that political pressure for legislation was increasing quite sharply. Sir Cyril Osborne, the leading figure in the anti-immigration campaign run from the Tory back benches, had already announced his intention to put down a motion at the Party Conference in October. Nonetheless, there was still outright opposition to the proposed legislation from within the Cabinet. Edward Boyle, the Financial Secretary to the Treasury, was not persuaded by the social argument and maintained that the economic advantage of present levels of immigration should be of over-riding importance. The Colonial Office in the shape of Hugh Fraser still argued for delay, this time on the grounds that if controls came before Caribbean independence it might be necessary to increase the level of financial aid given to West Indian governments as part of the independence arrangements. However, the majority of the Committee were persuaded of the need for legislation and of the attractiveness of the Working Party's proposals for controls based on employment. Butler was instructed to see to the drafting of a Bill and the linked Order in Council for approval by the Committee and Cabinet in time for the preparation of the Queen's Speech (in October) in which the intention to legislate during the next session of Parliament would be announced.[124]

The decision to go ahead with legislation to end the legal right of all British subjects to enter Britain freely was finally taken at the Cabinet

Committee on 29 September and confirmed by the full Cabinet on 10 October 1961. If there were any remaining doubts they were removed by the Home Secretary's report that the number of Asian and black immigrants entering Britain was continuing to rise sharply. The net inward movement during the last month had been almost 16,000. In the view of the Committee this level was 'too high for successful assimilation'. Consequently, a number of social problems had accumulated which produced a 'difficult situation'. The Committee recognised the general feeling in the country that 'too many coloured persons were settling here'. There was growing public anxiety and mounting pressure from government supporters. As administrative attempts to restrict the flow were clearly no longer effective, there was no alternative but to introduce controls. Iain Macleod, the Colonial Secretary who was reshuffled into the Leadership of the House of Commons the day before the Cabinet took the final decision, now accepted legislation as a 'sad necessity'. In the September referendum Jamaica had decided not to join the Federation and there was, therefore, no longer a case for further delay. The economic arguments against controls were acknowledged and the scheme proposed would allow the flow to continue, should it be needed, by adjusting the number of unskilled allowed to enter. The Cabinet did not expect that the legislation would lead to a drastic or immediate reduction in the number of Asian and black immigrants entering Britain. The Cabinet clearly expected that the announcement of the measure would be greeted by a storm of opposition. However, it was satisfied that, though the Bill, as Butler admitted to the Cabinet, was aimed at limiting 'coloured' immigration, there was no discriminatory element in it. Because it proposed to limit rather than eliminate 'coloured' immigration it was thought likely that it would satisfy middle-of-the-road and moderate opinion and meet the objections of those who argued for a continuation of immigration on economic grounds.[125]

In view of the long history of hostility to 'coloured' immigration perhaps it is surprising that the Bill took so long to emerge. That it eventually did so can be explained principally by the hugely increased numbers of immigrants entering Britain from the Caribbean, India, Pakistan and Africa which clearly made a crucial difference at all levels to the outcome of very long-running discussions about the need for legislation. Fears for the future – in employment, housing, social order and even racial and cultural survival – could much more easily be felt in 1961 than in 1958 or 1955. There was political advantage to be gained by putting through a measure which enjoyed popular support, but the influence of party and public opinion has often been overstressed in writing on the subject.[126] Though polls are notoriously difficult to interpret in this area, a large majority of the public were known to be in favour of strict controls, but they had been more strongly in favour of them in 1958 than they were in 1961. Many intellectuals and senior members of the clergy were strongly opposed to legislation. The newspapers were no more enthusiastic in 1961 than they had been in 1955, with most of the national press – including the opinion-forming broadsheets but excluding the *Daily Express*, indicating grave reservations about the need for legislation.[127]

Cyril Osborne had for many years been a lone, and often despised, voice in favour of controls. Joined from the mid-1950s by Norman Pannell, Martin Lindsey and Harold Gurden (Conservative) and John Hynd, Harry Hynd, Albert Evans and George Rogers (Labour) the pro-control lobby was boosted further by the 1959 elections which brought in to the Commons a bevy of West Midlands MPs whose support was sought by the Birmingham Immigration Control Association, the largest of the pro-control pressure groups. For the Annual Conservative Party Conference beginning on 11 October 1961 constituency associations had sent in thirty-nine motions advocating controls. In fact, the decision to legislate had been taken before the Conference began but government chose not to announce its intentions until after the conference was finished. Opinion at the party grassroots and within the parliamentary party could be, and was, managed effectively and outfaced. At the Conference the issue of immigration controls was briefly debated and assurances were forthcoming from R.A. Butler, the Home Secretary, that government was taking the matter seriously.

Though the Party at its conference in 1961 was convinced by a large majority of the need for controls, there was little enthusiasm among the main body of Conservative MPs – except for a small and vociferous minority on the right – to press the issue either in public debate or in elections. When attempts were made by Conservative candidates to exploit the issue in by-election campaigns, for example, by Bernard Owens in Small Heath, Birmingham in 1961 and by Brimmacombe in Deptford and Hawkins in West Bromwich in 1963, there was evidence only of a negative impact on their chances of success.[128] Indeed, even in the general election of 1964, when there was a party difference that might have been exploitable, the instruction given to Conservative MPs was to avoid the issue of race and immigration. Only late in the day when the campaign seemed to be going badly for the party did Alec Douglas-Home and Quintin Hogg attempt to develop the issue. Griffiths' campaign in Smethwick was very much an exception to the way in which the vast majority of Tory candidates fought the election in 1964. Central Office was opposed to the use of immigration as an electoral issue. Not only was it unproven as a vote-winner, it was also divisive for the party. The issue aroused powerful feelings on both the right and the left, among a band of

MPs strongly attached to the idea of empire for whom the open door was a symbol of its continuing importance, and on the liberal wing for men like Macleod and Boyle. It was better avoided.[129] It is, therefore, unlikely that the Cabinet in deciding in favour of controls in mid-1961 was much moved by the emergence of a vocal pro-immigration wing within the party or much attracted by the possibility of seeking and exploiting political advantage on this question.

It was a change of view at the centre – in Whitehall and in the Cabinet – rather than pressure of anti-immigration opinion in the country that brought the shift in policy in 1961. The strength of official support can be gauged from the urgent tone of the final Working Party reports. Butler reflected later that the dominant reaction of Whitehall to the Bill was that it was not strong or tough enough.[130] If the Cabinet minutes are to be taken as a fair reflection of the discussion which took place, members of it were concerned about liberal objections, which saw the proposed measure as being too restrictive, and not about any prospect that the provisions of the projected bill would not satisfy pro-immigration pressures. The timing of the announcement, after rather than during the Conservative Party Conference, again indicated an unwillingness on the part of the government to appease, or be seen to appease, the pro-immigration lobby. Whilst it is surely true that the support for immigration legislation by grassroots Conservatives as part of a wide swath of public opinion was a factor in government calculations, it is unlikely that the strength of public opinion was a dynamic element in the decision-making process. Only in the late 1960s did immigration become an important public and electoral issue. Given large-scale and increasing Asian and black immigration, Cabinet did not need to be convinced of the need for legislation – preventing the creation of an ethnically and racially diverse Britain had long been an objective of British governments. How it should be done and, if legislation was necessary to do it, what its terms would be and when it would be introduced were, since 1951, the questions government had tried to answer. On those occasions in the past when the government had seriously considered legislation, it had been an increase in 'coloured' immigration numbers which had clearly preceded and stimulated the discussion. So it was in 1961. Public and party opinion was one, but certainly not the crucial, element influencing the outcome of discussions about these questions.

The international constraints that had played such a key role in 1955 and 1958 were, in 1961, much less of a barrier to legislation. The hard lessons of Suez about the usefulness of the Commonwealth as an enhancement of Britain's status and standing in the international community had been absorbed and the now increasing pace of decolonisation was shifting the locus of power within the organisation away from the United Kingdom. If the 'disloyalty' of Canada over Suez had not already done so, the expulsion of South Africa in 1961 destroyed any last vestige of it as the white man's club it had once been, whose members might again in the future rally round the mother country in time of war. In 1960 the Cabinet had decided that closer association with the European Economic Community must be sought and on 9 August 1961 the first formal application for membership had been made. The costs of adverse Commonwealth reaction to legislation had been devalued.[131] Arguments about labour were not crucial; they were not even important. The 'reserve army of labour' was not being turned back because it was no longer needed. Immigrants from the Caribbean and the Indian sub-continent were still going straight into jobs; according to the Treasury, Asian and black labour was still required in 1961. It is clear that Cabinet took the decision to legislate despite the economic costs that the Treasury predicted it would impose. But 'coloured' immigrants had only constituted a quarter of annually imported labour and no proposals were made to control more tightly the import of white labour. The government concern since 1949, through a period of full employment, had been to find ways to control immigration from the Caribbean, Africa and the Indian sub-continent, not immigration in general. The timing of its discussions of the question had everything to do with the variations in the number of Asian and black immigrants arriving and nothing to do with population flows in general or the number of job vacancies in British industry.

So why was it not done sooner? Certainly, the decision was based upon a cost–benefit analysis whose terms shifted decisively in the early 1960s, but underlying the whole process of political calculation was, perhaps, a set of values, attitudes and assumptions which embraced a reluctance to enter new legislative territory, a liberal fear of the consequences of bringing race into politics and an unwillingness to discuss openly issues of race that were recognised by all to be at the centre of this debate.[132] Administrative measures had been preferred for many decades; they had apparently done the job of limiting the growth of the 'coloured' population of the country and they did not have to be debated. Whilst applying them with considerable rigour Britain could and did continue to enjoy the political benefits of its 'open door' stance. If legislation had to be introduced to slow or stop Asian and black immigration it had to be non-racial in appearance and justifiable in terms of the broad national interest. We have already observed the operation of the committee of officials whose central task from 1949 was to monitor 'coloured' immigration and, when necessary, advance a justification for the introduction of controls. Its failure in 1955 was significant; it did much better in 1961.

Though the justification for controls advanced in 1961 was no stronger than in 1955, the careful invention of a method of control which was apparently colour-blind but which, in effect, kept out 'coloured' people was an important part of the discussion that led up to the decision. As in 1955, Cabinet would not accept legislation that was discriminatory in appearance but would only approve legislation which would effectively keep out Asian and black immigrants. Throughout the debate on the Bill ministers continued to deny that the intention of the legislation was to keep out immigrants from Asia, Africa and the Caribbean. This distaste or embarrassment was linked to their strongly negative attitudes towards Osborne, Pannell and their supporters. Their overt approach to race issues was regarded with strong disapproval by ministers; they were an embarrassment to their party and their country.[133] Perhaps the operating rules of empire were deeply embedded. To maintain support, rulers must give the impression of fairness; to maintain control, rulers must retain essential colour distinctions.

5   The making of multi-racial Britain, 1962–91

THE IMPORTANCE OF THE COMMONWEALTH IMMIGRANTS ACT, 1962

The Act of 1962 made all those seeking to enter the United Kingdom for settlement from the Commonwealth and colonies after 1 July 1962 subject to rules which required them to have been issued with a job voucher in one of three categories: (A), (B) or (C). They could

- have a job to come to
- possess special skills which were in short supply or
- be part of a large undifferentiated group whose numbers would be set according to the labour needs of the United Kingdom economy.

Veterans were to receive priority in this last category. People born in the United Kingdom or holding United Kingdom passports issued by the British government were deemed to 'belong to' the United Kingdom and were, therefore, not restricted under the Act. The Act was of very great significance in the making of multi-racial Britain. If the footings of modern multi-racial Britain were dug during and immediately after the Second World War, then the Commonwealth Immigrants Act of 1962, the first legislation supposedly introduced to prevent multi-racial Britain from happening, in fact ensured that foundation stones were laid and the Asian and black communities transformed into populations of substantial proportions.

There has been a collective and persistent failure among writers on race and immigration in Britain to recognise the true position and importance of the 1962 Act. With the benefit of a longer temporal perspective it will be easier to appreciate that the Act was passed at the beginning, rather than at the end, of the process of large-scale Asian and black immigration and that the manner and timing of its introduction – as well as its terms and application – did a great deal, far more than its authors intended, to secure a multi-racial Britain. Of course it is possible to argue that, without the controls which the Act introduced, immigration from New Common-wealth sources would have increased more rapidly than it did; but against this must be weighed the very considerable significance of the beat-the-ban rush, which the early announcement and slow implementation of the Act allowed, and the relaxed regime that the Act initially established. With travel and communication between rich, developed countries of the West and poorer, less developed countries to the south and east becoming rapidly cheaper and easier, some form of immigration control was inevitable. Every industrialised country of the world had already raised or was about to raise such barriers.

The flows that were permitted under the Act and subsequent legislation were at levels – often over 30,000 a year and averaging over 20,000 a year – that legislators in the 1950s and the architects of the Act would have considered very high. For the purpose of broad comparison of pre- and post-Act flows, it is worth noting that the average Asian and black net immigration figure for the 1950s was less than 20,000. Table 7 indicates that, of the Asian and black immigrants who had arrived by 1982 – twenty years after the Act – only a small proportion, certainly no more than a fifth, had arrived before the impact of the Act began to be felt. The difference between the Caribbean and the South Asian figures is particularly marked. The proportion of the West Indian population that arrived before 1960 was about three times greater than for the groups from the Indian sub-continent. Over three-quarters of South Asian males and over nine-tenths of South Asian females arrived after the passage of the Act.

In practice the Act stimulated the growth of the Asian and black population in four ways. First, the expectation of its enactment was a

Table 7 Asian and black immigrants: date of settlement in Britain (percentages)[1]

	Before 1960	1 Jan. 1960–30 Jun. 1962	1 Jul. 1962–1982
West Indian men	40	33	26
West Indian women	28	30	43
Indian men	14	11	75
Indian women	8	7	85
Pakistani men	11	20	69
Pakistani women	2	3	95
Bangladeshi men	10	9	81
Bangladeshi women	0	0	100

Source: 1982 PSI Survey (researched over a period in 1982)

significant factor in explaining the rapid doubling of the Asian and black population between the middle of 1960 and the middle of 1962. According to Home Office figures, of the approximately half a million Asian and black immigrants to enter Britain between the end of the Second World War and the Act, about a quarter of a million came in the two years between July 1960 and the end of June 1962. The threat of controls was exploited by travel agents in emigration zones. Travel agents in north-west Pakistan, for example, may have induced some to travel to the United Kingdom who had not otherwise intended to do so. They would take advantage of a 'last-chance, never to be repeated opportunity' and establish a right to come to the United Kingdom.[2] The 'beat-the-ban rush' was by far the most important (but not the only) element in the rapid increase of immigration in the period 1960–2. Labour demand was buoyant during those years and immigration in general increased, though at a far lower rate than immigration from the Asian and black Empire/Commonwealth.

The response to the expectation and then the announcement of the Act was vigorous from both the Indian sub-continent and the Caribbean, but it was from the former that the reaction was greatest. Immigration from the Caribbean had dominated the pattern of Asian and black arrivals since the Second World War; in the two years before the Bill became law, immigration from the sub-continent increased at a pace sufficient to ensure that South Asian rather than Caribbean voices would be the most numerous in the future minority ethnic population of Britain. The Act was widely and frequently signalled. From the speech by Patricia Hornsby-Smith in the House of Commons in April 1958 expressing the hope that major legislation would not be necessary but indicating that the government was 'watching the situation closely' to the announcement in the House of Commons by Iain Macleod in December 1960 that administrative measures were no longer adequate to restrain immigration, the government seemed intent on issuing periodic warnings to those who wanted to emigrate to the United Kingdom that they should to do so before it was too late.[3]

From February 1961 the government ceased to deny without qualification that it was contemplating legislation. For example, in a press statement of 21 April 1961 – issued in response to Grantley Adams' public prediction that emigration from the West Indies to Britain would be stopped before the end of the year – Her Majesty's Government denied that it had plans 'at present' to introduce legislation to bring immigration from the Commonwealth to a halt, and indicated that it was keeping the situation 'under review'.[4] The gap of over eight months between the formal announcement of the legislation in the Queen's Speech in October

1961 and the beginning of the enforcement period of the legislation on 1 July 1962 was quite sufficient to allow a very large number of people to make and execute plans for emigration to the United Kingdom. It was not as if government was unaware of the dilemma in which it found itself.[5] Six years later, when movement to Britain from East Africa of people of Indian origin began to accelerate, the government passed legislation through both Houses of Parliament in three days to limit its scale.

Second, the Act encouraged those who had settled temporarily, or who were uncertain about how long they would stay, to decide to remain in Britain permanently. A large majority of the South Asian migrants who had arrived before the Act were adult males of working age whose intention was to earn money to remit to the sub-continent in order to improve the economic position of the family back home, often through the purchase of land. For many early settlers from the extreme north-eastern and extreme north-western areas of the Indian sub-continent the decision to locate themselves in Britain was a response to increasingly restricted opportunities in the arena they had originally selected, the sea. Viewed from a broader sub-continental perspective Britain was one of a wide range of destinations to which groups with an already established propensity for international migration, such as Jullunduris, Gujeratis and Mirpuris, had travelled in order to augment their income.[6] Their propensity to migrate was already established; their selection of destination depended largely on opportunity. The large majority of the men who came to Britain from the sub-continent in the fifteen years after the end of the Second World War almost certainly initially believed that they would return to their homeland once the target of earnings had been reached. Of course, those who did return were often replaced by another male from the extended family, so there is no case for arguing that without the Act the South Asian population would have fallen. Indeed, it would have probably continued to increase as some men decided to call their wives and families to join them in the United Kingdom. A significant proportion of Indian men (mainly Sikh) were joined by their wives and children before the Act was passed; very few Mirpuri and Kashmiri and almost no Sylhetti wives and children arrived before the Act, as Table 7 indicates. Prior to July 1962 the Asian population of Britain was overwhelmingly male and made up very largely of sojourners rather than permanent residents.

Though it was not the only factor involved and though it is likely that it would have eventually happened anyway, the Act stimulated the rate of increase of the South Asian population by removing the likelihood that a retiring male could simply be replaced by one of his kin.[7] If the source of family income from the United Kingdom was to be maintained the single sojourner had to become, in a more substantial sense, a settler. It may not have been the case that significant numbers of male immigrants from South Asia consciously and deliberately made a decision to stay permanently following the passage of the Act. The 'myth of return' survived in a powerful and influential form through the 1960s and 1970s and into the 1980s. It is more likely that the impact of the Act was felt through pressing a change of strategy on immigrant families which, in turn, had a marked effect on the rate of increase and likely future permanence of the South Asian communities. In order to ensure his replacement by another wage-earning member of the family many South Asian immigrants brought in their wives and children, especially male children and close relatives' sons.[8] For those who did make the decision to settle permanently, family reunification also became a strong objective. Further, there is some evidence that those already here thought the new rules would prevent them bringing in their wives and children should they wish to do so. There was a rush of women and children from India into the United Kingdom in the months before the Bill became law.

Third, and perhaps as importantly, the Act permitted the unification of families, which ensured that the future growth of the South Asian derived population could take place. Whereas settlers from the Caribbean were fairly evenly balanced by gender and included some children, migrants from South Asia who arrived before the 1962 Act were very largely adult males of working age.[9] The decision to admit wives (and unmarried partners) and children below working age of both existing and future immigrants was a decision taken without apparent consideration for the effect it would be likely to have on the size of Britain's future South Asian population.[10]

Fourth, the Act, far from excluding all future immigration from the Empire/Commonwealth, established a regime that allowed a substantial flow of Asian and black migrants into the United Kingdom. Though, compared to the beat-the-ban rush, the number of Asian and black immigrants entering Britain fell by a half, compared to any other period in the first sixty years of the twentieth century immigration from the Asian and black Empire/Commonwealth remained, after the 1962 Act, at historically high levels. During every single year bar two between 1963 and 1989, between 30,000 and 50,000 Asian and black immigrants arrived for settlement in Britain. The only exceptions were 1972 when numbers were swelled to over 60,000 by the sudden arrival of the Uganda Asians and 1984 when the level fell slightly below 30,000.[11] The government's continuing attempts to limit numbers coming from the New Commonwealth by introducing ever more restrictive legislation have succeeded in achieving only a gentle fall over the last thirty years. It is one of the great myths of recent British immigration history that the Act of 1962 brought a swift reduction in the number of Asian and black people settling in Britain; its influence as a stimulant to the growth of multi-racial Britain has been generally underplayed. It caused a reduction only in relation to the 'bulge' figures of 1960–2 which it did so much to create. As we have seen, the composition of the inward movement changed by gender, age and ethnicity, changes that were substantially related to impact of the Act.[12]

The Act's apparent significance lies in the fact that for the first time legislative powers were taken to restrict immigration from the Empire/Commonwealth but, except in a strictly legal sense, it was not the breach in the 'open door' regime that many at the time took it to be. That principle had been emphatically compromised by the administrative practice of immigration policy during the whole of the twentieth century. The effective collapse of the administrative arrangements under the weight of demand for entry precipitated the new legislation. The new legislation in itself did limit entry, but dependents and students could come in freely and vouchers, which did not have to be used, were initially issued quite liberally. The importance of the Commonwealth Immigrants Act of 1962 was that it became the basis for a schedule of restrictions that placed limitations on the rate of growth by immigration of Asian and black communities in Britain. To achieve this it introduced a crucially important distinction, never before admitted in law, between the rights of British subjects born in Britain and holding British-issued passports and British subjects who held passports issued by other Commonwealth governments.

CLOSING THE DOOR: NEW RULES, 1965

Though, when it was introduced, the 1962 Bill had been vigorously opposed by Labour under Gaitskell's leadership, the party, now led by Harold Wilson (following Gaitskell's untimely death in early 1963), began to shift its position. When the 1962 Act came up for the first of its required annual renewals in that year the Labour Party, apparently fearing the electoral unpopularity of a stance which opposed all entry controls, moved from outright opposition to support for the idea that immigration controls on British subjects should be negotiated with Commonwealth governments. The fact that there had been 319,000 applications for vouchers in sixteen months since the beginning of the new scheme and that net immigration from the New Commonwealth was running at about 10,000 a week seemed to cast some doubt on the realism of Labour's new approach. In its manifesto for the 1964 general election, Labour accepted the need to retain the Act until new agreements could be negotiated.[13]

In power from the summer of 1964 the Labour government of Harold

Wilson quickly set about changing its position again. The number of Asian and black immigrants entering Britain had already fallen quite sharply after the passage of the Act, due almost entirely to the delay in setting up the voucher issuing machinery. However, the number seeking entry to the United Kingdom appears, from the level of applications for vouchers, to have been at an all-time high. The notion that the beat-the-ban rush had exhausted the pool of those who wished to come to the United Kingdom and the proposition that immigration from the Commonwealth would be self-regulating according to the demands of the economy for labour were now difficult to sustain.[14] After some significant changes in the rate at which vouchers were issued and taken up, the rate of issue of vouchers settled down to 400 a week by the middle of 1964, of which about three-quarters were taken up. From September 1964 the priority categories (those with a job offer or special skills) took up the whole of the voucher issue and from then on no more vouchers were issued in the 'others' category in which a waiting list of 300,000 built up. The number of voucher holders admitted fell from nearly 30,000 in the first full year of their issue to almost 7,000 in the first half of 1965 and was quickly exceeded by the number of dependants. The Act of 1962 had given right of admittance to the wife and children up to the age of 16 of any Commonwealth citizen resident or taking up residence in Britain, but the Act had been applied in a relaxed manner to admit without vouchers a broader range of dependants including children up to the age of 18, children up to 16 coming to join close relatives other than parents, fiancées and common law wives, and elderly parents. Both dependants and students had been freely admitted with few, if any, checks made on the bona fides of either and without time limits being imposed on students' stays.

Wilson's government moved not just to accept the Act but also to tighten rules of entry under it. In February 1965 the intention was announced of reducing the evasion of immigration rules by taking powers to deport illegal immigrants, to tighten up the rules governing dependent relatives and to time-limit student visits. In the White Paper of August 1965, *Immigration from the Commonwealth*, the government announced the abolition of non-priority vouchers and the reduction in the total number of vouchers issued to those with a job offer or special skills to a maximum of 8,500 per year, 1,000 of which would be reserved for Malta. Of almost as much long-term significance for the making of multi-racial Britain, however, was the introduction of a stricter interpretation of who was to be admitted as a dependant and the announcement of much more rigorous means of enforcing the barriers erected in 1962. Restrictions on the entry of dependants were to be interpreted to exclude nephews and cousins and children over 16. In future, dependants would be expected to produce either an entry certificate or appropriate documents to establish identity at the port of entry. This was the origin of the system of entry control which saw the posting – to those Commonwealth countries that were sources of immigration – of Entry Control Officers whose job was to validate evidence of identity and issue entry certificates. By regulating the rate at which those waiting for interviews were seen they became an important agency for controlling access to the United Kingdom of potential immigrants. Entry certificates were introduced informally at first but became a legal requirement by the Immigration Appeals Act of 1969. Students would now be admitted only for a year and visitors for six months. The government took powers to deport those who sought to evade the new, stricter controls. The systematic and effective control of Asian and black immigration began in 1965 rather than 1962.[15]

At a time of labour shortage, and in view of the fact that the government contemplated no simultaneous action on Irish or alien immigration, it is difficult to interpret the White Paper proposals as anything other than an attempt to cut back sharply Asian and black immigration in order to appease political pressure. The Labour Party had completed a U-turn on immigration policy.[16] In line with the 1964 manifesto promise, Lord Louis Mountbatten had undertaken a tour of all the countries, except Pakistan, from which a significant flow of non-priority immigrants derived. He was apparently unsuccessful in persuading them to adopt self-regulating procedures which would have averted the need for the new British restrictions. Unwilling to face accusations of racial discrimination, the British government was once again trying to shift the burden of responsibility.[17] The introduction of these significant changes was clearly the second act of the play that had opened in 1962. Macmillan's government wanted – but had been too fearful of very strong adverse reaction – to ban entirely the entry to Britain of semiskilled and unskilled workers from the Caribbean and the Indian sub-continent. The motivation for the 1965 measures is neither difficult to define nor controversial. For the first time in a general election, immigration had been an issue in 1964. As was demonstrated by the defeat of Patrick Gordon Walker at the hands of Peter Griffiths in Smethwick, it was apparent that voter opposition to further Asian and black immigration could be exploited. By running an openly anti-Asian and black campaign Griffiths enjoyed a positive swing of 7.5 per cent compared to an average national drift of 3.2 per cent away from the Conservatives. Gordon Walker's subsequent defeat in Leyton in January 1965 rubbed the lesson in. Crossman's diaries set out the electoral calculations with great clarity.[18] The White Paper was endorsed by the Labour Party at conference and became the basis of a bipartisan approach to immigration questions.

It now appeared that, leaving aside natural means and barring unforeseen circumstances, from now on existing minority ethnic communities could grow largely through settled migrants exercising their right to bring in their wives and children. A small skilled and professional cadre would be admitted each year. Setting aside consideration of the still largely unforeseen developments which brought East African Indians to Britain, this change in rules was very important for its impact on the ethnic balance of Asian and black Britain and on the scale and nature of the future contribution of ethnic minorities to British society and its economy. The change ensured that the large majority of future migrants would be from the Indian sub-continent. This was so because, first, the large majority of South Asian immigrants living in Britain in 1965 were males, while the migration from the Caribbean had been much more evenly balanced in terms of gender. Numerically speaking, with the number of vouchers for primary immigrants set so low, migration from 1965 onwards would be dominated by the arrival of dependants who would be mainly South Asian females and children. From 1965 the rate of immigration into each of the established South Asian communities depended on the capacity and desire of each community to bring about family unification. These rates varied very significantly over the next thirty years. Historically, the Sikh community had settled in number first and had both the economic means and the willingness to finance family movement from Jullundur and Hoshiapur. The Mirpuri and Kashmiri communities were later arrivals, their settlement concentrated chronologically in the late 1950s and early 1960s. They were more reluctant to bring their women and children to the United Kingdom and much less well able to fund expensive air tickets. The Sylhetti community, chronologically the last to arrive and by some margin the least successful in economic terms and the most reluctant to expose their women to the dangers of life in Britain, did not establish a clear pattern of family reunification until well after the Sikhs and Pakistani Muslims. The differential impact of the restrictions of 1962 and 1965 on the South Asian communities has had the effect of exaggerating their differing age profiles in contemporary Britain.[19]

Second, the available vouchers were taken up predominantly by males from the Indian sub-continent. There were far more skilled and professional people from India and Pakistan ready and willing to take up opportunities in Britain; the professional and managerial class in the Caribbean was not only far smaller in size but it had never been seized with enthusiasm for migration to Britain. In another way the measures affected the ethnic balance within the South Asian population. From 1965 onwards most of the new South Asian families establishing themselves in the United Kingdom were professional and drawn from the whole of India rather than just from the few small areas from which migration had traditionally come. The doctors, dentists and research scientists came from Kerala and Karnataka, from Madhya Pradesh and Bihar as well as from the traditional sources of Punjab and Gujerat.[20] The changes ensured much greater South Asian diversity. The highly skilled and professional East African Asian immigrants of the late 1960s and early 1970s added to the priority voucher category immigrants to provide a highly qualified group of new South Asian residents.

As it was applied from August 1965 the voucher scheme was much more restrictive of Asian and black immigration than it appeared to be and it steadily became more restrictive as tighter rules were drawn up. Of the maximum of 8,500 vouchers issued annually the Home Office anticipated that only half of the B (job-offer) vouchers and three-quarters of the A (special skills) vouchers would be taken up. However, those admitted with

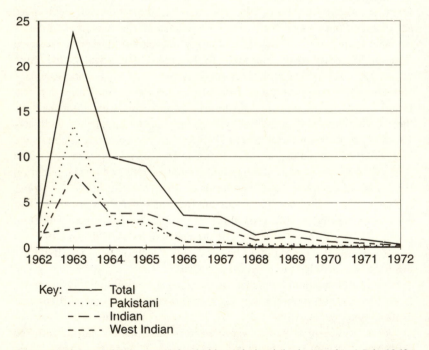

Key: —— Total
    ······ Pakistani
    – — – Indian
    – – – – West Indian

Figure 2 Ministry of Labour voucher holders admitted (in thousands), 1 July 1962–31 December 1972

Source: Adapted from the Home Office, *Commonwealth Immigrants Acts of 1962 and 1968: Control of Immigration, Statistics 1972*, Cmnd. 5285, London, HMSO, 1973; and previous volumes published annually in the same series

a voucher were heads of households with the right to bring in their partner and children. On average that meant that each voucher taken up added 3.7 persons to the country's population.[21] Further alterations were made to the voucher system, limiting the total granted to any one country to fifteen per cent of the whole and restricting the issue of category A (special skills) vouchers to workers in manufacturing industry, those who came as part of an approved recruitment scheme and those whose work was of 'substantial economic and social value'. From June 1969 Category A vouchers would not be issued if suitable labour was available locally. The issue of Category B vouchers was then restricted much more rigorously to doctors, dentists and trained nurses, qualified teachers acceptable to the Department of Education, science and technology graduates with qualifications acceptable to professional bodies and non-graduates with recognised professional qualifications and at least two years' experience. The largest occupational group applying for Category B vouchers was the doctors, but in June 1969 vouchers issued to them were limited to 2,000 a year.

So restrictive were these new rules that the long waiting lists of 1968 were quickly reduced. In 1969 only 6,769 of the permitted 8,500 vouchers were issued and of these only 4,010 were taken up. The suggestion that the immigration policy of these years was somehow designed to match labour supply with the economy's changing demands for labour is as wrongheaded applied to the policy of the period after the Act as it is applied to the Act itself. As the Department of Employment admitted, the voucher was simply a convenient device for limiting the number of Asian and black immigrants who would be allowed to enter Britain for the purposes of settlement. On no occasion was a decision about the number of vouchers to be issued correlated to changes in the demand for labour or shifts in other sources of labour supply. Nor was the abolition of Category A and B vouchers in the legislation of 1971 anything to do with changes in the conditions of labour supply and demand.[22]

Dependants of existing immigrants made up the large bulk of the immigrants even before the withdrawal of Category C vouchers in 1965. Dependants outnumbered voucher holders by almost three to one in the immigration figures of 1964. A calculation made at the end of 1967 indicated that there were close to 250,000 dependants of existing immigrants waiting to enter but the number qualifying was reduced by changes in the qualifying rules for entry certificates. In 1968, for example, the two-parent rule was introduced by which chidren under 16 were only entitled to an entry certificate if both of their parents were either resident in the United Kingdom or accompanying the child. When it was introduced this rule caused a sharp drop in the number of dependants entering from Pakistan. The practice had been for male children to join

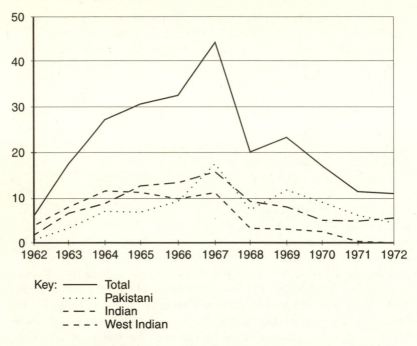

Key: ——— Total
······ Pakistani
– — – Indian
– – – – West Indian

Figure 3 Dependants admitted in Britain (in thousands), 1 July 1962–31 December 1972

Source: Adapted from the Home Office, *Commonwealth Immigrants Acts of 1962 and 1968: Control of Immigration, Statistics 1972*, Cmnd. 5285, London, HMSO, 1973; and previous volumes published annually in the same series.

their fathers with wives and girls often remaining behind in Pakistan. Over 200,000 dependants had arrived under the 1962 Act by May 1970.[23]

EAST AFRICAN ASIANS

By the latter half of 1967 immigration was again an issue in British politics. East African Asians were British subjects, in origin mainly from Gujerat, with significant minorities from Punjab and Goa, who had settled in Kenya, Uganda and Tanganyika as merchants, traders, clerks and artisans. At the time of independence in East Africa – Tanganyika in 1961, Uganda in 1962 and Kenya in 1963 – they were faced with a choice of either local or British citizenship. The significant proportion who, unsure of the future under African majority rule, had chosen British citizenship were not subject to the requirements of the 1962 Act once their British passports, after independence, were issued by the British High Commissions in East Africa. British subjects of Indian origin who retained British passports issued by the colonial governments or who had chosen local citizenship in the two-year period after independence when they had the choice, were subject to the Act. By contrast most whites who had been settled in Kenya and many of whom were also leaving Kenya at the same time were not so controlled. Under the Nationality Act of 1964 those with close connections to the United Kingdom – defined as a UK-born father or grandfather – were able to regain British citizenship if they had previously been forced to renounce it as a condition of obtaining another Commonwealth citizenship.

When the screws of nationalisation and Africanisation began to turn more sharply, non-African movement out of the three territories increased. Kenya's Immigration Act and Trade Licensing Act of 1967, which appeared to undermine the future economic prospects of the Indian communities, were generally credited with having precipitated a much more rapid emigration in late 1967. As in 1962 anticipation that further controls would be introduced by the British government was fuelled by a campaign, this time led by Enoch Powell and Duncan Sandys, which created anxiety and then a certain amount of panic among potential migrants. This had the effect of speeding the exodus from Nairobi, Kampala and Dar es Salaam. In the last two weeks of February 1968 10,000 East African Asians entered the United Kingdom, creating what the government thought of as a crisis and increasing pressure for further controls very considerably. Earlier in the month the British government had contributed to the sense of anxiety in East Africa by sending Malcolm MacDonald to Nairobi to try to find a way to decrease the rate of movement. He failed to secure Kenyatta's compliance.

The second Commonwealth Immigrants Act of March 1968, which was rushed through Parliament in only three days, subjected all holders of United Kingdom passports to immigration controls unless they, a parent or a grandparent had been born, adopted or naturalised in the United Kingdom. The legislation affected perhaps 200,000 people in all. The British High Commission-issued passports of the East African Asians were, despite the promises of 1963, rendered largely valueless by the Act which was passed with the full co-operation of the Conservative opposition though against a background of condemnation from the broadsheet press, the weeklies and the church. As a concession the government created a voucher scheme which would allow entry from East Africa at a carefully measured rate of 1,500 vouchers or about 5,000 people a year. Smuggled in with the new rules about the entry of United Kingdom citizens were new limitations on the immigration of children of Commonwealth citizens, which had the effect of preventing fathers from bringing in their sons for employment, and tighter controls in the rules on the admission of the elderly. Both had the effect of sharply reducing immigration.[24] Richard Crossman's view that the party's increased majority in the general election of 1968 was due in significant part to the firm stand the government had adopted on East African immigration was widely shared.[25]

There are many who would judge this episode to be the most dishonourable in the long history of dishonourable conduct in the area of immigration policy. It is true that those who were affected by the legislation had little previous direct contact with the United Kingdom. However, when the East African territories had been granted independence, not five or six years previously, East African Asians had received assurances about their rights as holders of British passports which were now being denied.[26] The Act of 1968 was not the first legislation to link rights to enter the United Kingdom with the place of birth of the applicants, their parents or grandparents – the Nationality Act of 1964 had already done so – but it was a straightforward device to deny rights to, amongst others, East African Asians without disenfranchising the numerous 'white' people of British origin settled outside Britain in the 'old' dominions and in Southern Rhodesia, Kenya or Argentina. The decision was as indefensible morally as it was irrational from a practical, self-interested British viewpoint. Collectively, East African Asians were a well educated, materially very successful group, containing an unusually high proportion of entrepreneurs and professionally qualified people. In signalling so plainly the fact that they were unwelcome in Britain the British government managed to divert to Canada many of those who could exercise a choice, namely the wealthiest and the best qualified. The legislation brought Britain into dispute with the East African states and with India and Pakistan over the question of responsibility for the migrants who were excluded from Britain. It caused widespread accusations of racial discrimination to be levelled at the British government.[27]

On the right the issue of continuing Asian and black immigration was taken up by Enoch Powell who briefly became a national figure following his 'rivers of blood' speech, given a month after the passage of the 1968 Commonwealth Immigrants Act. The speech was not just an attack on the bipartisan immigration policy, which seemed to Powell to be overly generous to potential Asian and black immigrants, but an assault on the proposed new Race Relations Act which was intended to provide a mechanism which would allow members of minority ethnic communities to achieve equality of treatment in key areas such as housing and employment. It was less the content of his speeches, which called for an end to non-white immigration and for organised and subsidised repatriation, than the alarmist tone of them that led directly to his exclusion from the Shadow Cabinet by the party leader, Edward Heath. There is little doubt that, briefly, Powell captured and expressed a widespead public mood that was hostile to continued Asian and black immigration. In 1969, 327 of 412 Conservative Constituency Associations polled wanted all 'coloured' immigration stopped indefinitely, while another 55 called for a five-year total ban. Edward Heath had already shifted Conservative Party policy to incorporate the ideas that dependants should be subject to more rigorous control and that, in general, potential immigrants from the Commonwealth should be dealt with on the same basis as those from the rest of the world. In the election campaign of 1970 voters regarded immigration as the fourth most important issue, but most Conservative and almost all Labour candidates failed to refer to it directly in their election addresses. Clear Conservative promises to end future large scale immigration almost certainly made a major contribution to the party's success, particularly in the West Midlands.[28]

THE IMMIGRATION ACT, 1971

The Immigration Act of 1971 (which became law in 1973) was the direct consequence of those Conservative promises. Except for the users of the vouchers issued under the Act of 1968, the annual issue of which the Conservative Government doubled to 3,000 per year, the effect of the new legislation was to bring new permanent primary migration from the Indian sub-continent, the Caribbean and Africa to the United Kingdom finally to a halt. In practical terms this made little difference to immigration flows, as the Acts of 1962 and 1968 and the rules applied under them had already almost achieved this. By preserving the existing rights of dependants the Act of 1971 ensured that a substantial Asian and black immigration, and in particular the reconstruction of South Asian families, would continue.

The Act was of considerable symbolic significance. The historic categories of 'alien' and 'British subject', that used to divide the world into those from the Empire/Commonwealth who had rights and privileges in the United Kingdom and those foreigners who did not, were replaced by the essentially racially-defined categories of 'patrial' and 'non-patrial'. Patrials were free from restrictions; non-patrials were all liable to controls. Patrials were defined as British or Commonwealth citizens who were born or naturalised in the United Kingdom or who had a parent (or grandparent in the case of British citizens) who had been born or naturalised in the United Kingdom. The category also included British and Commonwealth citizens who had been settled in the United Kingdom for five years and had registered or had applied to register as a British citizen. Thus, British citizens who were non-patrial were subject to controls, whereas non-citizens who were patrials were not subject to controls. From 1973 non-patrials seeking residence could apply for a work permit which carried neither the right of permanent residence or the right of entry for their dependants. The Act abolished the last vestiges of the old Empire-embracing concept of British subject or citizen. It also included modest, but in the event ineffective, financial assistance for repatriation and new powers to prevent illegal immigration. The rights of non-white Commonwealth citizens to migrate to and settle in United Kingdom were finally ended, whereas the rights of white settlers in the Empire/Commonwealth, so long as their settlement overseas had occurred in the last two generations, were strengthened. Overall, the Act increased the number of people entitled to enter Britain without restriction, but as these comprised almost entirely people of 'European extraction' who had 'special ties of blood and kinship' this caused no political difficulty.[29]

The Immigration Act of 1971 was closely associated, in its content and its timing, with Britain's moves towards Europe. Not only did the Act terminate the last rights to settle of those who belonged to the old all-embracing 'British subject' category, it also introduced for those non-patrial Commonwealth citizens who came to Britain to work a status which was closely akin to that enjoyed by guest workers in the Federal Republic of Germany and other European states. From 1971 non-patrial Commonwealth citizens and aliens came to Britain on the same terms. Neither had the right to settle or to bring their family.[30] By a highly symbolic coincidence, on the same day that the Immigration Act of 1971 became law, 1 January 1973, Britain entered the European Economic Community. In doing so Britain pledged itself to the principle of the free movement of labour within the community. As the restrictions were removed, citizens of the European Community – for example, Germans, Italians, Spaniards and Greeks – during the 1970s and 1980s gained the right to enter Britain freely for the purposes of settlement. The easing of immigration restrictions on over 200 million people, including the people of countries against which Britain had fought recent and bitter wars, caused very little public discussion. The change was symbolised by the new signs which appeared at the principal points of entry, such as Heathrow Airport: 'United Kingdom citizens and EEC nationals' now marked the channel for those entering free of restrictions.

THE UGANDAN EXODUS

If by the 1971 Act the Conservatives hoped to capitalise on the popularity of stricter immigration controls, they were unable to do so because of the

Ugandan Asian crisis of 1972. The exodus of people of Indian sub-continental origin from Uganda had followed the same broad pattern as movement from Kenya and Tanganyika in the decade following independence. President Obote's Trade (Licensing) Act of 1969 sharply limited the business opportunities of Asians who were not Ugandan citizens; and Uganda's new Immigration Act of 1969, which came into force the following year, considerably enhanced their feelings of insecurity. In 1970 Obote's announcement of his intention to work towards African socialism and new measures which brought importing and exporting into the government domain severely damaged Asian prospects. Increased pressure from East Africa caused the British government in 1971 to double the number of entry vouchers available to British passport holders in East Africa. A further special quota of 1,500 was offered in the latter half of 1971 in response to steadily increasing pressure. When the expulsion was first announced in August 1972 it affected Ugandan residents of Asian descent who were citizens of the United Kingdom or one of the countries of the Indian sub-continent. Rigorous checks on the papers of Asians who claimed Ugandan citizenship widened the scope of the expulsion and exemptions introduced by the Ugandan government for government employees and professionals were generally ignored. As the crisis deepened it became apparent that only very few people of Indian sub-continental origin, irrespective of their citizenship, would be both willing to stay and be accepted as residents in Idi Amin's Uganda.

Idi Amin's ejection of Uganda's Asian population at short notice created a very lively debate in Britain. Though entitled under the 1968 Act to limit severely the entry of the large majority who were British passport holders, the British government under Edward Heath decided to accept responsibility for those it could not persuade other governments to take. Its energetic campaign to gain help from other governments resulted in about 23,000 Uganda Asians, including many of the best qualified, settling in other countries, particularly Canada, which arranged an airlift for the large number of Ismailis who decided to settle there in preference to the United Kingdom. Just under 29,000 Uganda Asians arrived in the United Kingdom, the majority of whom were people who held British passports issued by the colonial government of Uganda. Elaborate, if unsuccessful, arrangements were made by the Uganda Resettlement Board to encourage East African Asians to settle in Britain away from existing centres of Asian settlement.

The effect of the Ugandan expulsion, added to the continuing movement of Asians from other East and Central African territories and the migration of dependants of settlers from India, Pakistan and Bangladesh, gave the figures for Asian and black immigration of 1972 a boost just before the

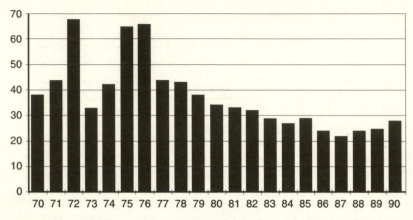

Figure 4 New Commonwealth acceptances for settlement in Britain, 1970–90 (in thousands)

Source: *Control of Immigration: Statistics, UK 1990*, Cm. 1571, HMSO, 1991

impact of the Act of 1971 began to be felt. A brief examination of the figures for the decade of the 1970s provides evidence for the continuing steady growth through immigration of Britain's new black and Asian communities. At the beginning of the decade the Asian and black population numbered some 1.2 million; the 1981 Census recorded an increase to 2.1 million. About a third of the increase can be accounted for by net immigration which, together with differential fertility rates, quite sharply changed the balance of the ethnic composition of black and Asian Britain. Inward movement from the Caribbean had already declined to below 5,000 a year by the end of the 1960s; during the 1970s it fell to negligible levels. On the other hand, inward movement of Indians (including East Africans) on the other hand had increased sharply through the 1960s to reach a peak of over 25,000 in 1968. The year 1972 saw an exceptional immigration of close to 40,000, but the figure did not fall significantly below 20,000 for the rest of the decade. Pakistani migration also peaked in the 1970s rising to an average of close to 10,000 a year. The smaller communities, Bangladeshis, Chinese and Africans all showed steady growth compared to the 1960s. The shift in the ethnic balance was remarkable. At the beginning of the 1970s the Caribbean community was comfortably the largest single component, making up about half of Asian and black Britain. By 1981 the Indian population had overtaken the Caribbean, and the total South Asian population was heading quickly for a figure double that of the West Indian community.[31]

THE BRITISH NATIONALITY ACT, 1981

The last parts of the process of restricting entry to the United Kingdom of 'coloured' immigrants from the Empire/Commonwealth occurred between 1980 and the beginning of 1983. New immigration rules, described as 'tough but fair', and the British Nationality Act of 1981, which became law in 1983, were really only footnotes to a work that had, to all intents and purposes, already been completed. In practice the changes had only a marginal impact on the rate of immigration from the new Commonwealth to Britain. Race, having emerged in the late 1960s with Enoch Powell into the public arena as a focus for open political discussion, was a subject which both parties attempted to exploit. They sought benefit by playing on what they believed to be popular anxieties about the impact of continuing large-scale Asian and black immigration. Just as Labour in the period before the 1970 election had both sharpened and emphasised its rigorous anti-'coloured' immigration stance so Margaret Thatcher, in the run-up to the 1979 election, in her famous 'swamping' statement made known her sympathy and understanding for what she believed were 'people's fears on numbers'. Despite the warning of the previous leader of the Conservative Party that little could be done to reduce even further the number of Asian and black immigrants, the Conservative manifesto of 1979 contained reference to a number of ways in which this would be done – all, of course, in the interests of good future community relations.[32]

Though more draconian as they were originally proposed – they included a register of dependants and the withdrawal of the right of husbands and (male) fiancés of British citizens to enter – the new immigration rules, as introduced in 1980, had the effect of limiting the right of entry for settlement of fiancées or spouses and dependants of resident British citizens. They established the 'Primary Purpose Rule' which forbade the entry of affianced or spouses unless the British citizen partner could show that the primary purpose of marriage was not settlement. For elderly dependants to be allowed in they had to show that they had no relatives in their own country who could support them, that they lived abroad at a standard substantially below the average and they had to be mainly or wholly dependent on their children in Britain. New rules made it much more difficult for people entering as students or visitors to obtain permission to settle. Neither the proposal for a register of dependents nor the idea that new Commonwealth immigration should be subject to an overall quota survived the drafting and debating stages. Proposals on partners and dependents were both modified following vigorous criticism in Parliament. Rules subsequently passed under the Act in 1982 appeared to ease the restrictions on women bringing their husbands or fiances into Britain. The new rules of 1980 and 1982 were in general considerably tighter than those they replaced.

The intention behind the British Nationality Act of 1981 was to bring nationality and immigration legislation into line. The rights of entry of certain classes of British subject had been so eroded as to make their possession of British status virtually meaningless. The Act was intended to rationalise and legitimise immigration rules by bringing Britain into line with Europe. It introduced a simplified definition of citizenship which created a new narrower definition of British citizenship for those with close (parental and grandparental) ties to the United Kingdom who would have right of entry and the right of abode. In effect it replaced the composite citizenship of the United Kingdom and colonies created by the Nationality Act of 1948 which had been gradually rendered obsolete by decolonisation, the change in Britain's position in the world and the growing political distance between Britain and many of its ex-colonies. The Act created two additional and much smaller categories of British citizenship neither of which enjoyed the right of abode. Citizenship of British Dependent Territories was created for those born or naturalised, or descended from those born and naturalised, in the few remaining dependencies. Residents of Hong Kong and the Falkland Islands shared this category but neither could use it to enter the United Kingdom or any other British territory. British Overseas Citizenship was a kind of dustbin category intended for those who, like the holders of dual citizenship in Malaysia, did not qualify for either of the first two categories. East African Asians holding British passports and waiting in India to come to the United Kingdom under the special voucher scheme found that, on replacing their passports, they had become British Overseas Citizens. It was essentially a transitional category which conferred no rights on the holder and could not be passed on to children. In effect, the Act disposed of remaining claims to enter the United Kingdom from groups who were not recently descended from British emigrants.[33]

Two further sets of changes must be noted. In 1988 the Immigration Act introduced changes designed to limit the right of entry of dependants of Commonwealth citizens who settled before 1973 and to make it easier for the authorities to deal with overstayers and illegal immigrants. The second set of changes related to the citizenship and immigration status of Hong Kong residents who had British Dependent Territory Citizenship. Under the Hong Kong Act of 1985 the long-term arrangements for Hong Kong residents were defined, by which those with British Dependent Territory Citizenship would lose their status in 1999, from which point they could apply for consular protection. However, anxieties about the future of the colony, following the Tiananmen Square incident in 1989 and the resulting exodus, caused the British government to enact the British Nationality (Hong Kong) Act under which the right of abode was granted to a highly selected and highly qualified minority of Hong Kong residents. The idea behind the legislation was that, by granting this economically vital segment of the population the right to come to Britain, they would be induced to stay in Hong Kong.[34] Measures to impose harsh penalties on carriers of passengers not qualified for entry (the Immigration Carriers Liability Act of 1987), legislation to curtail the rights of asylum seekers and the government's refusal to accept the abolition of passport controls for internal European Community frontiers are other expressions of a continuing acute concern with the level of Asian and black immigration into Britain.

These measures completed the transformation of British immigration policy from a set of administrative arrangements and practices – which after many years of use were finally proved to be ineffective in the years 1960–2 at keeping Asian and black British subjects out of Britain – to a rigorous and complex set of rules and laws which were intended to bring to an end Asian and black entry into Britain for the purposes of settlement. But the scale of Asian and black entry for settlement in Britain over the decades following the Act of 1962 depended not just on the broad outline of the law as set out here but very substantially on the rules and on how they were applied. This was so because those making the laws tended not to entrench the rights of partners and dependants in legislation but to define them by rules which were formulated and applied by the Home Office. For example, from the 1971 Immigration Act onwards no mention at all was made of the rights of partners of Commonwealth citizens to join their resident spouse. The rules which govern the right of entry of dependent children of residents have been steadily tightened. For example, whereas the rules in 1970 allowed the admission of a wholly dependent unmarried son or daughter under 21 if the whole family was coming to settle in the United Kingdom, a decade later children over the age of 18 had to qualify for settlement in their own right.[35]

From 1969, according to the Immigration Appeals Act of that year, dependants of existing residents who wished to gain entry had to obtain an entry clearance certificate, a stamp endorsed on the passport of the prospective immigrant by the relevant office of the High Commissioner. Standards of documentation and standards of proof of family relationships, rates of processing applications and refusal rates in categories where discretion was available could all be varied in order to depress or liberalise the entry regime. There is evidence of a steady tightening of the administration in order to reduce numbers further. For example, refusal rates for applications for family renewal from the Indian sub-continent rose from 30 per cent to 44 per cent between 1981 and 1983.[36] Executive discretion appears to have permeated immigration law, with the broadest legal powers bestowed on officials. The close questioning of spouses who applied to enter from the sub-continent by Entry Clearance Officers in order to elicit an answer designed to disqualify under the 'primary purpose' rule has been well documented. The long waiting lists for interviews with Entry Clearance Officers, especially marked in Dacca and Islamabad have appeared to operate as a method of keeping numbers down.[37] The degree of enthusiasm with which the rules were enforced could also be varied as far as illegal entrants and overstayers were concerned. Tough enforcement was, however, somewhat limited by the capacity of communities to campaign effectively against the harsh treatment of individuals and by the occasional public rejection of over-zealous methods, such as the 'virginity test' scandal of 1979. From 1983, so completely had the drawbridge been raised against the possibility of new Asian and black immigration that the degree of enthusiasm with which the rules were enforced was the only area left for public and political debate.

The changes in immigration law and practice since 1945 have perfectly mirrored the change in Britain's international position. By 1983 citizens of the Commonwealth were in a position broadly equivalent to the one aliens had been in 1945. Europeans, who in 1945 had no rights to enter and settle in the United Kingdom, by 1981 were at liberty to do so. In 1945 Britain was still the head of a vast Empire; scarcely more than a generation later Britain was becoming integrated into a European Community heading fitfully and uncertainly towards closer political unity. Decolonisation and the movement away from the Commonwealth and into Europe was always an essential part of the background to the making of immigration policy. In the 1950s governments had considered it politically too damaging to introduce immigration restrictions that would be received unfavourably by fellow states in the Commonwealth, whether that legislation was openly discriminatory or not. By 1962 when the first Commonwealth Immigrants Act was finally introduced the cost of Commonwealth objections had fallen. The decision to make the first application to enter the EEC had already been made, the decolonisation process was largely completed and there was a widespread public perception that Britain's future lay at least as much with Europe as with the old Empire/Commonwealth.

But more fundamental was the consideration that Britain should avoid the racial problems that had affected the United States of America and which had begun to appear in a serious form in British cities in 1958 and then in 1980, 1981 and 1985. The immigration legislation of the 1960s, 1970s and 1980s was clearly, incontestably and unsuccessfully designed to limit and then stop the movement into Britain of people of colour from Africa, the Caribbean and the Indian sub-continent. The introduction of new legislation did not signal a departure for the British government with regard to the objectives of immigration policy. For many decades Britain had striven to keep out its Asian and black subjects. It did represent a departure in the sense that from 1962 the British government used administrative methods set within a legal framework; the procedures used before 1962 were founded on nothing more than political and administrative preference. What did continue were the denials, more and more muted over time, that the British government sought to limit entry for settlement to Britain on the grounds of colour.

Conclusion

For three centuries 'black' British history, hidden or visible, was the history of a very small fragment of the total population whose collective impact on British society was slight and, owing to its relative poverty, not even commensurate with its small number. The settlers of the mid- and late 1950s changed this position radically. Within a generation, between the late 1950s and the late 1980s, major Asian and black communities established themselves in most major cities of the United Kingdom, while the Asian and black population increased tenfold from a quarter of a million to two and a half million, from 0.5 per cent to over 5 per cent. A reconsideration of the chronology of the making of multi-racial Britain would place the Commonwealth Immigrants Act of 1962 closer to the beginning of the process than to its end. Its role in that process was a crucial one. Multi-racial Britain is a very recent phenomenon.

The main body of this book has been concerned with the making and implementation of government policy towards the immigration of people from the Indian sub-continent, the Caribbean and Africa. During the inter-war years, when the number attempting to enter Britain from the colonies was very small, British governments acted to obstruct the movement of Asian and black people from the Empire/Commonwealth to the United Kingdom for the purpose of settlement. In the post-war years British governments, both Labour and Conservative, attempted with some success to maintain and expand the restrictive arrangements previously imposed by colonial governments at London's request. They made considerable efforts to find new ways to prevent the movement of Asian and black British subjects to the United Kingdom for settlement and to block loopholes as they appeared. Though they enjoyed some success for a decade or more, their endeavours ultimately failed, a failure recognised by the acceptance of the need to legislate. In line with repeated official assurances, all British subjects, irrespective of colour or country of origin enjoyed the right of free entry into the United Kingdom until 1962. In practice the white inhabitants of the 'old' dominions found that right much easier to exercise than Asian and black British subjects from the New Commonwealth.

During the whole of the tortuous and lengthy debate about 'coloured' immigration leading up to the 1962 Act, the approach of Britain's policy makers was always 'racialised', as indeed it was before the post-war debate began in earnest. The only aspect of immigration from the Empire/Commonwealth which was regarded by the government as 'a problem' (and which had to be dealt with) was, in practice, 'coloured' – or Asian and black – immigration. The Irish and Commonwealth immigrants of European origin, who were more numerous during almost every post-war year, barely merited a mention at the higher levels of government except in relation to the political difficulties that would be caused by attempting to keep out Asian and black migrants without agreeing to restrict those of European origin. In fact, during the 1950s Asian and black immigration averaged considerably less than a quarter, and was in most years less than a fifth, of immigration as a whole. Governments and their civil servants understood very well the racial basis of discussion about 'colonial' immigration policy. The officials were men (with only the occasional woman) who had raised the invention of techniques to keep Britain white without using legislation almost to the level of an art-form. The contrast between the public face of a mother country open to all and the private calculation to exclude was sharp, from the Commons welcome to the Windrushers through to the constant denial that the Act of 1962 was intended specifically to keep out Asian and black subjects. Appearances were of critical importance for a country attempting, in a hostile Cold War setting, to retain its world role at the head of a multi-racial Commonwealth in an era of rapid decolonisation.

The type of immigration with which the British officials were concerned was explicitly and openly described, in the language of the day, as 'coloured'. The relevant assumptions on which the officials and their political masters operated were relatively few, quite simple and widely shared and understood. They were that the permanent settlement of 'coloured' immigrants in any significant number would constitute 'a problem', particularly if the geographical pattern of settlement was concentrated in a small number of cities. The creation of communities of different racial origins living side-by-side which would be the consequence of large-scale 'coloured' immigration, would almost certainly result in racial tension and a colour problem on American lines. The settlement in Britain of a large number of people from the Caribbean, Africa or the Indian sub-continent was, therefore, to be avoided. The acid test of the acceptability of immigration was whether the groups entering Britain could be 'assimilated'. It was accepted without question, and usually without saying, that 'coloured' immigrants in large numbers could not be assimilated.

In the end, as the 'crisis' debates of 1954–5 and 1958–61 showed so clearly, questions of policy hinged on questions of numbers. There was little dissent in the post-war debate from the view that 'colonial', or 'coloured' or 'new Commonwealth', immigration was undesirable and no question that white immigration from the Commonwealth and Eire was, and continued to be, desirable. The debate about immigration controls was not a debate about controls in general but only about the control of coloured 'immigration'. In fact, for a time in the 1960s and 1970s 'immigration' came to mean 'coloured immigration', as if there were no other kind. It was not a debate about the supply of labour either. Consideration of Britain's labour needs played virtually no part in the discussion about immigration policy. Nor was it a debate about whether controls should be introduced, but a debate about how and when. The study of the making and implementation of immigration policy in the twentieth century reveals a consistent 'racialisation' and a constant hostility to the immigration and settlement of 'coloured' Asian and black British subjects.

To a significant degree the shape, form and extent of multi-racial Britain was the result, both intended and unintended, of British immigration policy and in particular of the 1962 Commonwealth Immigrants Act. The unannounced but clearly defined goal of its architects was to restrict the size of Britain's Asian and black population. Its consequences were to increase hugely the number of those who would leave Africa, Asia and the Caribbean to settle in Britain. Many thousands came because they feared that the Act would exclude them for ever, while many thousands more decided that they would stay and would bring their families when the Act made it difficult or impossible for them to maintain the original purpose of their decision to settle, albeit temporarily, in Britain. After the Act was passed immigration from the Caribbean quickly came to a halt, whereas the peak years of immigration of people from the Indian sub-continent followed, rather than preceded the passage of the Act. Contrary to popular mythology many more people, males as well as females and children, arrived for settlement from the Indian sub-continent and Africa after the Act than before.

The shaping of minority ethnic communities in contemporary Britain cannot be understood without an examination of how the Act caught different minority ethnic communities at different stages of their migration – movement from Bangladesh had hardly started, but Caribbean migration had reached a mature stage. Also important in this process were the ways in which the rules were written and applied throughout the 1960s, through to the abolition of the voucher system in 1971, as well as of the legislation that supplemented and then replaced it, the 1968 Commonwealth Immigrants Act, the Immigration Act of 1971 and the British Nationality Act of 1981. The making and implementation of British immigration policy from 1962 until 1981 eventually ended the possibility that Asian and black Britain could continue to grow significantly from external sources, but did so in a manner and over a timescale that enabled multiracialism to become an established and important fact of British life. Of those recorded in the 1981 Census, well over three-quarters of all the immigrants of the major Asian and black minority ethnic communities, except one (Afro-Caribbean), arrived in Britain after the Commonwealth Immigrants Act of 1962 and not before.

One of the most popular explanations for the attempt to shift to restrictive immigration legislation in 1962 is that government policy sought to serve the labour demands of the economy. It is argued that Britain, in the period of post-war reconstruction, required additional sources of labour which it sought in part from its Empire/Commonwealth. When that demand for labour turned down at the beginning of the 1960s, government began to contemplate the imposition of legislative restrictions on the freedom of movement of British subjects from the Empire/Commonwealth.[1] Not only had government for a long time been trying to limit entry by non-legislative means but, far from its actions showing that labour demand issues had been at all a significant factor, it had also seriously contemplated legislation at times when such issues would not have been even close to the national agenda. It also knew perfectly well that newly arrived Asian and black labour was being absorbed very speedily into the workforce. At the critical Cabinet meeting in 1961 the Treasury were very clear that Asian and black immigration was of continuing benefit to the British economy and that grounds of economic self-interest could not be used to justify the introduction of restrictions. Numbers were what counted in 1961; but not numbers of unemployed, or numbers seeking benefit, or numbers spreading disease, or numbers involved in crime or disorder. It was what might happen in the future that counted; it was fear of 'swamping', of loss of identity and of the 'magpie society'. 'Assimilibility' was the issue; controls over 'coloured' immigrants were introduced despite labour needs, not because of them.

Related to the notion that immigration policy was closely linked to the labour demands of the economy is the idea that Asian and black immigrants from the Caribbean, the Indian sub-continent and Africa came to Britain mainly or in substantial part as invitees, as the result of the direct recruitment of labour, often to fill the most menial, undesirable and low paid of jobs, those that white British workers in an era of full employment would no longer occupy. It is clear that only a very small minority of Asian and black immigrants came as a direct result of recruitment activities by British employers, many of which were nationalised industries or public concerns, acting with either the tacit or direct approval of government. Direct recruitment from the Caribbean, often cited as the principle example of this process, was almost entirely confined to Barbados, which sent less than 10 per cent of the total number to arrive in Britain from that region. The best known and probably the largest and most sustained of the recruitment initiatives was British Transport's recruitment in Barbados from 1956 to 1968. It recruited, on average, just over 300 men a year.[2] The overwhelming majority of Asian and black immigrants and their families came to Britain, not as recruits to a reserve army of labour but as self-selected volunteers intent on using their skills and qualifications to the best possible effect to raise their income and status.

The portrayal of Asian and black immigration as substantially – or even significantly – the result of labour recruitment is often associated with the notion that Asian and black immigrants comprised an imported underclass occupying a rung of the ladder of British society below that of the poorest white workers. They were broadly characterised as unskilled and semiskilled workers who came to Britain to fill jobs which white people were too proud or over-qualified to fill.[3] At the most simple level the assertion conceals the huge diversity of socio-economic backgrounds from which Asian and black migrants came.[4] Characteristically, works that make these assumptions about Asian and black immigrants concentrate their analysis or draw their illustrations from the period of migration just before 1962 and tend also to focus on the Caribbean experience. During those years a substantial percentage of South Asian migrants were from poor, and often illiterate, peasant backgrounds and Caribbean migrants tended to be less well qualified and educated than the earlier post-war arrivals.[5] Peach's highly influential research on immigration from the Caribbean in the period up to the Commonwealth Immigrants Act of 1962 examined a movement of immigrants into job vacancies in non-growth and low-growth industries at the lower end of the occupational ladder.[6] The results of his analysis of a movement over a relatively short period of time from one sending area appear to have been a major influence on thinking about Asian and black immigration in general.

There is a very large body of evidence which suggests that immigrants from the Caribbean brought to Britain a high level of skill and enterprise, the levels of skill comparable with – and the levels of enterprise considerably in excess of – 'native' standards. Fisher's report in 1955 suggested that the departure of emigrants from the Caribbean represented a serious loss of skills to the island economies. At the peak of the migration Ruth Glass found that a quarter of arrivals had professional or managerial experience, almost half were skilled workers and only one-eighth were unskilled. Roberts and Mills' study of Jamaican migrants of 1953–5, Cumper's study of emigrants from Barbados in 1955 and Francis' sample from 1962 all point to a high, if declining proportion of skilled workers.[7] After arrival, Asian and black immigrants often found jobs in industries that were declining or unpleasant, or which involved long or awkward hours, because that type of employment was readily available. Of the West Indians who came to Britain in the 1950s just over a fifth had worked in unskilled or semiskilled capacities, yet almost two-thirds did so in Britain. Over a quarter of the emigrants had left skilled or professional jobs, yet only a tenth found equivalent employment in the United Kingdom.[8] Most employers discriminated against job applicants from the New Commonwealth; those employers who had the fewest applicants were the least able to discriminate. Asian and black immigrants often found their qualifications either ignored or downgraded. Partly as a result of the more highly qualified migrants entering after 1962, Asian and black immigrants into the United Kingdom over the whole period since 1945 were, taken together, little different in terms of the level and quality of their skills and qualification from the indigenous population of the British Isles. A survey carried out in 1982 by the Policy Studies Institute showed that Asian men over the age of 44, almost all of whom were immigrants, were more likely to be well educated than white males, but also were more likely to possess no qualifications at all. West Indian males fared less well in both categories than either white or Asian.[9]

Available data about the levels of education and skill of Asian and black immigrants indicate that, taken as a whole, they were not significantly below those of the population of the United Kingdom as a whole. There were evidently very large differences – in levels of education, skills and previous property ownership – between minority communities of different geographical, cultural and linguistic origins. Considering the background of communities from the Indian sub-continent, there was (and still is) a very large gulf between standards of living and standards of literacy, education and skill in, for example, Jullundur District in Punjab, from which many Sikh immigrants came, and those in Sylhet District in Bangladesh, from which most Bengali-speaking migrants came. The size and cultural and linguistic complexity – as well as the very large differences in standards of living between different parts – of the Indian sub-continent are seldom fully appreciated by those writing about immigration and settlement in the United Kingdom. On arrival in Britain a large proportion of the Sylhetti migrants were illiterate, unable to speak English and lacking in skills which had a direct commercial or industrial application. By contrast some of the East African and Indian derived Gujerati-speaking communities, the Shahs and the Ismailis for example, possessed very high levels of literacy in both Gujerati and English (usually Swahili and Hindi as well), a very high average level of academic and professional qualifications and often acutely developed commercial skills. But generalisations about South Asian immigrant based communities are very dangerous. There is a very clear differentiation between economically successful Gujerati-speaking communities like the Jains and the Bohras on the one hand and Sunni Muslim communities (Surati in origin) based on towns like Bolton on the other. At another level the Gujerati-speaking Patel community, most of whom have come to Britain from East Africa, have enjoyed substantial success in London high streets as confectioners, tobacconists and newsagents.[10]

Not only were immigrants from the New Commonwealth and Pakistan, taken together, better qualified than is normally acknowledged, but their success in Britain, despite discrimination, has been considerable. Perhaps the tendency to group all Asian and black communities together and the concentration of so much research and writing on issues relating to discrimination have tended to conceal the very considerable economic and social achievements of many minority ethnic communities. Immigrants from South Asia, the Caribbean and Africa, whether from illiterate peasant or professional backgrounds, were economic migrants who saw migration – with the huge costs (for them) that it imposed – as an investment in the future which would result in an increase in status for themselves and their families. The aim of migration was not limited merely to gaining employment and enjoying a higher standard of living. Whatever their class and caste background, South Asian migrants were willing to undertake menial jobs in the short term and at the same time to live very frugally in order to place themselves in a position where status ambitions could be realised, usually through starting a business.[11]

The speed with which a number of Asian and black immigrant derived communities have acquired the key markers of high status – educational qualifications and property – has been breathtaking. Most of the crude indicators of success in contemporary Britain – rates of home owner occupancy and car ownership, distribution between occupational cat-egories and levels of educational achievement – rank African, Indian and Chinese communities as more successful than the average for the country whereas Caribbean, Pakistani and Bangladeshi communities, as yet, enjoy less success than the average. The 1991 census revealed that a higher proportion of Indian than white males were classified as professionals and as managers or proprietors (twice as many), though in the third high-status employment category, corporate managers and administrators, whites were

Table 8 Measures of economic success of minority communities

	White	Indian	Pakistani	Bangladeshi	African	Caribbean	Chinese
Corporate managers and administrators (% of males)	12.4	8.2	4.9	3.0	8.0	4.9	5.9
Managers and proprietors (% of males)	7.1	14.8	16.0	13.6	4.0	3.5	20.5
Professionals (% of males)	9.6	13.5	7.8	6.8	17.1	4.3	17.1
Self-employed with employees (% of active males)	5.1	9.6	7.1	10.6	2.2	1.6	17.8
Qualification of A-Level equivalent (% of males)	13.4	15.0	7.0	5.2	26.5	9.2	25.4
Owner occupied home (% of households)	66.6	81.7	76.7	44.5	28.0	48.1	62.2
Car ownership (% of households)	67.0	76.8	63.7	39.1	38.0	45.2	70.6

Source: Office of Population and Census Surveys

better represented than Indians. Indians take up a relatively greater share of university places than whites, and Indian graduates enjoy higher levels of income than whites. Indians are proportionately over-represented in the ranks of British millionaires.[12] There were, however, very large differences in the levels of skill, education and income of different immigrant-based communities.[13]

As countless pieces of research testify, however, the common experience of Asian and black employees in Britain is of racial discrimination and the undervaluing of – or refusal to recognise – their qualifications. People from Asian and black communities have always been disproportionately over-represented in the ranks of the unemployed, a phenomenon that is less clearly related to levels of qualification than to levels of discrimination. Qualifications may increase the prospects of finding a job, but those with higher qualifications do not necessarily experience less discrimination than those with poor or no qualifications.[14] In the longer term the high levels of academic success by the children of all of Britain's minority ethnic communities and the marked trend into self-employment may do something to limit the deleterious effects of discrimination on the economic fortunes of those communities.[15]

Britain became multi-racial during a period in which, except for the years of the beat-the-ban rush, net emigration exceeded net immigration and during which Asian and black immigration was a fraction of total immigration. For the early part of the post-war period the availability of employment in Britain was one of the key circumstances that encouraged the growth of Asian and black immigration. Aside from the increasing difficulty of controlling movement into Britain in the face of rapid decolonisation, there were other important changes which made movement from the Caribbean, Africa and the Indian sub-continent to Britain much cheaper, easier and attractive than it had ever been before. In the Indian sub-continent the increasing availability of passports from independent governments, the introduction of charter flights, and the rapid fall in the price of air travel all made a major contribution to the increasing movement. The growing availability through the 1950s of cheap sea passages from the Caribbean, added to new opportunities for air travel, provided means of movement where none had been practical before.

The decisions of Asian and black subjects of the Empire/Common-wealth to move to the United Kingdom were almost always the result of the determination of individuals and families to improve their income and status. Those that entered Britain did so, not as an underclass recruited to poorly paid jobs, but as members of a highly diverse set of communities with a very wide range of qualifications and experience that were, taken as a whole, of a level broadly comparable to those of the 'white' inhabitants of Britain. To characterise Asian and black immigrants as an imported underclass of unskilled labour is inaccurate. Such generalisations provide little help towards an understanding of the migration as a whole and fail to prepare Britain to understand the scale of the contribution that minority ethnic communities are likely to make to British society in the next generation. The persistence of those generalisations does however underscore the fact that after arrival Asian and black immigrants were very often forced by discrimination into roles for which they were over-qualified.

Asian and black migration to Britain since 1945 was the migration of a complex mosaic of communities of highly diverse backgrounds and qualifications. British policy grouped them together as 'coloured' and resisted their entry. Perhaps there is a parallel between the 'racialised' outlook of those British governments and the attitudes and assumptions of academics and commentators who have persistently classified these communities as 'black' and described them as collectively located in the lower reaches of British society. Each community that makes up the minority ethnic population of Britain has a distinctive character and role formed substantially by its own particular ethnic and cultural origins as well as by its immigration history and by the interaction of it with British immigration policy.

Notes

PREFACE

1 The 1991 Census question on 'ethnic group' asked people who did not describe themselves as 'White' to classify themselves as Black – Caribbean; Black – African; Black – Other; Indian; Pakistani; Bangladeshi; or Chinese. Ethnicity, according to the authors of the question, was clearly a matter of skin colour or nationality or continental origin, or a combination of the three. The term 'race' was carefully avoided. The courts, wrestling with questions of recognition of ethnic groups in cases brought under the Race Relations Acts of 1968 and 1976, have come to quite different conclusions.

2 R. Ballard and V.S. Kalra, *The Ethnic Dimensions of the 1991 Census: A Preliminary Report*, Census Microdata Unit/University of Manchester, Manchester, 1994.

3 Whereas in the Census of 1961 there were roughly twice as many people in Britain who had been born in the Caribbean as there were born in the Indian sub-continent, by the 1991 Census the position had been reversed. People who identified themselves as Indian, Pakistani and Bangladeshi in origin were twice as numerous as Caribbean derived people. Asian communities have been growing much faster than black ones.

1 THE ORIGINS OF MULTI-RACIAL BRITAIN

1 Typical of this approach is Nigel File who asserts that a certain amount of re-education is necessary for those who believe that Britain became a multi-racial society only in the early 1950s; N. File, 'History', in A. Craft and G. Bardell (eds), *Curriculum Opportunities in a Multicultural Society*, London, Harper and Row, 1984, p. 14.

2 R. Visram, *Ayahs, Lascars and Princes: Indians in Britain, 1700–1947*, London, Pluto, 1986; P. Fryer, *Staying Power: The History of Black People in Britain*, London, Pluto, 1984; and R. Ramdin, *The Making of the Black Working Class in Britain*, Aldershot, Hampshire, Gower, 1987. Other important works are J. Walvin, *Black and White: The Negro in English Society, 1555–1945*, London, Allen Lane, 1973; E. Scobie, *Black Britannia: The History of Blacks in Britain*, Chicago, Johnson, 1972; and F.O. Shyllon, *Black People in Britain, 1555–1958*, London, Oxford University Press for the Institute of Race Relations, 1978.

3 The claim is made by Folarin Shyllon, 'The black presence and experience in Britain: an analytical overview', in J.S. Gundara and I. Duffield, *Essays on the History of Blacks in Britain: From Roman Times to the Mid-Twentieth Century*, Aldershot, Hampshire, Avebury, 1992, p. 203. James Walvin has recently warned of the dangers of exaggerating the importance of black history in Britain; J. Walvin, 'From the fringes: the emergence of British black historical studies', in Gundara and Duffield, *Essays*, p. 239.

4 See N. Myers, 'Reconstructing the black past: blacks in Britain, *circa* 1780 to 1830', unpublished Ph.D. Thesis, University of Liverpool, 1990, p. 71.

5 For a convenient summary see J. Walvin, *Passage to Britain: Immigration in British History and Politics*, Harmondsworth, Middlesex, Penguin, 1984, pp. 31–47. The *Gentleman's Magazine* is the source of the contemporary estimate, see Walvin, p. 33. Fryer (*Staying Power*, p. 235) puts the number of 'black' people living in Britain at about 10,000 at the beginning of the nineteenth century; and Shyllon at 'not less than 10,000' in 1772, see Shyllon in Gundara and Duffield, *Essays*, p. 203.

6 Visram, *Ayahs, Lascars and Princes*. Originally denoting an Indian seaman, by the mid-nineteenth century the term 'lascar' came to include Burmese, Siamese, Malay and Chinese. See N. Myers, 'The black poor of London: initiatives of eastern seamen in the eighteen and nineteenth centuries', *Immigrants and Minorities*, 1994, vol. 13 (nos. 2 and 3), p. 9.

7 This figure is frequently repeated in post-war official papers. See, for example, 'Report of the Working Party on coloured people seeking employment in the United Kingdom', 17 December 1953. p. 5 in CAB124/1191. For the early history of dockland communities in London and Liverpool, see Myers, 'The black poor', pp. 7–21 and I. Law and J. Henfrey, *A History of Race and Racism in Liverpool, 1660–1950*, Liverpool, Merseyside CRC, 1981.

8 From personal experiences recorded by the author. For half the population never having met a black person, see A.H. Richmond, *Colour Prejudice in Britain: A Study of West Indian Workers in Liverpool, 1942–1951*, London, Routledge & Kegan Paul, 1954, pp. 104–7.

9 T. Lane, 'The political imperatives of bureaucracy and empire: the case of the Coloured Alien Seamen Order, 1925', *Immigrants and Minorities*, 1994, vol. 13 (nos. 2 and 3), pp. 108–10. 'Seedee' became the widely used term for all Arab and Somali seamen and 'Kru' the generic term for West African seamen, though Kru also denoted an ethnic group, active as seamen, who derived from eastern Liberia. See D. Frost, 'Ethnic identity, transience and settlement: the kru in Liverpool since the late nineteenth century', *Immigrants and Minorities*, 1993, vol. 12 (no. 3), pp. 88–106.

10 For the early history of lascars in the UK see Myers, 'Reconstructing the black past', pp. 174–95; Visram, *Ayahs, Lascars and Princes*, pp. 34–54; and Lane, 'Political imperatives', pp. 114–15. For Glasgow see B. Maan, *The New Scots: The Story of Asians in Scotland*, Edinburgh, John Donald, 1992; and A. Dunlop and R. Miles, 'Recovering the history of Asian migration to Scotland', *Immigrants and Minorities*, 1990, vol. 9 (no. 2), pp. 151–2.

11 Kenneth Little's quaintly named pioneering study of Cardiff, *Negroes in Britain: A Study of Race Relations in English Society*, London, Routledge & Kegan Paul, 1948 stands out as one of the very few that looks in detail at the development of the black communities in British ports. Disappointing from this point of view is Laura Tabili, *"We Ask for British Justice": Workers and Racial*

Difference in Late Imperial Britain, Ithaca, New York, Cornell University Press, 1994, a very well-researched study of the dockland communities and of the attitudes of government, organised labour and capitalists towards them. She uncovers a mountain of relevant official sources but seems intent on using them to demonstrate the validity of a set of general propositions about the methods and techniques of exploitation of 'colonised workers' and to challenge explanations for conflict 'that rest on ahistorical assumptions about the universality and naturalness of xenophobia and racism'. Her comment, that the use of the term 'black' to refer to all of Britain's minority ethnic communities is justified by the fact that they prefer it, is indicative of her level of knowledge and understanding of those diverse communities. Much more useful are P.B. Rich, *Race and Empire in British Politics*, Cambridge, Cambridge University Press, 1990, pp. 120–144; and an excellent and detailed article by N. Evans, 'Regulating the reserve army: arabs, blacks and the local state in Cardiff, 1919–1945', *Immigrants and Minorities*, 1995, vol. 14 (no. 2), pp. 68–115. For the growth and size of dockland communities, see Lane, 'Political imperatives', pp. 106–10.

12 Report of the Cardiff City Police, 2 December 1930, HO45/14299/2; and Little, *Negroes in Britain*, pp. 57, 130–8. The figures for 1930 are reproduced by Evans, 'Regulating the reserve', p. 71. For Liverpool see Richmond, *Colour Prejudice*, p. 20.

13 D. Lawless, 'The role of seamen's agents in the migration for employment of Arab seafarers in the early twentieth century', *Immigrants and Minorities*, 1994, vol. 13, (nos. 2 and 3), pp. 35–7. South Shields was the second largest 'Adenese' settlement, numbering about 700 in 1930. See also Lane, 'Political imperatives', pp. 105–7. In July 1931 Arabs and Somalis made up just over a half of those in Britain of defined ethnicity who registered under the 1925 Order.

14 Little, *Negroes in Britain*, p. 78.

15 Maan, *New Scots*, pp. 98–148 provides sufficient detail about early Asian settlement in Scotland to be able to link it to post-war migration patterns. See also J.A.G. Griffiths *et al.*, *Coloured Immigrants in Britain*, London, Oxford University Press for the Institute of Race Relations, 1960, p. 27.

16 H. Joshua and T. Wallace (with H. Booth), *To Ride the Storm: The 1980 Bristol Race 'Riot' and the State*, London, Heinemann, 1983, pp. 14, 17–20.

17 For the riots of 1919 see J. Jenkinson, 'The 1919 race riots in Britain: a survey,' in R. Lotz and I. Pegg (eds), *Under the Imperial Carpet: Essays in Black History, 1780–1850*, Crawley, Sussex, Rabbit Press, 1986 and N. Evans, 'Across the universe: racial violence and the post-war crisis in imperial Britain, 1919–1925,' *Immigrants and Minorities*, 1994, vol. 13 (nos. 2 and 3), pp. 59–88. For Liverpool see R. May and R. Cohen, 'The interaction between race and colonialism: a case study of the Liverpool riots of 1919', *Race and Class*, 1974, vol 16 (no. 2).

18 Evans, 'Across the universe', pp. 75–7.

19 Ibid., pp. 72–3, 75–6; Tabili, *'We Ask'*, pp. 119–20, 137–8; and Lane, 'Political imperatives', pp. 120–1.

20 Tabili, *'We Ask'*, pp. 151–2.

21 Excellent background to these developments is provided by C. Holmes, *John Bull's Island: Immigration and British Society, 1871–1971*, London, Macmillan, 1988, chapter 1.

22 Evans, 'Across the universe', pp. 74–5. Evans quotes a Board of Trade official

writing in 1920: 'It is most desirable that the number of coloured seamen coming into this country should be restricted as much as possible, as it is extremely difficult for these men to obtain employment in the United Kingdom either on board ship or ashore and their presence is a cause of serious unrest among British seamen and has led to disturbances and breaches of the peace in British ports.' (Asst. Secretary, Marine Department to British Consul, Marseilles, 20 September 1920, HO45/11897).

23 For these measures see HO45/11897/19, 20 and 22. See also Tabili, *'We Ask'*, pp. 118–9.

24 Little, *Negroes in Britain*, pp. 86–9; Evans, 'Across the universe', pp. 80–1; and Tabili, *'We Ask'*, pp. 121–2, 128.

25 Immigration Officers Report, 1921 in HO45/11897/332087, quoted in D. Frost, 'Racism, work and unemployment: West African seamen in Liverpool, 1880s to 1960s', *Immigrants and Minorities*, 1994, vol. 13 (nos. 2 and 3), p. 28.

26 See Circular to Chief Constables, 23 March 1925, HO45/12314; Evans, 'Across the universe', pp. 80–1; and P. Gordon and D. Reilly, 'Guestworkers of the sea: racism in British shipping', *Race and Class*, 1986, vol. 28 (no. 2), pp. 76–7. Parallels between the application of the 1925 Order and later immigration controls are drawn by Joshua and Wallace, *To Ride the Storm*, pp. 32–3.

27 Evans, 'Across the universe', p. 83 and D. Byrne, 'The 1930 "Arab riot" in South Shields: a race riot that never was', *Race and Class*, 1977, vol. 18 (no. 3).

28 Little, *Negroes in Britain*, pp. 96–7 and Evans, 'Across the universe', pp. 84–6.

29 Aliens Department (Home Office) to Chief Constable of South Shields 20 June 1934, HO213/242. For early evidence of Sikh pedlar activity, see D.S. Tatla, 'This is our home now: reminiscences of a Punjabi migrant in Coventry', *Oral History*, 1993, vol. 21 (no. 1) and V. Davis, 'A sweet prison', unpublished MA Dissertation, University of Leicester, 1993, pp. 12–15.

30 Aliens Department (Home Office) to Chief Constable of South Shields 20 June 1934, HO213/242.

31 The Resident, Aden to Secretary of State for the Colonies, 16 April 1935, CO725/31/3 (quoted in Lawless, 'Seamen's agents', p. 55).

32 See Ramdin, *Black Working Class*, pp. 76–9. His account is largely based on Little, *Negroes in Britain*.

33 Frost, 'Racism', p. 29.

34 Sylhettis, Mirpuris, Gujeratis and Sikhs from the Indian sub-continent and Caribbeans, African and Chinese from the basis of Britain's contemporary Asian and black population. The notion that the minority ethnic population of Britain is made up of a relatively small number of distinct communities from a series of very precisely definable geographical locations in the Caribbean, Africa and South Asia was developed in, for example, E.J.B. Rose and others, *Colour and Citizenship: A Report on British Race Relations*, London, Institute of Race Relations/Oxford University Press, 1969. Figures for the size of minority communities are from R. Ballard and V.S. Kalra, *Ethnic Dimensions of the 1991 Census: A Preliminary Report*, Manchester, Census Microdata Unit/University of Manchester, 1994, p. 11.

35 For West African seamen settling after the war see, Frost, 'Ethnic identity', p. 93.

36 Caroline Adams' work records the stories of pioneer Sylhetti settlers in Britain: *Across Seven Seas and Thirteen Rivers: Life Stories of Pioneering Sylheti Settlers in Britain*, London, Tower Hamlets Arts Projects, 1987, pp. 39–43, 50–2.

37 Scottish Office Circular No. 2440 of June 1930 (quoted in Dunlop and Miles, 'Asian migration to Scotland', pp. 156–7). '

38 By 1942 the labour situation in Britain was desperate. Temporarily resident pedlar Sikhs also forsook more traditional occupations to work in munitions factories during the war. See V. Davis, 'Sweet prison', pp. 12–13 who notes that fifty Sikhs were resident in Coventry during the war. Duffield notes that several iron foundries in the West Midlands by the end of the war employed substantial numbers of Indians; M. Duffield, *Black Radicalism and the Politics of Deindustrialization*, Aldershot, Hampshire, Avebury, 1988, p. 32. In Glasgow in 1940 two-thirds of those who held pedlar licences were Indian Muslims, presumably ex-seamen. See E.W. McFarland, 'Clyde opinion on an old controversy: Indian and Chinese seafarers in Glasgow', *Ethnic and Racial Studies*, 1991, vol. 14 (no. 4), p. 511, who also indicates that the large number of Indian ex-sailors who settled in Glasgow during the war formed the basis for later permanent settlement. Scotland's largest city had acquired an Asian population of about 600 by 1941. See Dunlop and Miles, 'Asian migration to Scotland', p. 158 and Tabili, *'We Ask'* pp. 78, 162.

39 For changes in the treatment of 'coloured seamen', see 'Coloured people from British colonial territories', memorandum by the Secretary of State for the Colonies, 18 May 1950, CP(50)113, CAB 129/40; and memorandum by Howard (Home Office) 15 February 1949. in HO 213/869. See also M. Sherwood, 'Race, nationality and employment among Lascar seamen, 1660–1945', *New Community*, 1990, vol. 17 (no. 2), pp. 229–44.

40 This information was revealed in correspondence between the Home Office and the Ministry of War Transport in HO 213/820. Part of the explanation for the growth of numbers in towns with munitions factories may also have been the relocation there of Indians who had previously been pedlars, unable to carry on with their traditional role during a period of wartime shortages. See, for example, the growth of Glasgow's Asian population in Maan, *New Scots*, pp. 149–50.

41 Minutes of meeting at the Home Office to discuss the problem of Indian seamen deserters, 4 June 1943, HO213/869.

42 Kneale (Ministry of War Transport) to Harrison (Home Office) 10 May 1943, HO213/869.

43 See A. Shaw, 'The Pakistani community in Oxford', in R. Ballard (ed.), *Desh Pardesh: The South Asian Presence in Britain*, London, Hurst, 1994, pp. 37–40. For the importance of one pioneer in shaping the Indian community in Glasgow, see Maan, *New Scots*, pp. 105–122.

44 See M.M. Islam, 'Bengali migrant workers in Britain', unpublished Ph.D. Thesis, University of Leeds, 1976, p. 58. The British Labour Attaché in Pakistan reported that the position of Muslim seamen employed in Bombay and Calcutta was being made very difficult by the introduction (by the Government of India) of a regulation which insisted that at least 25 per cent of the sailors employed in the two ports were Indian born. Report of Labour Attaché, Pakistan, 1948–9, LAB13/524. See also Adams, *Across Seven Seas*, pp. 61–2.

45 See, for example, M. Sherwood, *Many Struggles: West Indian Workers and Service Personnel in Britain, 1939–1945*, London, Karia Press, 1985 and Richmond, *Colour Prejudice*.

46 See 'Wartime recruitment from the West Indies', CO323/1863/5. Sherwood notes that 872 Hondurans actually arrived in Scotland in two contingents, *Many Struggles*, pp. 100, 104.

47 See 'Civil manpower: recruitment of labour for the UK 1942', CO323/1863/2; 'Note by J.L. Keith on his visit to the West Indies, September 1947', in CO318/476/1; 'Coloured people from British colonial territories', memorandum by the Secretary of State for the Colonies, 18 May 1950, CP(50)113, CAB 129/40; and Richmond, *Colour Prejudice*, p. 26. For the British Guiana figure see Officer Administering British Guiana to Creech Jones, 3 April 1947, CO318/476/1. Sherwood, perhaps keener to identify racism than to assess the contribution of West Indians to the winning of the war, appears seriously to underestimate the number who served. See Sherwood, *Many Struggles*, footnote 75 on p. 45.

48 See P. Noel Baker (Ministry of War Transport) to H. Macmillan (Colonial Office) 17 June 1942 in CO323/1863/2.

49 Details of the *Almanzora* are in Sir J. Huggins (Governor, Jamaica) to Secretary of State, Colonial Office 24 November 1947 and of the *Empire Windrush* in A.W. Peterson (Home Office) to F. Graham-Harrison (Prime Minister's Office) 5 July 1948, in HO213/244. For the *Georgic*, see Huggins to Griffiths, 16 June 1949, in MT9/5463. See also *Forty Years On*, Lambeth Borough Council, 1988. Numbers of Jamaicans demobbed are given by Keith in 'Note by J.L. Keith', CO318/476/1) and civilians staying on are estimated by Richmond, *Colour Prejudice*, p. 24. Further figures are provided by Griffiths in his 1950 memorandum to the Cabinet, CP (50)113, CAB 129/40. Sherwood has useful references on discharge policy from CO968, and believes that most of the Honduran foresters returned home; see *Many Struggles*, pp. 39, 121.

50 See, for example, Officer Administering the Government of British Guiana to the Colonial Secretary, A. Creech Jones 3 April 1947 and Sir H. Blood (Governor of Barbados) to A. Creech Jones 2 August 1947 in CO/318/476/1.

51 A. Creech Jones (Colonial Office) to Governor of Jamaica 28 July 1947 and minute by J.L. Keith 3 October 1947 in CO/318/478/1.

52 It should be pointed out that under the 1962 Act, veterans were to be allowed preference in the allocation of work vouchers in Category C. This provision operated for three years. See below, Chapter 5.

2 IMMIGRATION POLICY IN PRACTICE, 1945–55

1 For emigration and population figures, see 'Report of the Interdepartmental Committee on Migration Policy', 7 September 1956 in CAB139/399. As late as 1956 the government decided to continue subsidising emigration schemes to the 'white' dominions.

2 Almost all of the writing on this subject subscribed to the view that a *laissez-faire*, open-door immigration policy was followed in the period up to 1962 until the important 1987 article appeared by B. Carter, C. Harris and S. Joshi, 'The 1951–55 Conservative government and the racialization of black immigration', reproduced in W. James and C. Harris (eds), *Inside Babylon:The Caribbean Diaspora in Britain*, London, Verso, 1993, pp. 55–72.

3 House of Commons debate of 5 November 1954 quoted in LAB26/259. In 1954 when the British government was examining the possibility of introducing restrictions on the entry of British subjects from South Asia, the Caribbean and Africa, the Commonwealth Relations Office was asked to survey the procedures used by members of the 'old' Commonwealth; see

CAB124/1191. Each had effectively prevented any significant immigration from non-white countries by employing discriminatory regulations.

4 The question of where the borders of 'colouredness' lay is an interesting one which deserves some exploration. Cypriots, Maltese and Gibraltarians were affected by some – but not – all of the measures alluded to here. They were usually seen as both less undesirable and much smaller sources of unwanted immigration than the Indian sub-continent and the Caribbean.

5 See R. Oakley, 'The Control of Cypriot migration to Britain between the wars', *Immigrants and Minorities*, 1987, vol. 4 (no. 1), pp. 30–43.

6 See 'Report of the Working Party on Coloured People Seeking Employment in the United Kingdom', 17 December 1953 in CAB124/1191.

7 There is ample evidence in the British government record that officials thought the system to be effective. See, for example, H.W. Savidge (Home Office) to T. Heiser (Colonial Office) 22 October 1955, DO35/10372. Many immigrants from India and Pakistan who arrived in the period 1958–62 have related to the author in interviews the often expensive difficulties experienced in obtaining passports. These additional costs provided another barrier to movement.

8 See below Chapter 4.

9 Blackwell (High Commission, New Delhi) to Ashford (CRO) 21 September 1950 in DO35/3567. The words quoted are Blackwell's.

10 This issue is dealt with in DO35/6437. See also Memorandum by Smedley (High Commission, New Delhi) 21 May 1958, DO35/6163.

11 Morley (Dominion Office) to Murray (High Commission, Karachi) 21 April 1954, DO35/6437.

12 Harrison (Dominion Office) to Sykes (High Commission, New Delhi) 13 July 1954, DO35/6437.

13 Gibson (CRO) to Smedley (High Commission, New Delhi) 13 February 1958 in DO35/6163.

14 Figures are provided in Annex B, 'Measures taken by the governments of India and Pakistan to restrict emigration', Cabinet memorandum by Lord Hailsham, 20 June 1958, p. 3 in CAB129/93.

15 Minute by Sidgewick, 26 March 1954, DO35/6437.

16 Heiser (CO) to Wickson (CRO), 15 December 1954, confirms that most of the forgeries took place in India and in four out of five cases the place of birth of the passport holder was Jullundar. See also G.S. Aurora, *The New Frontiersman: A Sociological Study of Indian Immigrants in the United Kingdom*, Bombay, Popular Prakashan, 1967, pp. 41–4; and M. Duffield, *Black Radicalism and the Politics of Deindustrialization*, Aldershot, Hampshire, Avebury, 1988, p. 42. For alleged forgery of endorsements on Indian passports in Singapore, see DO35/6444.

17 This remarkable story was told by Mohammed Keyani to the Buckinghamshire Constabulary, 8 March 1959. See H.W. Savidge (Home Office) to M.P. Preston (CRO) 22 April 1959. DO35/7986. For further evidence of organised movement from Pakistan via the Middle East, this time Teheran, see Regional Controller, Manchester to Ministry of Labour Headquarters, London, 21 November 1961 in LAB8/2490.

18 Savidge (Home Office) to Heiser (Colonial Office), 22 October 1955, DO35/10372.

19 Wickson (High Commission, New Delhi) to Preston (CRO), 1 September 1958, DO35/10372.

20 Minute by Morley, 26 March 1954 on DO35/6437.

21 Minute by Morley, 18 March 1954 and Morley to Murray (High Commission, Karachi) 21 April 1954 in DO35/6437.

22 See Cabinet Memorandum, 'Immigration of British subjects into the UK, 1950–51', 2 January 1951, CAB130/61; and Appendix 3, 'Immigration of British subjects into the United Kingdom', CP(51)51, 12 February 1951, CAB129/44. Useful contributions to the debate about the responses to the arrival of the *Empire Windrush* and the *Orbiter* can be found in K. Lunn, 'The British state and immigration, 1945–51: new light on the *Empire Windrush*', *Immigrants and Minorities*, 1989, vol. 8 (nos. 1 and 2), pp. 161–74; and M.M. Smith, 'Windrushers and Orbiters: towards an understanding of the "official mind" and colonial immigration to Britain, 1945–51', *Immigrants and Minorities*, 1991, vol. 10 (no. 3), pp. 3–17.

23 Cabinet Memorandum, 'Immigration of British subjects into the UK, 1950–51', 2 January 1951 in CAB130/61.

24 The film was shown on *Timewatch*, BBC2, May 1994. Secretary of State for the Colonies to Governors of Jamaica and Trinidad, 17 October 1949, LAB26/259.

25 'Arrival in the United Kingdom of Jamaican unemployed', CP(48)154, 18 June 1948, CAB129/28.

26 Secretary of State for the Colonies to Governor of Jamaica, 20 October 1950, LAB26/259.

27 Governor of Jamaica to Secretary of State for the Colonies, 12 November 1948, and Secretary of State for the Colonies to Governor of Jamaica, 24 November 1948, HO213/868.

28 'Coloured people from British colonial territories', notes on the memorandum by the Secretary of State for the Colonies, n.d. [but datable by internal evidence to 1950], in MT9/5463.

29 The minutes for 1949–50 of the Interdepartmental Committee on Colonial People in the United Kingdom provide a reflection of the nature of official concern. The minutes of the Interdepartmental Committee, figures for stowaways and an estimate of the number of immigrant workers arriving from the Caribbean (see draft of Cabinet Memorandum 'Coloured people from British colonial territories' by Secretary of State for the Colonies, 29 March 1950) are to be found in MT9/5463. Earl Howe, a first cousin of Winston Churchill, expressed publicly his concern in the House of Lords and sought and received assurances that something was being done. Extract from Hansard, 11 April 1951, in MT9/5463.

30 The relationship is clear from the minutes of the first five meetings of the Interdepartmental Committee held between May and October 1949. See MT9/5463.

31 Frequent references to repatriation can be found in MT9/5463 which contains the minutes for 1949 and 1950 of the Interdepartmental Committee on Colonial People in the UK. Particularly interesting documents (on which the following paragraphs are based) include 'Report on a visit to Tyneside', by V. Harris, Welfare Officer, Colonial Office, 13 October 1949 and E. Barry to J.L. Keith, 12 November 1949. Barry was a retiring Chief Secretary to the Somali government who spoke the language of the sailors and provided a somewhat sympathetic perspective on their plight. All references are to MT9/5463.

32 See Ministry of Transport Memo, 'Unemployed colonial seamen', 9 October 1950, in MT9/5463.

33 'The repatriation of colonials', National Assistance Board Memorandum, 6 September 1950, in MT9/5463.

34 Only 64 applications were submitted to the National Assistance Board in the scheme's first year of operation. See 'Unemployed colonial seamen', Memo by D.C. Haselgrove, Ministry of Transport, 9 October 1950, MT9/5463.

35 Minister of Transport to all Maritime Colonies, Draft Dispatch, April 1950 and 'Coloured people from British colonial territories', notes on the memorandum by the Secretary of State for the Colonies, n.d. [1950] in MT9/5463.

36 See Appendix 3, 'Immigration of British subjects into the United Kingdom', CP(51)51, 12 February 1951, CAB129/44.

37 J.B. Howard (Aliens Dept, Home Office) to M.B. Churchyard (Ministry of Transport), 27 June 1949, enclosing a copy of the new instructions to immigration officers in MT9/5463. See also Secretary of State for the Colonies to Colonial Governors, 26 January 1950, LAB26/259.

38 Secretary of State for the Colonies to Governors of Gold Coast, Gambia, Sierra Leone and Nigeria, 11 July 1950 and Minutes of Interdepartmental Committee on Colonial People in the UK, 19 July 1950, LAB26/259.

39 Garnett (CRO) to Murrie (Home Office), 17 March 1949, HO213/869.

40 Appendix 3, 'Immigration of British subjects into the UK', CP(51)51, 12 February 1951, CAB129/44.

41 See below, Chapter Four.

42 E. Cashmore and B. Troyna, *Introduction to Race Relations*, London, Routledge & Kegan Paul, 1983, p. 47.

43 For post-war emigration see LAB13/281. On European sources of labour see C. Holmes, *John Bull's Island: Immigration and British Society, 1871–1971*, London, Macmillan, 1988, pp. 210–14. The 180,000 figure comes from the 'Report of the Working Party on employment in the UK of surplus colonial labour' of July 1949, LAB13/42. On the Cabinet and labour shortages see B. Carter and S. Joshi, 'The role of Labour in the creation of a racist Britain', *Race and Class*, 1984, vol. 25 (no. 3), pp. 55–7.

44 Minute of 27 April 1945 in LAB26/134. See also M. Sherwood, *Many Struggles: West Indian Workers and Service Personnel in Britain, 1939–1945*, London, Karia Press, 1985, pp. 86–90; and E. Pilkington, *Beyond the Mother Country: West Indians and the Notting Hill White Riots*, London, Tauris, 1988, pp. 16–18.

45 The handling of this question by the Ministry of Labour is dealt with in LAB26/134.

46 See Governor of Barbados to Secretary of State for the Colonies, 8 March 1947; Officer Administering British Guiana to Secretary of State for the Colonies, 3 April 1947; Governor of Trinidad to Secretary of State for the Colonies, 1 May 1947; and Governor of Jamaica to Secretary of State for the Colonies, 1 May 1947, all in CO318/476/1.

47 Secretary of State for the Colonies to Governor of Jamaica (copy to all West Indian territories), 28 July 1947, CO318/476/1.

48 'Working Party on the employment in the UK of surplus colonial labour', 1948, CO1006/1.

49 See the views of Bevan (Ministry of Labour) at the first meeting of the Working Party, 6 October 1948 in ibid.

50 'The possibilities of employing colonial labour in the UK', Ministry of Labour memorandum, September 1948, CO1006/2. Duffield, *Black Radicalism*,

contains much interesting material on the negative approach of unions to the employment of Asian and black labour in the West Midlands in the fifties and sixties.

51 Memo by MacMullan, 2 October 1948, LAB13/42.

52 'Report of the Working Party on employment in the UK of surplus colonial labour', July 1949, Ibid.

53 The analysis is found in Governor of Jamaica to the Secretary of State for the Colonies, 8 June 1949 and 16 June 1949 in MT9/5463. It was copied to the Ministries represented on the Working Party.

54 The problem faced by many of the skilled was that their skills would not be recognised because they had not completed apprenticeship requirements. See, for example, 'Report on a visit to Tyneside', V. Harris, 13 October 1949, in MT9/5463.

55 'Notes of a conference held with representatives of the regions on 20th January 1949 to discuss the placing of colonial negroes', in MT9/5463.

56 Details are contained in two Colonial Office Memoranda, 'Employment of Barbadian women as domestic helpers in UK hospitals', 31 October 1949; and 'Interdepartmental Committee on Colonial People in the United Kingdom. Employment of St Helenian agricultural workers in the UK', 14 September 1949, both in MT9/5463.

57 Minute by Goldberg, 10 May 1950; in Ibid. His immediate senior Hardman minuted on the following day, 'We do not want officially to encourage West Indians to come to Great Britain, but they are not so difficult as some of the less civilized from Africa.'

58 For an example of the open contrast between the desirability of white (Irish) as against the undesirability of 'coloured' immigration, see 'Report of the Working Party on coloured people seeking employment in the United Kingdom', 17 December 1953, CAB124/1191. Apparently twenty times more Irish than 'coloured' immigrants presented no assimilation difficulties.

59 Notes of a meeting held at the Home Office to discuss the problems of persons from the colonies and British Protectorates, 18 February 1949, in MT9/5463.

60 See, for example, Garnett (CRO) to Murrie (Home Office), 17 March 1949, DO35/3566.

61 Minute by Garnett (CRO), 23 March 1949, ibid.

62 Harrison (CRO) to Head (High Commission, New Zealand), 25 August 1954, DO35/6457.

63 Memo by Howard (Home Office), 15 February 1949, refers to communists being 'a large element in the coloured population.' See also minute to Howard (signature illegible), 12 March 1949, HO213/869.

64 Note by MacMullan, 2 October 1948, LAB13/42.

65 G.D.N. Worswick',The British Economy, 1950–1959', in G.D.N. Worswick and P.H. Ady (eds), *The British Economy in the 1950s*, Oxford, Oxford University Press, 1962, p. 75.

66 N. Deakin argues this in 'The politics of the Commonwealth Immigrants Bill', *Political Quarterly*, 1968, vol. 39, pp. 35–6, 44. His views are challenged by Ira Katznelson, *Black Men, White Cities: Race, Politics and Migration in the United States, 1900–30 and Britain, 1948–68*, London, Oxford University Press for the Institute of Race Relations, 1973, p. 128; Katznelson does not appreciate the extent of Cabinet and official discussion of the issue or the reasons why external appearances of indifference should have been maintained.

3 THE MAKING OF POLICY, 1945-55

1 For the origins of the Working Party, see MT9/5463. Murrie was Deputy Under-Secretary of State at the Home Office until 1952.

2 *Hansard*, 451 H.C. Debs., cols. 1852–3, 8 June 1948.

3 'Arrival in the United Kingdom of Jamaican unemployed', Memorandum by the Secretary of State for Colonies, 18 June 1948, CP(48)154, CAB129/28.

4 Letter from J.D. Murray *et al.* to C. Attlee, 2 June 1948 and draft letter to Murray from Attlee [n.d.] in HO213/244. Subsequent government moves to restrict the availability of cheap passages from the Caribbean are outlined above in Chapter 2.

5 Ibid., and A.W. Peterson (Home Secretary's PPS) to F.L.T. Graham Harrison (Prime Minister's Assistant PS) 5 July 1948, in HO213/244.

6 Among those who should know better, Enoch Powell castigated the 1948 Act for opening the flood gates to Asian and black immigration, *Timewatch*, BBC2, May 1994. Edward Pilkington – in an otherwise well researched and interesting book – writes that before 1948 West Indians, though technically British subjects, were restricted in their entry to Britain. The Act removed an anomaly. He is apparently unaware of the boats that arrived in 1947; E. Pilkington, *Beyond the Mother Country: West Indians and the Notting Hill White Riots*, London, Tauris, 1988, p. 37. Deakin argues very persuasively that, as far as rights of entry were concerned, the legislators of 1948 were doing nothing but preserving the *status quo* with the warm approval of the Opposition. See N. Deakin, 'The British Nationality Act of 1948: A brief study on the political mythology of race relations', *Race*, 1969, vol. 11, pp. 77–83.

7 W. Ormsby-Gore, quoted in the House of Lords debate, 11 May 1948, *Hansard*, col. 795. See N. Deakin, 'The immigration issue in British politics, 1948–1964', unpublished Ph.D. thesis, University of Sussex, 1972, p. 49.

8 Andrew Roberts misleadingly refers to the British Nationality Act (1948) as giving 'over eight hundred million Commonwealth citizens the perfectly legal right to reside in the United Kingdom.' He also claims, quite inaccurately, that: 'The holes in Labour's cumbersome legislation allowed hundreds of thousands to enter Britain.' See A. Roberts, *Eminent Churchillians*, London, Phoenix, 1995, p. 216. For a treatment based on research, see Z. Layton-Henry, *The Politics of Race in Britain*, London, Allen and Unwin, 1984, pp. 11–13. See also V. Bevan, *The Development of British Immigration Law*, London, Croom Helm, 1986; J.M. Evans, *Immigration Law*, London, Sweet and Maxwell, 1983; A. Dummett, *Citizenship and Nationality*, London, Runnymede Trust, 1976; H. Tinker, *Separate and Unequal: India and Indians in the British Common-wealth, 1920–1950*, London, Hurst, 1976; and most importantly Deakin's Ph.D. Thesis, 'The immigration issue', pp. 42–64. *Hansard* for 7 July 1948 is very useful.

9 Deakin, 'The immigration issue', pp. 60–1. Lord Simon for the Liberals agreed that: 'It is one of the finest things in the whole of our British Commonwealth that anyone who is a British citizen knows that, without challenge or question, he will be admitted here; and that we reserve for aliens our powers of exclusion.' See *Hansard*, 155 H.L. Debs., col. 1031, 11 May 1948.

10 *Report of the Royal Commission on Population*, London, HMSO, 1949, Cmd.7695, para.329.

11 Cabinet Minutes CM13(50)7, 20 March 1950. CAB 128/17.

12 'Coloured people from British colonial territories', 18 May 1950, CP(50)113, CAB 129/40.

13 Ibid.

14 CM37(50)2, 19 June 1950, CAB 128/17.

15 'Immigration of British subjects into the United Kingdom', CP (51)51, 12 February 1951, CAB129/44. The paper was discussed at the Cabinet meeting on 22 February 1951; see CM15(51)4, CAB128/19. The only dissenting voice among the ministers was that of Aneurin Bevan, who was apparently unprepared to see his socialist paradise enjoyed by 'coloured' Britons; see 'Stowaways – Murrie Committee', 11 January 1951 in MT9/5463. On the other hand he appeared keen to persuade the unions to accept foreign workers from Europe. See B. Carter and S. Joshi, 'The role of Labour in the creation of a racist Britain', *Race and Class*, 1984, vol. 25 (no. 3), pp. 56–7.

16 This is the language of the Report. For an appreciation of what this meant in practice see below, Chapter 2.

17 The minutes of the Interdepartmental Committee for 1949 and 1950 can be found in MT9/5463.

18 Roberts, *Eminent Churchillians*, p. 211. Churchill's atypical views about race and white supremacy are confirmed by, for example, C. Thorne, *Allies of a Kind*, London, Hamish Hamilton, 1978, pp. 724, 730; and S. Gopal, 'Churchill and India' in R. Blake and W.R. Louis (eds), *Churchill*, Oxford, Oxford University Press, 1993, pp. 457, 470–1.

19 Ian Gilmour was then the editor and owner of the *Spectator*. See Ian Gilmour, *Inside Right: A Study of Conservatism*, London, Hutchinson, 1977, p. 134 and I. Bradley, 'Why Churchill's plan to limit immigration was shelved', *The Times*, 20 March 1978. Churchill is also quoted as saying to Hugh Foot, then Governor of Jamaica in 1954, 'We would have a magpie society: that would never do', in Deakin, 'The immigration issue', p. 32.

20 CC100(52)8 (Cabinet Conclusions) on 25 November 1952, CAB128/25. His papers for November contain three other separate attempts to generate material on the subject of black immigration. His staff were asked to provide details of difficulties or alleged difficulties in Lambeth, Brixton and Cardiff; see PREM11/824. His enquiries produced a paper on 'The coloured population in the United Kingdom', from B.G. Smallman, PS to the Colonial Secretary, which put the 'coloured' population of the UK at 40–50,000, including about 6,000 students.

21 CC106(52)7, 18 December 1952, CAB128/25.

22 'Report of the Working Party on coloured people seeking employment in the United Kingdom', 17 December 1953, Appendix III, p. 2. CAB124/1191. It is very likely that the government significantly underestimated the size of the Asian population, by failing to take into account the significant number of 'middle-class' Indian professional people dotted across the country. Rose recalculates the Census figures to exclude the 'white' returnees from the Indian sub-continent, but there are still very great differences between the Census figures and the Government's own estimates. Rose put the total 'coloured' population of Britain in 1951 at 74,500: see E.J.B. Rose *et al.*, *Colour and Citizenship: A Report on British Race Relations*, London, Oxford University Press, 1969, pp. 96–7, 769–71.

23 Ibid., p. 7. The year 1954 was to prove a watershed in the pattern of migration from the Caribbean to the UK when the effect of the 'McCarren–Walter Act'

and its restrictions on movement to the USA worked through. In 1954 the total of immigrants from the Caribbean suddenly doubled to over 8,000. See Boothroyd to Quirk, 29 October 1954, CAB124/1191.

24 This was said to be due to the difficulty in finding accommodation and 'their general inability to become assimilated with the white community.' 'Report of the Working Party on coloured people seeking employment in the United Kingdom', 17 December 1953, Appendix II, p. 3, CAB124/1191. Over half the black and Asian population lived in London, including three-quarters of West Indians and two-thirds of West Africans. Birmingham, London, Coventry, Manchester and Glasgow were, in that order, the five most important centres of Asian settlement.

25 Ibid.

26 See note by P.G. Oates (Prime Minister's PS) to R.J. Guppy (Home Office), 29 January 1954, PREM11/824.

27 CC7(54)4, 3 February 1954, CAB128/27.

28 See Appendix 2, 'Immigration of British subjects into the United Kingdom', CP(51)51, 12 February 1951, CAB129/44.

29 'Immigration of coloured people', memorandum by the Home Secretary, 9 March 1954, CP(54)94, CAB129/66. The Earl of Munster, the Parliamentary Under-Secretary of State at the Colonial Office wrote to Salisbury, the Lord President of the Council and the leader in the Cabinet of the advocates of control, on 12 March 1954, telling him of four approaches by members of the Lords and Commons and enclosing a paper on 'The problem of colonial immigration', authored by the Liverpool Group of the Conservative Commonwealth Association. Deakin charts the growth of interest by Parliament in 'The immigration issue', pp. 76–80.

30 CC17(54)6, 10 March 1954.

31 The same notion of 'unmanageability' is referred to in the Cabinet minutes of 10 March 1954 and in almost exactly contemporary letters from Salisbury to Munster (Parliamentary Under-Secretary, Colonial Office), 14 March 1954, and Salisbury to Swinton, 20 March 1954, in CAB124/1191.

32 Salisbury was also a man with a strong South African connection. After his resignation from the government in 1957 he became a director of the British South Africa Company. For his influence see, for example, J. Colville, *The Fringes of Power: 10 Downing Street Diaries, 1939–1955*, London, Hodder and Stoughton, 1985, pp. 642, 765; and R. Rhodes James, *Anthony Eden: A Biography*, London, Weidenfeld and Nicolson, 1986, who describes him as 'the truest and best of his [Eden's] political friends', p. 616. His influence within the party is best illustrated by his key role in the determination of a successor to Eden, see James, *Eden*, pp. 596–7. See also D.W. Dean, 'Conservative governments and the restriction of Commonwealth immigration in the 1950s: the problems of constraint', *Historical Journal*, 1992, vol. 35 (no. 1), pp. 183–4.

33 Salisbury to Swinton, 12 March 1954, CAB124/1191.

34 Salisbury to Munster, 14 March 1954, CAB124/1191.

35 'The problem of colonial immigration', Conservative Commonwealth Association, Liverpool Group, January 1954, enclosed in Munster to Salisbury, 12 March 1954, CAB124/1191. Salisbury's comments on it are to be found in Salisbury to Munster, 14 March 1954, ibid.

36 Salisbury to Swinton, 20 March 1954, CAB124/1191.

37 Swinton to Salisbury, 15 March 1954, CAB124/1191.

38 For Swinton's views on India and the Commonwealth, see J.A. Cross, *Lord Swinton*, Oxford, Oxford University Press, 1982, pp. 261–2, 274, 279. According to Swinton's valedictory speech following Salisbury's death in 1972, he never disagreed with him on policy or on the handling of policy; Cross, p. 257.

39 For an excellent summary of Britain's relationship to the Commonwealth in 1953 see the opening chapters of J.D.B. Miller, *Survey of Commonwealth Affairs: Problems of Expansion and Attrition, 1953–69*, London, Oxford University Press, 1974. Franks is quoted on p. 13. For a very influential contemporary, mid-fifties view of the advantages Britain hoped to gain from increased Commonwealth membership see 'The future of Commonwealth membership', Report by the Official Committee, 21 January 1954, CAB134/786. The report was subsequently endorsed by the Ministerial Committee and went to Cabinet.

40 This is wonderfully well expressed by Woodrow Wyatt who, as a young Labour M.P. went on a lecture tour of the USA in 1952: 'I was shocked by the low regard for Britain. . . . I looked one night at the stars and wept: this vast country thought my darling England was not worth bothering about, equating her to a poor old aunt out of the mainstream. I was a long way from adjusting to Britain's loss of status, and hence mine, and it hurt'; W. Wyatt, *Confessions of an Optimist*, London, Collins, n.d., p. 187.

41 Miller, *Survey*, p. 18.

42 Swinton to Salisbury, 7 April 1954 in CAB124/1191. As Chapter 2 demonstrates, British policy was already discriminatory in practice in a number of respects.

43 'Report of the Working Party on coloured people seeking employment in the United Kingdom', 17 December 1953, p. 12, CAB124/1191.

44 Swinton's views are summarised in 'Brief for meeting of Committee on Colonial Immigrants', 19 May 1958, DO35/7987.

45 Swinton to Salisbury, 23 March 1954, CAB124/1191. See also Swinton to Liesching (Permanent Under-Secretary of State for Commonwealth Relations), 11 November 1954, DO35/5217.

46 Note of a meeting held in Lord Munster's room, 6 April 1954, CAB124/1191.

47 Note of an informal meeting held in the Home Office on 12 April 1954, CAB124/1191.

48 The Chair of the working party was W.H. Cornish, Assistant Under-Secretary of State at the Home Office, who had been educated at Wesley College and Trinity College, Dublin. 'Report of the Working Party to consider certain proposals to restrict the right of British subjects from overseas to enter and remain in the United Kingdom', 10 July 1954, CAB124/1191. The Working Party delivered a second report in October dealing with the issues that arose from the decision to enact legislation to deport Commonwealth subjects. It looked at the question of 'belonging'. There had to be clear and agreed criteria in order that those liable to deportation could be identified as well as a territory which would be prepared to take them. Grounds for deportation for conviction of a criminal offence and undesirability were fairly straightforward but dependence on public funds was more difficult to define. The committee recommended 'substantial dependence on public funds for twelve months' as the criterion. 'Second Report of the Working Party to consider certain proposals to restrict the right of British subjects from overseas to enter and remain in the United Kingdom', 22 October 1954, CAB124/1191.

49 Note by Lord Salisbury, 8 August 1954, on memorandum by A.H.K. Slater, 5 August 1954, CAB124/1191.
50 *The Times*, 28 September 1954.
51 E. Boothroyd (Treasury) to R.N. Quirk (Secretary to the Lord President of the Council), 7 October 1954, CAB124/1191. The term 'ammunition' (which Salisbury was 'anxious for') is used by Quirk in a note on Guppy to Slater, 9 October 1954, CAB124/1191.
52 A. Montague-Browne (Prime Minister's Office) to R.J. Guppy (Home Office), 5 October 1954; and Guppy to Montague-Browne, 12 October 1954, both in PREM11/824.
53 CC65(54)2, PREM11/824.
54 Slater to Colville (Prime Minister's Private Secretary), 14 October 1954, PREM11/824.
55 'Second Report of the Working Party to consider certain proposals to restrict the right of British subjects from overseas to enter and remain in the United Kingdom. Deportation of British subjects', 22 October 1954, CAB124/1191.
56 Memorandum, Quirk to Salisbury, 29 October 1954, in ibid.
57 Memorandum by Boothroyd on the 'Second Report of the Working Party. . . .' 29 October 1954, in ibid.
58 Slater to Quirk, 2 November 1954, CAB124/1191; and 532 H.C. Debs., cols. 824–36, 5 November 1954.
59 See Sir Frank Newsam (Permanent Under-Secretary of State, Home Office) to Sir Thomas Lloyd (Permanent Under-Secretary, Colonial Office), 8 November 1954; and Lloyd George to Swinton, 19 November 1954, both in CAB124/1191.
60 Churchill had been stimulated by a report in the *Daily Telegraph* of 19 October 1954 of a statement by the Jamaican Minister of Labour to the effect that no steps would be taken by the Jamaican Government to counter immigration because there were plenty of jobs available in Britain. Montague-Brown to J.B. Johnston (Colonial Office), 2 November 1954, PREM11/824.
61 Swinton to Lloyd George, 16 November 1954, DO35/7987. Britain had, of course, long practised administrative discrimination by, for example, making arrangements with the governments of India and Pakistan to require their citizens coming to Britain to have their access to employment and housing checked. See below, Chapter 2.
62 Minute by Alan Lennox-Boyd, 17 November 1954, CAB124/1191.
63 CM78(54)4, 24 November 1954, CAB128/27 and 'Colonial immigrants', memoranda by the Home Secretary, 22 November 1954, C(54)354 and the Secretary of State for Commonwealth Relations C(54)356, 23 November 1954, PREM11/824.
64 Minute by Norman Brook, 23 November 1954, PREM11/824.
65 CM82(54)7, 6 December 1954.
66 *Daily Herald*, 19 and 20 October 1954. Cuttings in CAB124/1191 read by the Lord President. Deakin cites the lack of public interest and absence of an effective lobby for control as one of the explanations for the decision not to legislate; Deakin, 'The immigration issue', p. 83.
67 *The Star*, 10.11.54. p. 5.
68 *New Statesman and Nation*, 13.11.54.
69 *Sunday Times*, 14.11.54.
70 *Daily Sketch*, 3, 4 and 6 January 1955.

71 See 'Colonial immigrants', memorandum by the Home Secretary, 3 May 1955, CP(55)16, PREM11/824.

72 See CM14(55)4 of 14 June 1955, PREM11/824.

73 Lennox-Boyd spelled out his position in 'Colonial immigrants', memorandum by the Colonial Secretary, 1 November 1955, CP(55)167, PREM11/824. See also R. Lamb, *The Failure of the Eden Government*, London, Sidgwick and Jackson, 1987, p. 22. However, Salisbury was also very close to Eden, see Rhodes James, *Eden*, p. 616.

74 For Home's views see 'Colonial immigrants', memorandum by the Secretary of State for Commonwealth Relations, 2 September 1955, CP(55)113, PREM11/824. The British communities in India and Pakistan, only 26,000 strong, evidently made a substantial contribution to Britain's overseas earnings, and therefore to its balance of payments. See G.W. Chadwick (CRO) to All High Commissions, 12 September 1958, DO35/7987.

75 R.A. Butler, *The Art of the Possible*, London, Hamish Hamilton, 1971, p. 173. Churchill's decline can be followed in the Colville diaries. As early as 9 November 1952 he noted that 'He (W.) is getting tired and visibly ageing. He finds it hard work to compose a speech and ideas no longer flow. He has made two strangely simple errors in the House of Commons recently'; Colville, *Fringes of Power*, p. 654.

76 For Eden's belief in the Commonwealth see Rhodes James, *Eden*, p. 441. From the side of his predecessor Colville observed: 'I don't myself quite see how he can prove a very good successor to Winston when he has no knowledge or experience of anything except foreign affairs.' Colville, *Eden*, p. 645.

77 See Lamb, *Failure of Eden*, p. 23.

78 CC3(55)6 of 13 January 1955, PREM11/824; and 'Colonial Immigrants', memorandum by the Home Secretary, C(55)5, 11 January 1955, PREM11/824. In September 1955 at its annual conference the TUC agreed a resolution without discussion which urged that steps be taken to develop colonial economies, welcomed workers from 'undeveloped' Commonwealth areas and opposed any attempts to employ a colour bar to deny Commonwealth citizens their accepted rights. See H.O. Hooper (Cabinet Office) to A. Eden, 14 September 1955, PREM11/824.

79 Minutes of the Commonwealth Affairs Committee, 27 January 1955, and the covering note with them, P. Buchan-Hepburn (Government Chief Whip) to Churchill, 27 January 1955, PREM11/824. Andrew Roberts finds it puzzling that Osborne did not proceed with his bill and speculates that he was persuaded to feign illness. He finds in the Cabinet minutes the implication that Osborne had been put under pressure not to proceed; see Roberts, *Eminent Churchillians*, pp. 235–6.

80 See CC26(55)3 of 16 March 1955. The Council supported a deportation bill but was divided on the issue of more far-reaching legislation.

81 Lamb, *Failure of Eden*, p. 15. See also memorandum, 'Colonial immigrants', Cabinet Election Business Committee, 30 April 1955, PREM11/824.

82 CC3(55)6 of 13 January 1955, PREM11/824.

83 Memorandum to the Prime Minister, 'Coloured immigrants', Norman Brook, 17 February 1955, PREM11/824. Canadian regulations distinguished between, on the one hand, people who were British subjects by birth or naturalisation in the UK, Australia, New Zealand, South Africa and citizens of Eire and, on the other hand, British subjects from other parts of the Commonwealth. Non-

European British subjects were kept out of Australia by the administrative use, without statutory authority, of dictation and medical tests. Special restrictions were applied by New Zealand to all British subjects who were not born in Britain of parents who were of British stock. British subjects not of European race were excluded from South Africa by regulation as 'persons who on economic grounds or on account of standards or habits of life are deemed unsuitable to the requirements of the Union'.

84 CC15(55)4, 17 February 1955, PREM11/824.

85 The proposal was originally made in November 1954, see Cabinet Memorandum, 'Colonial immigrants', memorandum by the Home Secretary, C(54)354, 22 November 1954, PREM11/824.

86 Lloyd George's memos are both entitled 'Colonial immigrants': CP(55)16 of 3.5.55 and CP(55)32 of 11 November 1955. Cabinet discussion occurred on 14 June 1955, CM14(55)4, PREM11/824.

87 'Report of the Committee on the social and economic problems arising from the growing influx into the United Kingdom of coloured workers from other Commonwealth countries', 3 August 1955, and Appendix, Draft Statement on Colonial Immigrants, PREM11/824.

88 CM31(55)4 of 15.9.55.

89 Confirmation of the political difficulties of introducing a bill which limited immigration from the Caribbean can be found in Nigel Fisher's report, 'West Indian migration to the UK', written after a visit to the Caribbean as a member of the Parliamentary delegation in the summer of 1955. At the time he was Parliamentary Private Secretary to the Home Secretary, Gwilym Lloyd-George. His report was read at a critically important stage of the discussion, October 1955, by Lloyd-George, Lennox-Boyd and Eden. Fisher concluded that though a measure identifying the West Indies would be 'simple, easy and effective from our point of view' and would avoid embarrassment and difficulty in the Commonwealth generally, it would have serious repercussions in the Caribbean and adversely effect the future of the Federation. He did not think it would be either morally right or politically expedient. His view, shared by all the members of the delegation, was that restrictions, if they were imposed, would have to apply fairly to all parts of the Empire/Commonwealth irrespective of race and colour; PREM11/824.

90 Roberts and Lamb are both of this school of thought. Lamb confines himself to the statement that 'The nation might have been spared many tears if his [Lloyd George's] draft bill had been put to Parliament'; Lamb, *Failure of Eden*, p. 24. Roberts, in this instance neither judicious nor well-researched and who might be accused of reading history backwards, blames the Churchill and Eden governments for not consulting the electorate and failing to devise a policy in the face of 'a post-imperial implosion' and a 'major ethnological alteration'; Roberts, *Eminent Churchillians*, pp. 211–42. Excerpts from *Eminent Churchillians* dealing with immigration policy were published in the *Sunday Times* in November 1994.

91 'West Indian migration to the UK', by Nigel Fisher, see PREM11/824. The report emphasised the loss the emigrants represented to the islands, their high levels of skill and their sense of enterprise.

4 POLICY AND PRACTICE UNDER STRAIN, 1955–62

1 See Minute no. 10 of 48th Cabinet Meeting on 11 July 1956 [hereafter CM48(56)10], CAB128/30.
2 Minute by Norman Brook, 'Colonial immigrants', 2 November 1955, PREM11/824.
3 CM39(55)7 of 3 November 1955, PREM11/824.
4 Draft Statement on colonial immigrants, 3 August 1955, PREM11/824.
5 Minute by Norman Brook, 'Colonial immigrants', 10 November 1955, PREM11/2920. Brook, who filled the very influential post of Secretary of the Cabinet from 1947 to 1963, and his successor Burke Trend were both great enthusiasts for the Commonwealth. See P. Lyon, 'The Commonwealth and the Suez crisis', in W.R. Louis and R. Owen (eds), *Suez 1956: The Crisis and its Consequences*, Oxford, Oxford University Press, 1989, p. 260.
6 Minute by H.O. Hooper (Cabinet Office), 4 July 1956, PREM11/2920.
7 CM48(56)10, 11 July 1956, CAB128/30.
8 CM85(56)8, 20 November 1956, CAB128/30.
9 200 H.L. Debs., col. 420, 20 November 1956.
10 Both quotations are from A. Horne, *Macmillan, 1957–1986*, London, Macmillan, 1989, p. 83. See also pp. 80–1, 423.
11 CC57(57)5, 25 July 1957, CAB128/31.
12 See, for example, G.R. Elton, *The Unarmed Invasion: A Survey of Afro-Asian Immigration*, London, Geoffrey Bles, 1965, pp. 26–32. Elton was opposed to large-scale Asian and black immigration not on the grounds of race or colour but on the grounds of number. The much larger numbers of Irish, European and white Commonwealth immigrants do not appear to have attracted his attention in the same way.
13 E.J. Toogood (Ministry of Labour) to I. Watt (Colonial Office), 4 December 1958, in CAB13/1005.
14 E.J. Toogood (Ministry of Labour) to R.C.H. Greig (Colonial Office), 26 January 1959, in CO1031/2946. The National Insurance and Home Office figures cited by Toogood show a fairly close relationship.
15 J. Wickenden, 'Colour in Britain', London, Institute of Race Relations Pamphlet, 1958.
16 'West Indian migration to the UK', Colonial Office memorandum annexed to Progress Report by the Interdepartmental Working Party, 7 February 1961, CAB134/1489.
17 'Coloured immigration to the UK: problem of Indian and Pakistani immigrants', (n.d. – January 1959?), DO35/7987. The term 'alarming' is used by Home in a letter to all High Commissioners, 21 April 1958, DO35/7987.
18 See Annex 1, 'Commonwealth immigrants', memorandum by the Lord President of the Council, C(58)129, 20 June 1958, CAB129/93. For press coverage see, for example, *The Times*, 7 April 1958: '1,100 Workless Pakistanis Stranded in Bradford.'
19 Home to all High Commissioners, 21 April 1958, DO35/7987. The view that newcomers from the Indian sub-continent 'cannot be assimilated anywhere near so easily as the useful West Indian' was fairly common among officials. For this example, see Minute by A.W. Snelling (Assistant Under-Secretary of State, CRO), 31 July 1958, in DO35/6163.

20 'Immigration into the United Kingdom from India and Pakistan, 1957/58', Report by H. Arthington-Davy (n.d. – probably January 1959), DO35/7983. The application of a little thought to this appreciation might have led officials to the conclusion that most of the new arrivals were likely to be very tenacious in their efforts to find employment. Having mortgaged their land they would be keen to meet payments and none would want to return without being able to demonstrate his success. If high unemployment was to be a feature of this group's experience it might have been fair to conclude that it was not a result of their lack of effort and commitment.

21 An Indian had been arrested in Glasgow just before Easter having tried to persuade a local printer to produce 45,000 Indian passports for him. Minute by A.W. Snelling, 9 April 1958, DO35/7987. The involvement of agents recruiting labour in Pakistan for less than the rate prevailing in Britain was suggested, but as most Pakistani new arrivals were apparently going straight on to the unemployment register this seems unlikely. Secretary of State, CRO to High Commissioners, New Delhi and Karachi, 2.4.58. The organised racket is suggested in Sir G. Laithwaite (Permanent Under-Secretary of State, CRO) to All High Commissioners (except India and Pakistan), 21 April 1958, DO35/7987.

An element that puzzled officials was the ability of the migrants to afford the estimated £135 fare and £80 deposit required by the Pakistan Government before it issued a passport. The foreign exchange idea was an attempt to explain this. As departing emigrants from Pakistan were allowed to convert £150 worth of rupees to sterling, and yet very few immigrants appeared to arrive with any sterling, it was inferred that substantial profits were available from sterling obtained in this way and later sold on the black market in the sub-continent: 'Apparently some of the migrants are furnished with rupees for this purpose by the entrepreneurs organising the traffic', Minute by A.W. Snelling, 9 April 1958, DO35/7987.

22 Home to all High Commissioners, 21 April 1958, DO35/7987. The figures are reproduced in 'Commonwealth immigrants', Memorandum by the Lord President of the Council, Annex C, C(58)129, 20 June 1958, CAB129/93. Unemployment – at 244,000 in July 1957 – had risen to 412,000 by July 1958, apparently failing to act as a damper on enthusiasm for migration. 'Employment position in Great Britain', enclosure in J. Chadwick (CRO) to H. Smedley (High Commission, New Delhi), 29 August 1958, DO35/7987.

23 Snelling to High Commissioners, New Delhi and Karachi, 20 March 1958; and Home to High Commissioners, New Delhi and Karachi, 2 April 1958, DO35/7987.

24 Minute by A.W. Snelling, Assistant Under-Secretary of State, CRO, 9 April 1958, DO35/7987.

25 Minute by A.W. Snelling, 16 April 1958; and 'Brief for meeting of Committee on colonial immigrants', 19 May 1958, in DO35/7987.

26 Minute by A.W. Snelling, 16 April 1958, DO35/7987. Their hopes were not disappointed; most Commonwealth governments strongly opposed legal restrictions on entry to Britain, see DO35/7981.

27 Minute by A.W. Snelling, 7 May 1958, DO35/7987.

28 Brief for the Secretary of State, A.W. Snelling 25 June 1958, DO35/7987.

29 P. Carrington (High Commissioner, Canberra) to Sir G. Laithwaite, 6 May 1958, DO35/7981.

30 A. Clutterbuck (Ambassador, Dublin) to Sir H. Lintott (Deputy Under-Secretary of State, CRO), 12 May 1958, DO35/7981.

31 R.W.D. Fowler (Deputy High Commissioner, Karachi) to Sir G. Laithwaite, 11 July 1958; and M. MacDonald (High Commissioner, New Delhi) to Sir G. Laithwaite, 12 July 1958, DO35/7987.

32 High Commissioner, Colombo to Sir H. Lintott, 6 May 1958, DO35/7981.

33 Indians arriving in Britain were required to prove only that they were British subjects, which they could do by producing a valid passport or other forms of documentary evidence. Yet, immigration officers reported that only a very small fraction of the arrivals from India did not have the appropriate endorsement – 524 in 1955 (out of 18,470 arrivals), 187 in 1956 (out of 20,000) and 147 in 1957 (out of 20,160). This provides some prima facie evidence for the potential effectiveness of controls from the Indian end. See J. Chadwick (CRO) to H. Smedley, High Commission, New Delhi, 18 August 1958, DO35/7987. For Indian policy on passport issue see 'Note on the Government of India's policy in relation to the issue of passports for the UK with particular reference to the migration of Indians', by Ranbir Singh, Chief Passport Officer, enclosed in Smedley to Chadwick 17 November 1958, DO35/7986.

34 'Commonwealth immigrants', memorandum by the Lord President of the Council (Lord Hailsham) C(58)129, 20 June 1958, CAB129/93; D.W.H. Wickson, (High Commission, New Delhi) to M.P. Preston (CRO) 30 August 1958, and H. Smedley (High Commission, New Delhi) to G.W.S. Chadwick (CRO) 24 September 1958, DO35/7986.

35 'Note on the Government of India's policy in relation to the issue of passports for the UK with particular reference to the migration of Indians', by Ranbir Singh, Chief Passport Officer, enclosed in Smedley to Chadwick 17 November 1958, DO35/7986.

36 See Snelling to Fowler and Rob, 19 September 1958, DO35/7986. Financial deposits were already required of prospective emigrants by Ghana (£100) and by Ceylon (Rs.4,000).

37 'Commonwealth immigrants', memorandum by the Lord President of the Council (Lord Hailsham) C(58)129, 20 June 1958, CAB129/93.

38 Minute on Commonwealth immigrants, [signature illegible], 27 June 1958, PREM11/2920.

39 Minute by M.P. Preston (CRO) 19 September 1958, DO35/7995.

40 CC51(58)6 of 1 July 1958, CAB128/32 part 2.

41 See, for example, the treatment of the riots by Peter Fryer, *Staying Power: The History of Black People in Britain*, London, Pluto Press, 1984, pp. 376–81. D.W. Dean, 'Conservative governments and the restriction of Commonwealth immigration in the 1950s: the problems of constraint', *Historical Journal*, 1992, vol. 35 (no. 1), p. 188 also argues that they were a constraint.

42 Home to all High Commissioners, 26 August 1958, DO35/7992.

43 'Summary of UK editorial comment concerning immigration policy following incidents in Nottingham and London' [No date, no author, Sep. 1958?], DO35/7987.

44 Deputy to the Governor-General (Federation of the West Indies) to Secretary of State for the Colonies, 2 September 1958, DO35/7992; H. Macmillan to R.A. Butler, 2 September 1958, PREM11/2920; and Minute by A.W. Snelling, 'Race riots', 3 September 1958, DO35/7992.

45 CC69(58)3, 8 September 1958, and CC71(58)1, 11 September 1958, CAB128/32.

46 Press Statement of 4.9.58 in PREM11/2920. Both the Commissioner of the Metropolitan Police and David Renton, the Parliamentary Under-Secretary of State at the Home Office, went some way at an interdepartmental meeting – held just after the riots ended – to justify the thuggish behaviour of white youths. Renton was reported as saying that white people in Notting Hill felt they had long been subjected to provocation by coloured people living disreputable lives in appalling conditions. The chief of London's police reported that local residents resented the influx of coloured people because they had reduced the amenities of the areas in which they had settled, lived in conditions that would not be tolerated by white people and behaved as landlords and pimps in an unacceptable manner. See Note for Record of meeting with Home Secretary of 3 September 1958, PREM11/2920.

47 See, for example, E. Pilkington, *Beyond the Mother Country: West Indians and the Notting Hill White Riots*, London, Tauris, 1988, p. 138; Z. Layton-Henry, *The Politics of Race in Britain*, London, Allen and Unwin, 1984, p. 35–6; and J. Solomos, *Race and Racism in Contemporary Britain*, London, Macmillan, 1989, pp. 48–9.

48 See above, Chapter 2.

49 Layton-Henry argues that the riots 'put black immigration on the national political agenda' and that it was only after the riots that the word 'immigration' became associated in the public mind with non-white immigration. A more careful examination of the public debate of 1954–5 might result in some modification of that view; see Z. Layton-Henry, *The Politics of Immigration: Immigration, 'Race' and 'Race' Relations in Post-war Britain*, Oxford, Blackwell, 1992, p. 73.

50 See Brief by A.W. Snelling for the Secretary of State: 'Race Riots' (for Cabinet, 8 September 1958), 5 September 1958, DO35/7987.

51 Minute by Sir H. Lintott, 5 September 1958, DO35/7987.

52 See Brief by A.W. Snelling for the Secretary of State: 'Race Riots' (for Cabinet, 8 September 1958), 5 September 1958, DO35/7987.

53 J. Chadwick (CRO) to W.A.W. Clark (High Commission, New Delhi) and R.W.D. Fowler (High Commission, Karachi) 29 August 1958; and enclosure 'Employment position in Great Britain', DO35/7986.

54 See Brief by A.W. Snelling for the Secretary of State: 'Race Riots' (for Cabinet, 8 September 1958), 5 September 1958, DO35/7987. For CRO 'departmentalism' and criticism of the CO see also Snelling to Fowler (Karachi) and Rob (Delhi) 19.9.58. DO35/7986.

55 'Racial disturbances. Note of a meeting held in the Home Secretary's room on 8 September, 1958', PREM11/2920.

56 Confidential note, A.T. Lennox-Boyd to R.A. Butler, 10 September 1958, PREM11/2920; and Home to Governor-General, the West Indies, 24 September 1958, DO35/7995.

57 *The Times*, 13 September 1958.

58 'West Indian migration to the UK: local assessment of the position by West Indian governments', Memorandum by the Colonial Office attached as Annex 2 to the Progress Report of the Working Party . . . 1 February 1961, CAB134/1469.

59 Snelling to Fowler and Rob, 19 September 1958, DO35/7986. The CRO was also nagging the CO at Permanent Under-Secretary level to put its house in order, citing its effective work in Pakistan and India. Sir G. Laithwaite to Sir J. Macpherson, 22 September 1958, DO35/7995.

60 D.W.H. Wickson (High Commission, New Delhi) to H. Arthington-Davey (CRO) 4 October 1958; and Smedley to Chadwick, 24 September 1958, DO35/7986.

61 'Note on the Government of India's policy in relation to the issue of passports for the UK with particular reference to the migration of Indians', by Ranbir Singh, Chief Passport Officer, enclosed in Smedley to Chadwick 17 November 1958, DO35/7986.

62 See S. Josephides, 'Towards a History of the Indian Workers Association', Research Paper in Ethnic Relations No. 18, Coventry, Centre for Research in Ethnic Relations, 1991, pp. 10–14, R. Desai, *Indian Immigrants in Britain*, Oxford, Oxford University Press for the Institute of Race Relations, 1963, p. 105; and G.S. Aurora, *The New Frontiersman: A Sociological Study of Indian Immigrants in the United Kingdom*, Bombay, Popular Prakashan, 1967, p. 45.

63 J.A. Molyneux (High Commission, Karachi) to M.P. Preston (CRO) 5 December 1958, DO35/7986.

64 'Immigration into the United Kingdom from India and Pakistan, 1957/58', Report by H. Arthington-Davy [n.d., probably Jan. 1959], DO35/7983.

65 Brief for the Secretary of State on the deportation of British subjects from the UK, 23 October 1958, DO35/7987.

66 N. Deakin, 'The immigration issue in British politics', unpublished Ph.D. Thesis, University of Sussex, 1972, p. 116.

67 Ibid., pp. 120–1.

68 Brief for the Secretary of State, Cabinet Legislative Committee, 25 November 1958, DO35/7987.

69 Lord Hailsham, *A Sparrow's Flight: The Memoirs of Lord Hailsham of St Marylebone*, London, Collins, 1990, p. 323.

70 The arguments are set out in 'Draft Report by the Vice Chancellor', 14 January 1959, attached to Minutes of the Cabinet Committee on Colonial Immigrants, 13 January 1959, CAB134/1467.

71 CC11(59)8, 19.2.59.

72 Minutes of the Cabinet Committee on Colonial Immigrants, 22 July 1959, CAB134/1467.

73 Sir Norman Brook (Secretary of the Cabinet) to Eden, 24 November 1960 in PREM 11/3238. Brook told Eden that Enoch Powell, the Minister of Health, had apparently expressed a keen desire to become a member of the committee, 'because the problem arises in a particularly sharp form in his constituency.'

74 Cochrane, an Antiguan, was murdered in Kensington, apparently by a gang of white youths. The police suggested that robbery was a more likely motive for the stabbing than racial feeling.

75 'Progress Report of the Working Party on the social and economic problems . . .' 3 July 1959, CAB134/1467.

76 'Progress Report of the Working Party on the social and economic problems . . .' 22 June 1960, DO35/7991.

77 Report of the Interdepartmental Working Party, 25 July 1961, p. 3, CAB134/1469. The 'disorders' which took place in Middlesborough on 19–21 August 1961 were reported to the Ministerial Committee in the Working Party Report of 26 September 1961. However, the view of the local Chief Constable that the disturbances were not racial was accepted. The Report noted that the murder of an Arab boy had been seized upon by criminal elements as an excuse to settle

old scores. No coloured person was injured, involved or arrested in any of the incidents. Report of the Interdepartmental Working Party, 26 September 1961, p. 3, CAB134/1469; but see P. Panayi, 'Middlesborough 1961: a British race riot of the 1960s?' *Social History*, 1991, vol. 16 (no. 2), pp. 139–53 who describes the episode as 'a race riot'.

78 For the Working Party's treatment of crime see Report of January 1960, pp. 6–7 and June 1960, pp. 4–5, DO35/7991.

79 'Progress Report of the Working Party . . .' 1 February 1961, p. 14, CAB134/1469.

80 Report by the Interdepartmental Working Party, 26 September 1961, p. 4, CAB134/1469.

81 Report by the Interdepartmental Working Party, 25 July 1961, p. 3, CAB134/1469.

82 'Progress Report of the Working Party . . .', 22 June 1960, p. 7, DO35/7991.

83 Ibid., p. 8.

84 Ibid., pp. 7–8.

85 Ibid., p. 9 and Report of the Interdepartmental Working Party, 25 July 1961, p. 3, CAB134/1469.

86 See, for example, the minutes of the Cabinet meeting of 16 February 1961 at which it was agreed that whereas there was no cause for serious disquiet in relation to employment or preservation of law and order, housing problems had become 'increasingly acute' and there was cause for some anxiety on grounds of public health, CC7(61)2, 16 February 1961.

87 Minute of the Commonwealth Migrants Committee, 16 February 61, CAB1311/1469.

88 See Minutes of the Cabinet Committee on Colonial Immigrants, 22 July 1959, CAB134/1467.

89 See Appendix B, 'Housing certificates for intending immigrants', in Report to the Ministerial Committee by the Working Party, 11 April 1961, CAB134/1469.

90 See Report of the Interdepartmental Working Party, 25 July 1961, pp. 2–3, CAB134/1469.

91 See Iain Macleod to Governors and Administrators in the West Indies, 30 January 1961, CO1031/3933. Terry, who drafted this despatch, had already expressed her disquiet about the accuracy of the Ministry of Labour predictions.

92 A brief history of the practice can be found in 'Counts of coloured workers registered as unemployed at employment exchanges', 7 August 1958, in LAB8/2360. For a routine denial of the existence of the figures, see speech of Patricia Hornsby-Smith, Under-Secretary of State at the Home Office, 3 April 1958 in 585 H.C. Debs., col. 1426.

93 'Progress Report of the Working Party on the social and economic problems . . .' 3 July 1959, p. 7. CAB134/1467.

94 Minutes by M.Z. Terry, 11 January 1961, 12 April 1961, 15 May 1961 and 26 May 1961 in CO1031/3933.

95 'Unemployment position among West Indians', 6 September 1961, CO1031/3933.

96 'Progress Report of the Working Party on the social and economic problems . . .' 22 June 1960, p. 17, DO35/7991.

97 'Progress Report. . . .' 1 February 1961, pp. 7–8, CAB134/1469.

98 'Progress Report. . . .' 3 July 1959, pp. 6–7, CAB134/1467. The CO prepared a paper in September 1961 which showed that West Indian women's performance in the job market was very similar to that of West Indian men and that long-term unemployment was not a large-scale problem: 'Employment position among West Indians', 6 September 1961, CO1033/3933.

99 Report of the Interdepartmental Working Party, 25 July 1961, pp. 3–7, CAB134/1469.

100 'Curtailment of immigration by employment control: note by the Ministry of Labour', Working Party Report. . . . 28 April 1961, in CAB134/1469.

101 The key document is the one cited in the previous footnote. It sets out the reasoning for the adoption of the three-tier permit system without prevarication or concealment as to the government's motive.

102 Report of the Interdepartmental Working Party, 25 July 1961, pp. 7–8; and Appendix A: 'Restriction of immigration by quota', p. 2, CAB134/1469.

103 The figures for the Asian and black population are estimates but any error will be consistent through the series and, therefore, will not invalidate the movement over time of the unemployment figures. The population figures for 1961 tally closely with the census estimate as amended by E.J.B. Rose *et al.* in *Colour and Citizenship: A Report on British Race Relations*, London, Oxford University Press, 1969, p. 97.

This sequence of figures, set against the figures for Asian and black immigration in Table 1, provides an interesting alternative to the figures – of job vacancies in selected industries – used by Ceri Peach to demonstrate the effectiveness of the relationship between employment opportunities in the UK and the rate of immigration from the Caribbean. News of job opportunities in the UK was transmitted to the Caribbean through the correspondence of black people already living here; virtually everyone coming from the West Indies did so to join a friend or relative already here. See C. Peach, *West Indian Migration to Britain*, London, Oxford University Press, 1968. For details of the counts, see confidential memorandum, 'Counts of coloured workers registered as unemployed at employment exchanges', in LAB8/2360.

104 Report of the Interdepartmental Working Party, 25 July 1961, p. 3, CAB134/1469.

105 'Progress Report . . .' 22 June 1960, p. 2, DO35/7991. Figure 1 is based on Home Office statistics reproduced in Davison, *Black British*, London, OUP/IRR, 1966, p. 3.

106 Minutes of the Working Party, 10 June 1960, DO35/7991.

107 'Progress Report . . .' 1 February 1961, p. 3, DO35/7991.

108 Report of the Interdepartmental Working Party, 26 September 1961, p. 3, CAB134/1469.

109 The statistical bases on which government decisions were founded are reproduced in the Working Party reports. See, for example, that for June 1960, p. 1.

110 'Progress Report of the Working Party . . .' 1 February 1961, pp. 1, 12 and 14, DO35/7991.

111 Report of the Interdepartmental Working Party, 25 July 1961, p. 20, CAB134/1469.

112 K. Young, *Sir Alec Douglas-Home*, London, Dent, 1970, p. 102.

113 Deakin, 'The immigration issue', pp. 125–31.

114 To his great surprise, in the general election of October 1959 Mosley lost his

deposit in North Kensington where he was defeated by George Rogers, a Labour MP who had been a leading advocate of immigration controls.

115 624 H.C. Debs., col. 111, 31 May 1960 and 631 H.C. Debs., col. 586, 1 December 1960.

116 'Coloured immigration', memorandum by the Home Secretary, 8 February 1961, CAB134/1469; and 'Coloured immigrants', memorandum by Sir Norman Brook, 25 July 1960, PREM11/2920.

117 CC7(61)2, 16 February 1961, CAB128/35.

118 Record of a meeting with Dr Eric Williams, Premier of Trinidad, 25 March 1961 in PREM11/3238.

119 Minutes of the Cabinet Commonwealth Migrants Committee, 17 May 1961, CCM(61)2, CAB134/1469. The figure for 1961 was 136,400. Butler emphasised the importance of fear of racial disturbances as a motivation for the Act in his memoirs: R.A. Butler, *The Art of the Possible*, London, Hamish Hamilton, 1971, p. 206.

120 For a fuller analysis of the West Indian factor see the briefing paper on Caribbean immigration prepared by the West Indian Department of the Colonial Office for the Constitutional Conference of June 1961, CO1031/3933.

121 Net Asian and black immigration into Britain in the first six months of 1962 was 94,890. When the number of dependents (of the largely male immigrants of this period) who were subsequently able to come to Britain are considered, the importance of the delay takes on much greater importance.

122 Minutes of the meeting of the Commonwealth Migrants Committee, 17 May 1961, CCM(61)2, CAB134/1469.

123 CC29(61)7, 30 May 1961, CAB128/35.

124 Minutes of the meeting of the Commonwealth Migrants Committee, 31 July 1961, CCM(61)3, CAB134/1469.

125 Minutes of the meeting of the Commonwealth Migrants Committee, 29 September 1961, CCM(61)4, CAB134/1469 and CC55(61)3, 10 October 1961, CAB128/35; and 'Commonwealth migrants', Minute for the Prime Minister by Norman Brook, 9 October 1961, PREM 11/3238.

126 Paul Foot's excellent and pioneering book, *Immigration and Race in British Politics*, Harmondsworth, Middlesex, Penguin, 1965 places much emphasis on the influence of party grassroots opinion, see pp. 130–8. So does Layton-Henry who writes (*Politics of Immigration* p. 75), that it was pressure from within the Conservative Party that 'made the Cabinet do' what it had discussed so often in the past.

127 A poll taken by the *Daily Express* in late 1958 showed that nationally 79 per cent favoured controls (Layton-Henry, *Politics of Immigration*, p. 73). In the summer of 1961 67 per cent favoured restrictions (R.A. Butler, *Art of the Possible*, pp. 205–6). When the 1962 Act was announced 76 per cent favoured controls, but two weeks after the second reading debate support had slipped to 62 per cent (Foot, *Immigration and Race*, p. 172). For press opinion see Deakin, 'The immigration issue', pp. 156–7, 187.

128 Foot, *Immigration and Race*, pp. 136, 142.

129 Ibid., 142–7, 189. Robin Turton and John Biggs-Davidson, who moved a pro-Commonwealth amendment to the 1962 Act, were examples of right-wingers upset by controls. The issue of immigration was mentioned in the 1964 general election campaign by 14 per cent of Labour candidates and 8 per cent of Conservatives, p. 181.

130 Report of an interview with R.A. Butler by Ira Katznelson, *Black Men, White Cities*, London, Oxford University Press for the Institute of Race Relations, 1973, p. 134.

131 Interviewed by Deakin in 1967, both Butler and Brooke stressed the importance of the Commonwealth factor in delaying the decision to legislate. Macleod, representing colonial interests, had been the last member of the Cabinet to be convinced. Deakin, 'The immigration issue', p. 138.

132 Deakin briefly discusses the widespread feeling that 'any discussion of race is in some way improper' ('The immigration issue', p. 2). Studlar finds a great deal of evidence to suggest that MPs regarded immigration as a 'nasty' subject which was best avoided at all times. D.T. Studlar, 'Elite responsiveness or elite autonomy: British immigration policy reconsidered', *Ethnic and Racial Sudies*, 1980, vol. 3 (no. 2), pp. 213–14. Several aspects of the argument in this section are owed to J. Bulpitt, 'Continuity, autonomy and peripheralisation: the anatomy of the centre's race statecraft in England', in Z. Layton-Henry and P.B. Rich (eds), *Race, Government and Politics in Britain*, London, Macmillan, 1986, pp. 17–44.

133 Deakin, 'The immigration issue', pp. 140–1.

5 THE MAKING OF MULTI-RACIAL BRITAIN, 1962–91

1 Source: 1982 Policy Studies Institute Survey. Adapted from C. Brown, *Black and White Britain: The Third PSI Survey*, Heinemann, London, 1984, p. 27.

2 The government was aware of this. See, for example, briefing papers for the UK delegation at the West Indies Constitutional Conference, June 1961 in CO1031/3933, which talk of immigration from the West Indies having been given a 'special boost' by the public discussion of the possibility of introducing controls. For an example of the impact of the expectation of legislation on the size of a South Asian community, see A. Shaw, *A Pakistani Community in Britain*, Oxford, Blackwell, 1988, pp. 25–7.

3 Patricia Hornsby-Smith was Under-Secretary of State at the Home Office. See 585 H.C. Debs., col. 1426, 3 April 1958.

4 Press statement by the Secretary of State for Colonies, 21 April 1961, in PREM11/3238.

5 Home Office papers show clearly that the government was aware that, following its announcement, the longer it was before the legislation took effect, the greater the rush would be. See HO/BSI, 1 January 1948. As early as May 1958, following Patricia Hornsby-Smith's speech which envisaged the possibility of immigration controls, officials predicted a resulting surge in immigration pressure. See DO35/7982.

6 For the range of destinations to which Jullunduris have travelled and usually settled, see T. Kessinger, *Vilyatpur, 1848–1968*, Berkeley, California, University of California Press, 1974.

7 The pattern of cyclical and replacement migration organised within the kin group was observed by J. Rex and R. Moore, *Race Community and Conflict: A Study of Sparkbrook*, London, Oxford University Press, 1967, p. 116. This period of South Asian migration is well covered in R. Desai, *Indian Immigrants in Britain*, Oxford, Oxford University Press, 1963 and G. Aurora, *The New Frontiersmen*, Bombay, Popular Prakashan, 1967.

8 Interesting arguments about the factors that account for the arrival of women

and children from the mid-1960s are set out in A. Shaw, *A Pakistani Community in Britain*, Oxford, Blackwell, 1988, pp. 44–9.

9 In the first half of 1960, for example, 6,400 of the 16,575 arrivals from the Caribbean were female. See Appendix A, Report of the Interdepartmental Working Party, 22 June 1960, DO35/7991. By 1967 only a small minority of Caribbean families still had children waiting to join them; see E.J.B. Rose *et al.*, *Colour and Citizenship: A Report on British Race Relations*, London, Oxford University Press, 1969, p. 433.

10 See, for example, Report of the Interdepartmental Working Party, 25 July 1961, pp. 17–18, CAB134/1469.

11 Since the Act of 1962 the government has published annual summaries of immigration statistics. See, for example, *Commonwealth Immigrants Act 1962: Statistics 1965*, Cmnd. 2979, London, HMSO, 1966; and *Control of Immigration Statistics, UK 1994*, Cm. 2935, London, HMSO, 1995.

12 While the scale of 'secondary immigration' can be expected to fall it will never end. The rules will continue to permit limited forms of entry, for example, for marriage. See V. Bevan, *The Development of British Immigration Law*, London, Croom Helm, 1986, pp. 36–7.

13 Reported in *Hansard*, 685 H.C. Debs., cols. 365–8, 373–5, 27 November 1963. See Z. Layton-Henry, *The Politics of Race in Britain*, London, Allen and Unwin, 1984, pp. 55–6; and P. Foot, *Immigration and Race in British Politics*, Harmondsworth, Middlesex, Penguin, 1965, pp. 173–81.

14 Foot argues that the number of applications for vouchers was stimulated by the methods of control employed and that only a small percentage of voucher applicants had any sustained and properly financed intention to use their vouchers. See Foot, *Immigration and Race*, pp. 187–9.

15 *Immigration from the Commonwealth*, Cmnd. 2739, London, HMSO, 1965 pp. 7–8. See Bevan, *Immigration Law*, pp. 79–80, 164–5.

16 Vaughan Bevan in his judicious review of the subject calls it a somersault: *Immigration Law*, p. 80. See also, A. Bottomley and G. Sinclair, *Control of Commonwealth Immigration*, London, Runnymede Trust, 1970, p. 15. Gerald Kaufman describes the process of deciding how many immigrants would be allowed to enter in 'Dutch auction on immigrants', *New Statesman*, vol. 35, 9 July 1965.

17 See P. Ziegler, *Mountbatten: The Official Biography*, London, Collins, 1985, pp. 633–6.

18 R. Crossman, *Diaries of a Cabinet Minister*, vol. 1, London, Hamilton and Cape, 1975, pp. 149–50, 299: 'Immigration can be the greatest potential vote loser for the Labour Party if we are seen to be permitting a flood of immigrants to come in.'

19 After the 1962 Act Indian immigration peaked in the sixties, Pakistani in the seventies and Bangladeshi in the eighties. Excellent graphs have been produced by D. Owen, *Ethnic Minorities in Great Britain: Patterns of Population Change, 1981–1991*, 1991 Census Statistical Paper No. 10, University of Warwick/Centre for Research in Ethnic Relations, Coventry, Warks., 1995. The differing composition by age group of the South Asian communities can be studied in R. Ballard and V.S. Kalra, *The Ethnic Dimensions of the 1991 Census: A Preliminary Report*, Manchester, Census Microdata Unit/University of Manchester, 1994, pp. 15–21.

20 V. Robinson, 'The new Indian middle class in Britain', *Ethnic and Racial Studies*, 1988, vol. 11 (no. 4), p. 461–3.

21 Bottomley and Sinclair, *Control*, pp. 9–10.
22 For an example of the assertion that changes in the supply of and demand for labour were linked to decisions about immigration, see M.D.A. Freeman and S. Spencer, 'Immigration control, black workers and the economy', *British Journal of Law and Society*, 1979, vol. 6, pt. 1, p. 66. For the Department of Employment's position see the summary of evidence taken by the Select Committee on Race and Immigration, 1969–70, in Bottomley and Sinclair, *Control*, p. 17.
23 Bottomley and Sinclair, *Control*, pp. 10–11.
24 See Bevan, *Immigration Law*, pp. 81–2.
25 Crossman argued that one of Callaghan's greatest achievements had been to get tough on Asian and black immigration and by doing so enhance Labour's chances in the general elections of 1966, 1968 and 1970. See R. Crossman, *The Diaries of a Cabinet Minister: Volume 3, Secretary of State for Social Services, 1968–70*, London, Hamish Hamilton, 1977, p. 941.
26 Even the judicious J.D.B. Miller considered that 'In the minds of many, both Britain and the Commonwealth were brought into disrepute.' See Miller, *Survey of Commonwealth Affairs: Problems of Expansion and Attrition, 1953–1969*, London, Oxford University Press, 1974, p. 345. The normally very sober Zig Layton-Henry called the government decisions 'a disastrous betrayal of principle . . . the result of which devalued British citizenship' in *Politics of Race*, p. 69.
27 Miller, *Survey*, p. 346.
28 There seems to be agreement among political scientists that the identification of the Conservative Party with tougher immigration controls made a crucial difference to the outcome of the closely fought 1970 general election. See D.E. Schoen, *Enoch Powell and the Powellites*, London, Macmillan, 1977, pp. 51–66; and Layton-Henry, *Politics of Race*, pp. 79–80.
29 See Bevan, *Immigration Law*, pp. 83–4 and S.S. Juss, *Immigration, Nationality and Citizenship*, London, Mansell, 1993, pp. 46–7.
30 Freeman and Spencer, 'Immigration control', pp. 69–70.
31 Figures are taken from Owen, *Ethnic Minorities*, pp. 3–6.
32 Z. Layton-Henry, 'Race and the Thatcher Government', in Z. Layton-Henry and P.B. Rich (eds), *Race, Government and Politics in Britain*, London, Macmillan, 1986, pp. 75–7.
33 See R. White and F.J. Hampson, 'The British Nationality Act, 1981', *Public Law*, 1982, pp. 6–20, and Juss, *Immigration, Nationality and Citizenship*, pp. 53–5. The British government changed its mind about Falkland Islanders in 1983 when it conferred British citizenship on them by the British Nationality (Falkland Islands) Act.
34 Juss, *Immigration, Nationality and Citizenship*, pp. 56–7.
35 Ibid., pp. 44–5.
36 Layton-Henry, 'Race and the Thatcher Government', pp. 91–2.
37 G. Robertson, *Freedom, the Individual and the Law*, Harmondsworth, Middlesex, Penguin, 1989, pp. 315, 330; and *The Guardian*, 27 January 1984, 21 March 1984 and 2 April 1984. On the wider question of the administration of immigration policy see R. Moore and T. Wallace, *Slamming the Door – The Administration of Immigration Control*, Oxford, Martin Robertson, London, 1975.

CONCLUSION

1   See for example, M.D.A. Freeman and S. Spencer, 'Immigration control, black workers and the economy', *British Journal of Law and Society*, 1979, vol. 6, pt. 1, p. 57.

2   See P. Fryer, *Staying Power: A History of Black People in Britain*, London, Pluto, 1984, pp. 372–4. He cites the figures but sustains the myths of official encouragement and the importance of recruitment.

3   This approach is most often associated with the work of J. Rex, 'Black militancy and class conflict', in R. Miles and A. Phizacklea (eds), *Racism and Political Action*, London, Routledge & Kegan Paul, 1979; and S. Castles and G. Kosack, *Immigrant Workers and Class Structure in Western Europe*, Oxford, Oxford University Press, 1973. Even Zig Layton-Henry, who is as fine a writer as any on race, immigration and politics in post-war Britain, frequently infers that Asian and black immigrants were collectively 'unskilled and semiskilled.'

4   Tariq Modood has led the way in criticising the practice of blocking the diversity of Asian and black groups into a single 'black' underclass. See T. Modood, *Not Easy Being British: Colour, Culture and Citizenship*, Stoke-on-Trent, Runnymede Trust and Trentham Books, 1992, pp. 27–43. For an understanding of the range and diversity of communities from the Indian sub-continent settled in Britain, R. Ballard (ed.), *Desh Pardesh: The South Asian Presence in Britain*, London, Hurst, 1994, is essential reading.

5   Robinson's analysis of *Indians in Britain's Who's Who* shows larger numbers of the Indian elite entering after the early 1960s. By the mid 1980s the percentage of employed Indians and East African Asians in non-manual employment compared favourably with the indigenous population and was more than three times higher than the figure for West Indians. See V. Robinson, 'The new Indian middle class in Britain', *Ethnic and Racial Studies*, 1988, vol. 11 (no. 4), pp. 458, 463.

6   C. Peach, *West Indian Migration to Britain: A Social Geography*, London, Oxford University Press, 1968.

7   All these surveys are referred to in E.J.B. Rose *et al.*, *Colour and Citizenship: A Report on British Race Relations*, London, Oxford University Press, 1969, pp. 49–51.

8   For Nigel Fisher's report see PREM11/824. See also R. Glass, *The Newcomers: West Indians in London*, London, Allen and Unwin, 1960, pp. 24, 31; E. Pilkington, *Beyond the Mother Country: West Indians and the Notting Hill White Riots*, London, Tauris, 1988, pp. 23, 31–2; and Fryer, *Staying Power*, p. 374.

9   The percentage of each group possessing qualifications at 'O' Level equivalent and above were 5 per cent West Indian, 16 per cent white and 19 per cent Asian. But 87 per cent of West Indian males over 44 possessed no qualifications, vocational or academic, whereas 74 per cent of Asians and 64 per cent of whites were similarly placed. See C. Brown, *Black and White Britain: The Third PSI Survey*, London, Heinemann, 1984, p. 145.

10 M.H. Lyon and B.J.M. West, 'London Patels: caste and commerce', *New Community*, 1995, vol. 21 (no. 3), pp. 399–419. These themes are dealt with very capably by Rose *et al.*, *Colour and Citizenship*, pp. 52–62, and are elaborated in Ballard, *Desh Pardesh*, and M.J. Taylor and S. Hegarty, *The Best of Both Worlds . . .?*, Windsor, NFER–Nelson, 1985. The House of Commons

Home Affairs Committee, *Bangladeshis in Britain: Vol. 1, Report together with the Proceedings of the Committee*, London, HMSO, 1986 provides a well researched picture of Bangladeshi economic and social difficulty which could be contrasted very sharply with portraits of highly successful Asian communities.

11 This theme is explored by B. Dahya, 'South Asians as economic migrants in Britain', *Ethnic and Racial Studies*, 1988, vol. 11 (no. 4), pp. 439–455. Robinson, 'New Indian middle class', p. 459, produces figures based on the Labour Force Survey which show rapid upward mobility among Indian settlers in the 1970s. Brown's study shows that, even by 1982, young Asian and Caribbean males were considerably more likely to possess high academic qualifications than whites. See Brown, *Black and White Britain*, p. 147. For a testament to the quality of early Caribbean migrants, see N. Fisher, 'West Indian migration to the UK', October 1955, PREM11/824.

12 For an account of some aspects of Indian success in contemporary Britain, see Modood, *Not Easy Being British*, pp. 33–9.

13 This is quite clear from the analysis of 1991 Census data carried out by David Owen for the National Ethnic Minority Data Archive, the Centre for Research in Ethnic Relations at the University of Warwick. See 1991 Census Statistical Papers Nos. 6, 7 and 8, 1994.

14 E. Clough and D. Drew, *Futures in Black and White*, Sheffield, Pavic Publications, 1985.

15 The body responsible for inspecting schools, OFSTED, now officially recognises that, comparing schools with intakes of similar socio-economic backgrounds, schools with high ethnic minority populations tend to have better examination results than schools with low ethnic minority populations. PICSI (Pre-Inspection Context and School Indicator) Annex for Secondary Schools, Summer Term 1996.

Bibliography

Apart from publications (listed under 'Government'), a great many internal government documents have been consulted at the Public Record Office, Kew. Some have titles but others are, for example, letters or memoranda, and they are far too numerous to mention here. They are cited in the Notes with the following prefixes:

CAB	Cabinet Office
CM	Cabinet Minutes
CO	Colonial Office
CRO	Commonwealth Relations Office
HO	Home Office
LAB	Ministry of Labour
MT	Ministry of Transport

Adams, C., *Across Seven Seas and Thirteen Rivers: Life Stories of Pioneering Sylheti Settlers in Britain*, London, Tower Hamlets Arts Projects, 1987.

Anwar, M., *The Myth of Return: Pakistanis in Britain*, London, Heinemann, 1979.

Aurora, G.S., *The New Frontiersmen: A Sociological Study of Indian Immigrants in the United Kingdom*, Bombay, Popular Prakashan, 1967.

Ballard, R. (ed.), *Desh Pardesh: The South Asian Presence in Britain*, London, Hurst, 1994.

Ballard, R. and Kalra, V.S., *The Ethnic Dimensions of the 1991 Census: A Preliminary Report*, Census Microdata Unit/University of Manchester, Manchester, 1994.

Banton, M., *The Coloured Quarter: Negro Immigrants in an English City*, London, Cape, 1955.

Bevan, V., *The Development of British Immigration Law*, London, Croom Helm, 1986.

Bhachu, P., *Twice Migrants: East African Sikh Settlers in Britain*, London, Tavistock, 1985.

Bottomley, A. and Sinclair, G., *Control of Commonwealth Immigration*, London, Runnymede Trust, 1970.

Bradley, I., 'Why Churchill's plan to limit immigration was shelved', *The Times*, 20 March 1978.

Brooks, D., *Race and Labour in London Transport*, Oxford, Oxford University Press, 1975.

Brown, C., *Black and White Britain: The Third PSI Survey*, London, Heinemann, 1984.

Brown, J.M. and Foot, R. (eds), *Migration: The Asian Experience*, London, Macmillan, 1995.

Bulpitt, J., 'Continuity, autonomy and peripheralisation: the anatomy of the centre's race statecraft in England', in Z. Layton-Henry and P.B. Rich (eds), *Race, Government and Politics in Britain*, London, Macmillan, 1986.

Butler, R.A., *The Art of the Possible*, London, Hamish Hamilton, 1971.

Byrne, D., 'Class, race and nation: The politics of the "Arab issue" in South Shields, 1919–1939', *Immigrants and Minorities*, 1994, vol. 13 (nos. 2 and 3), pp. 89–103.

——, 'The 1930 "Arab riot" in South Shields: a race riot that never was', *Race and Class*, 1977, vol. 18 (no. 3).

Campbell, J., *Edward Heath: A Biography*, London, Cape, 1993.

Carter, B., Harris, C. and Joshi, S., 'The 1951–55 Conservative government and the racialization of black immigration', *Immigrants and Minorities*, 1987, vol. 4 (no. 3).

Cashmore, E., *The Logic of Racism*, London, Allen and Unwin, 1987.

Cashmore, E. and Troyna, B., *Introduction to Race Relations*, London, Routledge & Kegan Paul, 1983.

Castles, S., *Here for Good: West Europe's Ethnic Minorities*, London, Pluto, 1984.

Castles, S. and Kosack, G., *Immigrant Workers and Class Structure in Western Europe*, Oxford, Oxford University Press, 1973.

Clarke, C., Peach, C. and Vertovec, S. (eds), *South Asians Overseas: Migration and Ethnicity*, Cambridge, Cambridge University Press, 1990.

Clough, E. and Drew, D., *Futures in Black and White*, Sheffield, Yorkshire, Pavic Publications, 1985.

Collins, S., *Coloured Minorities in Britain: Studies in British Race Relations Based on African, West Indian and Asian Immigrants*, London, Lutterworth, 1957.

Colville, J., *The Fringes of Power: 10 Downing Street Diaries, 1939–1955*, London, Hodder and Stoughton, 1985.

Cross, J.A., *Lord Swinton*, Oxford, Oxford University Press, 1982.

Crossman, R., *The Diaries of a Cabinet Minister*, vol. 1, London, Hamilton and Cape, 1975.

Crossman, R., *The Diaries of a Cabinet Minister*, vol. 3, London, Hamish Hamilton, 1977.

Dahya, B., 'The nature of Pakistani ethnicity in industrial cities in Britain', in A. Cohen (ed.), *Urban Ethnicity*, London, Tavistock, 1974.

——, 'South Asians as economic migrants in Britain', *Ethnic and Racial Studies*, 1988, vol. 11 (no. 4), 439–55.

Davis, V., 'A sweet prison,' unpublished MA Dissertation, University of Leicester, 1993.

Davison, R.B., *West Indian Migrants*, Oxford, Oxford University Press, 1962.

——, *Black British: Immigrants to England*, Oxford, Oxford University Press for the Institute of Race Relations, 1966.

Deakin, N., 'The politics of the Commonwealth Immigrants Bill', *Political Quarterly*, 1968, vol. 39, pp. 24–45.

——, 'The British Nationality Act of 1948: A brief study on the political mythology of race relations', *Race*, 1969, vol. 11, pp. 77–83.

——, *Colour, Citizenship and British Society*, London, Panther, 1970.

——, 'The immigration issue in British politics, 1948–1964', unpublished Ph.D. Thesis, University of Sussex, 1972.

Dean, D.W., 'Coping with colonial immigration, the Cold War and colonial policy: the Labour government and black communities in Britain, 1945–51', *Immigrants and Minorities*, 1987, vol. 6 (no. 3), pp. 305–34.

——, 'Conservative governments and the restriction of Commonwealth immigration in the 1950s: the problems of constraint', *Historical Journal*, 1992, vol. 35, (no. 1), pp. 171–94.

Desai, R., *Indian Immigrants in Britain*, Oxford, Oxford University Press for the Institute of Race Relations, 1963.

Duffield, M., *Black Radicalism and the Politics of Deindustrialization*, Aldershot, Hampshire, Avebury, 1988.

Dummett, A., *Citizenship and Nationality*, London, Runnymede Trust, 1976.

Dunlop, A., 'Aspects of Scottish migration history with particular emphasis on contemporary Pakistani and Bangladeshi migration', unpublished M.Litt. Thesis, University of Glasgow, 1988.

——, 'Lascars and labourers: reactions to the Indian presence in the west of Scotland during the 1920s and 1930s', *Scottish Labour History Society Journal*, 1990, vol. 25, pp. 40–57.

Dunlop, A. and Miles, R., 'Recovering the history of Asian migration to Scotland', *Immigrants and Minorities*, 1990, vol. 9 (no. 2), pp. 151–2.

Ebanks, G., George, P.M. and Nobbe, C.E., 'Emigration from Barbados, 1951–1970', *Social and Economic Studies*, 1979, vol. 28.

Elton, G.R., *The Unarmed Invasion: A Survey of Afro-Asian Immigration*, London, Geoffrey Bles, 1965.

Evans, J.M., *Immigration Law*, London, Sweet and Maxwell, 1983.

Evans, N., 'The South Wales race riots of 1919', *Journal of the Society for the Study of Welsh Labour History*, 1980, vol. 3 (no. 1), pp. 5–29.

——, 'Across the universe: racial violence and the post-war crisis in imperial Britain, 1919–1925', *Immigrants and Minorities*, 1994, vol. 13 (nos. 2 and 3), pp. 59–88.

——, 'Regulating the reserve army: Arabs, blacks and the local state in Cardiff, 1919–1945', *Immigrants and Minorities*, 1995, vol. 14 (no. 2), pp. 68–115.

File, N. and Power, C., *Black Settlers in Britain, 1555–1958*, London, Heinemann, 1981.

Fisher, N., *Iain Macleod*, London, André Deutsch, 1973.

Foner, N., *Jamaica Farewell: Jamaican Migrants in London*, London, Routledge & Kegan Paul, 1979.

Foot, P., *Immigration and Race in British Politics*, Harmondsworth, Middlesex, Penguin, 1965.

——, *The Rise of Enoch Powell*, Harmondsworth, Middlesex, Penguin, 1969.

Freeman, G.P., *Immigrant Labour and Racial Conflict in Industrial Societies: The British and French Experience, 1945–1975*, Princeton, New Jersey, Princeton University Press, 1979.

Freeman, M.D.A. and Spencer, S., 'Immigration control, black workers and the economy', *British Journal of Law and Society*, 1979, vol. 6, pt. 1, pp. 53–81.

Frost, D., 'Ethnic identity, transience and settlement: the Kru in Liverpool since the late nineteenth century', *Immigrants and Minorities*, 1993, vol. 12 (no. 3), pp. 88–106.

——, 'Racism, work and unemployment: West African seamen in Liverpool, 1880s to 1960s', *Immigrants and Minorities*, 1994, vol. 13 (nos. 2 and 3), pp. 22–33.

Fryer, P., *Staying Power: The History of Black People in Britain*, London, Pluto, 1984.

Ghai, D. (ed.), *Portrait of a Minority: Asians in East Africa*, Nairobi, Oxford University Press, 1965.

Gilmour, Sir I., *Inside Right: A Study of Conservatism*, London, Hutchinson, 1977.

Glass, R., *The Newcomers: The West Indians in London*, London, Allen and Unwin, 1960.

Gopal, S., 'Churchill and India' in R. Blake and W.R. Louis (eds), *Churchill*, Oxford, Oxford University Press, 1993.

Gordon, P., *Policing Immigration: Britain's Internal Controls*, London, Pluto, 1985.

Gordon, P. and Reilly, D., 'Guestworkers of the sea: racism in British shipping', *Race and Class*, 1986, vol. 28, (no. 2), pp. 73–81.

Goulbourne, H. (ed.), *Black Politics in Britain*, Aldershot, Hampshire, Avebury, 1990.

Government, H.M., *Report of the Royal Commission on Population*, Cmnd. 7695, London, HMSO, 1949.

——, *Immigration from the Commonwealth*, Cmnd. 2739, London, HMSO, 1965.

——, *Commonwealth Immigrants Act, 1962: Statistics, 1965*, Cmnd. 2979, London, HMSO, 1966.

——, *Control of Immigration Statistics, UK 1973*, Cmnd. 5285, London, HMSO, 1973.

——, *Control of Immigration: Statistics, UK 1990*, Cm. 1571, London, HMSO, 1991.

——, *Control of Immigration: Statistics, UK 1994*, Cm. 2935, London, HMSO, 1995.

Griffiths, J.A.G., Henderson, J., Usborne, M. and Wood, D., with Long, H.M., *Coloured Immigrants in Britain*, London, Oxford University Press for the Institute of Race Relations, 1960.

Gundara, J. and Duffield, I. (eds), *Essays in the History of Blacks in Britain: From Roman Times to the Mid-Twentieth Century*, Aldershot, Hampshire, Avebury, 1992.

Hailsham, Lord, *A Sparrow's Flight: The Memoirs of Lord Hailsham of St Marylebone*, London, Collins, 1990.

Harris, C., 'Configurations of racism: the Civil Service, 1945–60', *Race and Class*, 1991, vol. 33, (no. 1).

Helweg, A.W., *Sikhs in England: The Development of a Migrant Community*, Delhi, Oxford University Press, 1979.

Hepple, R., *Race, Jobs and the Law*, Harmondsworth, Middlesex, Penguin, 1968.

Hinds, E., *Journey to an Illusion: The West Indian in Britain*, London, Heinemann, 1966.

Hiro, D., *Black British, White British: A History of Race Relations in Britain*, London, Grafton Books, 1991.

Holmes, C. (ed.), *Immigrants and Minorities in British Society*, London, Allen and Unwin, 1978.

Holmes, C., *John Bull's Island: Immigration and British Society, 1871–1971*, London, Macmillan, 1988.

Horne, A., *Macmillan, 1957–1986*, London, Macmillan, 1989.

Humphrey, D. and Ward, M., *Passports and Politics*, Harmondsworth, Middlesex, Penguin, 1974.

Husband, C. (ed.), *Race in Britain: Continuity and Change*, London, Hutchinson, 1982.

Islam, M.M., 'Bengali migrant workers in Britain', unpublished Ph.D. Thesis, University of Leeds, 1976.

James, W. and Harris, C. (eds), *Inside Babylon: The Caribbean Diaspora in Britain*, London, Verso, 1993.

Jenkinson, J., 'The 1919 race riots in Britain: a survey', in R. Lotz and I. Pegg (eds), *Under the Imperial Carpet: Essays in Black History, 1780–1950*, Crawley, Sussex, Rabbit Press, 1986.

——, 'The black community of Salford and Hull, 1919–1921', *Immigrants and Minorities*, 1988, vol. 7.

Josephides, S., 'Towards a history of the Indian Workers Association', Research Paper in Ethnic Relations No. 18, Coventry, Warwickshire, Centre for Research in Ethnic Relations, 1991.

Joshi, S. and Carter, B., 'The role of Labour in the creation of a racist Britain', *Race and Class*, 1984, vol. 25, pt. 3, pp. 57–70.

Joshua, H. and Wallace, T. (with H. Booth), *To Ride the Storm: The 1980 Bristol Race 'Riot' and the State*, London, Heinemann, 1983.

Juss, S.S., *Immigration, Nationality and Citizenship*, London, Mansell, 1993.

Kanitkar, H., 'An Indian elite in Britain', *New Community*, 1972, vol. 1, pp. 378–83.

Katznelson, I., *Black Men, White Cities: Race, Politics and Migration in the United States, 1900–30 and Britain, 1948–68*, London, Oxford University Press for the Institute of Race Relations, 1973.

Kaufman, G., 'Dutch auction on immigrants', *New Statesman*, vol. 35, 9 July 1965.

Kessinger, T., *Vilyatpur, 1848–1968: Social and Economic Change in a North Indian Village*, Berkeley, California, University of California Press, 1974.

Killingray, D., 'All the king's men? Blacks in the British army in the First World War', in R. Lotz and I. Pegg (eds), *Under the Imperial Carpet: Essays in Black History, 1780–1950*, Crawley, Sussex, Rabbit Press, 1986.

Labour Party, *Citizenship, Immigration and Integration: A Policy for the 1970s*, London, Labour Party, 1972.

Lamb, R., *The Failure of the Eden Government*, London, Sidgwick and Jackson, 1987.

Lane, T., 'The political imperatives of bureaucracy and empire: the case of the Coloured Alien Seamen Order, 1925', *Immigrants and Minorities*, 1994, vol. 13 (nos. 2 and 3), pp. 104–29.

Law, I. and Henfrey, J., *A History of Race and Racism in Liverpool, 1660–1950*, Liverpool, Merseyside Community Relations Commission, 1981.

Lawless, D., 'The role of seamen's agents in the migration for employment of Arab seafarers in the early twentieth century', *Immigrants and Minorities*, 1994, vol. 13 (nos. 2 and 3).

——, *From Taiz to Tyneside: An Arab Community in the North-East of England*, Exeter, University of Exeter Press, 1995.

Lawrence, D., *Black Migrants, White Natives: A Study of Race Relations in Nottingham*, Cambridge, Cambridge University Press, 1974.

Layton-Henry, Z., *The Politics of Race in Britain*, London, Allen and Unwin, 1984.

——, 'The State and New Commonwealth Immigration, 1951–56', *New Community*, 1987, vol. 14.

——, *The Politics of Immigration: Immigration, 'Race' and 'Race' Relations in Post-war Britain*, Oxford, Blackwell, 1992.

Layton-Henry, Z. and Rich, P.B., (eds), *Race, Government and Politics in Britain*, London, Macmillan, 1986.

——, 'Race and the Thatcher government', in Z. Layton-Henry and P.B. Rich (eds), *Race, Government and Politics in Britain*, London, Macmillan, 1986.

Little, K., *Negroes in Britain: A Study of Race Relations in English Society*, London, Routledge & Kegan Paul, 1948.

Lotz, R. and Pegg, I. (eds), *Under the Imperial Carpet: Essays in Black History, 1780–1950*, Crawley, Sussex, Rabbit Press, 1986.

Louis, W.R. and Owen, R. (eds), *Suez 1956: The Crisis and its Consequences*, Oxford, Oxford University Press, 1989.

Lunn, K. (ed.), *Race and Labour in Twentieth-Century Britain*, London, Cass, 1985.

Lunn, K., 'The British state and immigration, 1945–51: new light on the *Empire Windrush*', *Immigrants and Minorities*, 1989, vol. 8 (nos. 1/2), pp. 161–74.

Lyon, M.H. and West, B.J.M., 'London Patels: caste and commerce', *New Community*, 1995, vol. 21 (no. 3), pp. 399–419.

Maan, B., *The New Scots: The Story of Asians in Scotland*, Edinburgh, John Donald, 1992.

Macleod, I., 'The shameful and unnecessary Act', *Spectator*, 1 March 1968.

May, R. and Cohen, R., 'The interaction between race and colonialism: a case study of the Liverpool riots of 1919', *Race and Class*, 1974, vol. 16 (no. 2).

McFarland, E.W., 'Clyde opinion on an old controversy: Indian and Chinese seafarers in Glasgow', *Ethnic and Racial Studies*, 1991, vol. 14 (no. 4).

Miles, R., *Racism and Migrant Labour*, London, Routledge & Kegan Paul, 1982.

Miles R. and Phizacklea, A., (eds), *Racism and Political Action*, Routledge & Kegan Paul, London, 1979.

Miles, R. and Phizacklea, A., *White Man's Country*, London, Pluto Press, 1984.

Miller, J.D.B., *Survey of Commonwealth Affairs: Problems of Expansion and Attrition, 1953–69*, London, Oxford University Press, 1974.

Modood, T., *Not Easy Being British: Colour, Culture and Citizenship*, Stoke-on-Trent, Runnymede Trust and Trentham Books, 1992.

Moore, R., *Racism and Black Resistance in Britain*, London, Pluto Press, 1975.

Moore, R. and Wallace, T., *Slamming the Door – The Administration of Immigration Control*, Oxford, Martin Robertson, 1975.

Morris, H.S., *The Indians in Uganda*, London, Weidenfeld and Nicolson, 1968.

Myers, N., 'Reconstructing the black past: blacks in Britain, *circa* 1780 to 1830', unpublished Ph.D. Thesis, University of Liverpool, 1990.

——, 'The black poor of London: initiatives of eastern seamen in the eighteenth and nineteenth centuries', *Immigrants and Minorities*, 1994, vol. 13 (nos. 2 and 3), pp. 7–21.

Oakley, R., 'The control of Cypriot migration to Britain between the wars', *Immigrants and Minorities*, 1987, vol. 4 (no. 1), pp. 30–43.

Owen, D., *Ethnic Minorities in Great Britain: Patterns of Population Change, 1981–1991*, 1991 Census Statistical Paper No. 10, University of Warwick/Centre for Research in Ethnic Relations, Coventry, Warwickshire, 1995.

Panayi, P., 'Middlesborough 1961: a British race riot of the 1960s?', *Social History*, 1991, vol. 16 (no. 2), pp. 139–53.

Pannell, N. and Brockway, F., *Immigration: What is the Answer? Two Opposing Views*, London, Routledge & Kegan Paul, 1965.

Parliament: House of Commons Home Affairs Committee, *Bangladeshis in Britain* (3 vols), London, HMSO, 1986.

Patnaik, A., 'Indian elites in Britain', *Institute of Race Relations Newsletter*, 6–8 January 1968.

Patterson, S., *Immigration and Race Relations in Britain, 1960–67*, London, Oxford University Press, 1969.

——, *Dark Strangers: A Study of West Indians in London*, Harmondsworth, Middlesex, Penguin, 1965.

Paul, K., 'The politics of citizenship in post-war Britain', *Contemporary Record*, Winter 1992, vol. 6, pp. 452–73.

Peach, C., *West Indian Migration to Britain: A Social Geography*, London, Oxford University Press for the Institute of Race Relations, 1968.

——, 'British unemployment cycles and West Indian immigration', *New Community*, 1978–9, vol. 7.

Philpott, S., *West Indian Migration: The Monserrat Case*, London, Athlone Press, 1973.

Pilkington, E., *Beyond the Mother Country: West Indians and the Notting Hill White Riots*, London, Tauris, 1988.

Ramdin, R., *The Making of the Black Working Class in Britain*, Aldershot, Hampshire, Gower, 1987.

Rex, J. and Moore, R., *Race Community and Conflict: A Study of Sparkbrook*, London, Oxford University Press, 1967.

Rex J. and Tomlinson, S., *Colonial Immigrants in a British City: A Class Analysis*, London, Routledge & Kegan Paul, 1979.

Rhodes James, R., *Anthony Eden: A Biography*, London, Weidenfeld and Nicolson, 1986.

Rich, P.B., *Race and Empire in British Politics*, Cambridge, Cambridge University Press, 1990.

Richmond, A.H., *Colour Prejudice in Britain: A Study of West Indian Workers in Liverpool, 1942–1951*, London, Routledge & Kegan Paul, 1954.

Roberts, A., *Eminent Churchillians*, London, Phoenix, 1995.

Robertson, G., *Freedom, the Individual and the Law*, Harmondsworth, Middlesex, Penguin, 1989.

Robinson, V., 'Correlates of Asian immigration, 1959–1974', *New Community*, 1980, vol. 8 (nos. 1 and 2), pp. 115–22.

——, 'The development of South Asian settlements in Britain and the myth of return', in C., Peach, V. Robinson and S. Smith (eds), *Ethnic Segregation in Cities*, London, Croom Helm, 1981.

——, *Transients, Settlers and Refugees: Asians in Britain*, Oxford, Clarendon Press, 1986.

——, 'The new Indian middle class in Britain', *Ethnic and Racial Studies*, 1988, vol. 11 (no. 4), pp. 456–73.

Rose, E.J.B. and associates, *Colour and Citizenship: A Report on British Race Relations*, London, Institute of Race Relations/Oxford University Press, 1969.

Rose, H., 'The Immigration Act, 1971: a case study', *Parliamentary Affairs*, 1972–3, vol. 26, pp. 69–91.

——, 'The politics of immigration after the 1971 Act', *Political Quarterly*, 1973, vol. 44, pp. 183–96.

Schoen, D.E., *Enoch Powell and the Powellites*, London, Macmillan, 1977.

Scobie, E., *Black Britannia: The History of Blacks in Britain*, Chicago, Johnson, 1972.

Shaw, A., *A Pakistani Community in Britain*, Oxford, Blackwell, 1988.

Shepherd, R., *Iain Macleod: A Biography*, London, Hutchinson, 1994.

Sherwood, M., *Many Struggles: West Indian Workers and Service Personnel in Britain, 1939–1945*, London, Karia Press, 1985.

——, 'Race, nationality and employment among Lascar seamen, 1660–1945', *New Community*, 1990, vol. 17 (no. 2), pp. 229–44.

Shyllon, F.O., *Black People in Britain, 1555–1958*, London, Oxford University Press for the Institute of Race Relations, 1978.

——, 'The black presence and experience in Britain: an analytical overview', in J.S. Gundara and I. Duffield, *Essays on the History of Blacks in Britain*, Aldershot, Hampshire, Avebury, 1992.

Sivanandan, A., *A Different Hunger: Writings on Black Resistance*, London, Pluto, 1983.

Smith, M. M., 'Windrushers and Orbiters: towards an understanding of the official mind and colonial immigration to Britain, 1945–51', *Immigrants and Minorities*, 1991, vol. 10 (no. 3), pp. 3–18.

Solomos, J. (ed), *Migrant Workers in Metropolitan Cities*, Strasbourg, European Science Foundation, 1982.

——, *Race and Racism in Contemporary Britain*, London, Macmillan, 1989.

Studlar, D.T., 'Elite responsiveness or elite autonomy: British immigration policy reconsidered', *Ethnic and Racial Studies*, 1980, vol. 3 (no. 2), pp. 207–23.

Tabili, L., *'We Ask for British Justice': Workers and Racial Difference in Late Imperial Britain*, Ithaca, New York, Cornell University Press, 1994.

Tatla, D.S., 'This is our home now: reminiscences of a Punjabi migrant in Coventry', *Oral History*, 1993, vol. 21 (no. 1).

Taylor, M. and Hegarty, S., *The Best of Both Worlds . . .?*, Windsor, Berkshire, NFER–Nelson, 1985.

Thorne, C., *Allies of a Kind: The US, Britain and the War against Japan, 1941–1945*, London, Hamish Hamilton, 1978.

Tidrick, G., 'Some aspects of Jamaican emigration to the UK, 1953–1962', *Social and Economic Studies*, 1966, vol. 15, pp. 22–39.

Tinker, H., *Separate and Unequal: India and Indians in the British Commonwealth, 1920–1950*, London, Hurst, 1976.

Vadgama, K., *India in Britain: The Indian Contribution to the British Way of Life*, London, Royce, 1984.

Vertovec, S. (ed.), *Aspects of the South Asian Diaspora*, New Delhi, Oxford University Press, 1991.

Visram, R., *Ayahs, Lascars and Princes: Indians in Britain, 1700–1947*, London, Pluto, 1986.

Walvin, J., *Black and White: The Negro in English Society, 1555–1945*, London, Allen Lane, 1973.

——, *Passage to Britain: Immigration in British History and Politics*, Harmondsworth, Middlesex, Penguin, 1984.

——, 'From the fringes: the emergence of British black historical studies', in J.S. Gundara and I. Duffield, *Essays on the History of Blacks in Britain*, Aldershot, Hampshire, Avebury, 1992.

Ward, R., Nowikowski, S. and Sims, R., 'Middle-class Asians and their settlement in Britain', in J. Solomos (ed.), *Migrant Workers in Metropolitan Cities*, Strasbourg, European Science Foundation, 1982.

Watson, J.L. (ed.), *Between Two Cultures: Migrants and Minorities in Britain*, Oxford, Blackwell, 1977.

Werbner, P., 'Avoiding the ghetto: Pakistani migrants and settlement shifts in Manchester', *New Community*, 1979, vol. 7, pp. 376–89.

——, 'From rags to riches: Manchester Pakistanis and the textile trade', *New Community*, 1980, vol. 8, pp. 84–95.

——, *The Migration Process: Capital, Gifts and Offerings among British Pakistanis*, Oxford, Berg, 1990.

White, R. and Hampson, F.J., 'The British Nationality Act, 1981', *Public Law*, 1982, pp. 6–20.

Wickenden, J., 'Colour in Britain', London, Institute of Race Relations Pamphlet, 1958.

——, *West Indian Migration to Britain*, London, Oxford University Press, 1968.

Wilson, C.O., 'A hidden history: the black experience in Liverpool, England, 1919–1945', unpublished Ph.D. Thesis, University of North Carolina, 1991.

Worswick, G.D.N. and Ady, P.H. (eds), *The British Economy in the 1950s*, Oxford, Oxford University Press, 1962

Wyatt, W., *Confessions of an Optimist*, London, Collins, n.d. [*c.* 1984].

Young, K., *Sir Alec Douglas-Home*, London, Dent, 1970.

Ziegler, P., *Mountbatten: The Official Biography*, London, Collins, 1985

Index